PENGUIN COOKERY LIBRARY

IN PRAISE OF THE POTATO

Lindsey Bareham is a restaurant critic turned food writer. Twenty years of reviewing the best, and many of the worst, restaurants has provided her with a unique background for cookery writing. As well as broadcasting weekly on London's restaurants for London Radio, she is the restaurant critic for *Homes & Gardens*, writes a monthly food page for *She* magazine and is food adviser to *Pie in the Sky*, the BBC series starring Richard Griffiths as the chef-detective, Henry Crabbe. She is the author of *Onions Without Tears*, *A Celebration of Soup*, shortlisted for the 1993 André Simon Award, *Sainsbury's Good Soup Book*, *Paupers' London* and *A Guide to London's Ethnic Restaurants*. She co-wrote *Roast Chicken and Other Stories*, which won the 1994 André Simon Award and the 1995 Glenfiddich Award for Food Book of the Year, with Simon Hopkinson, co-founder of *Bibendum* and food writer for the *Independent*. She is a member of the Guild of Food Writers and lives in London with her two sons.

In Praise
of the
POTATO

Recipes from around the World

LINDSEY BAREHAM

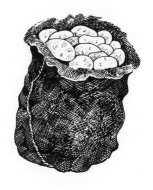

PENGUIN BOOKS

PENGUIN BOOKS

Published by the Penguin Group
Penguin Books Ltd, 27 Wrights Lane, London W8 5TZ, England
Penguin Books USA Inc., 375 Hudson Street, New York, New York 10014, USA
Penguin Books Australia Ltd, Ringwood, Victoria, Australia
Penguin Books Canada Ltd, 10 Alcorn Avenue, Toronto, Ontario, Canada M4V 3B2
Penguin Books (NZ) Ltd, 182–190 Wairau Road, Auckland 10, New Zealand

Penguin Books Ltd, Registered Offices: Harmondsworth, Middlesex, England

First published by Michael Joseph 1989
Published in Penguin Books 1995
1 3 5 7 9 10 8 6 4 2

Printed in England by Clays Ltd, St Ives plc

Contents

<u>Methods of Cooking</u>

The Recipes

Acknowledgements

Once I began talking about this book it became clear that potatoes are a national passion. I've discovered that to be writing a book about potatoes is a great social leveller and never fails to excite descriptions of favourite recipes or anecdotes, usually related to greed. The potato I now know inspires ardour in otherwise reticent folk and the collection and then collation of recipes very quickly became an unwieldy task. Credits appear throughout the book for specific recipes but there are a number of people whom I would like to thank for their more general contribution to this book. Had it not been for my column in *Time Out* and Tony Elliott's support this book might never have happened. Richard Shepherd, chef and part-owner of Langan's Brasserie in Piccadilly, shared his wealth of expertise of potato cookery as did chefs Alastair Little, Sally Clarke of Clarke's and Simon Hopkinson of Bibendum. The Potato Marketing Board showered me with leaflets and potato propaganda, Dudley Payne provided a diligent newspaper cutting service, and Henrietta Green allowed me the use of her photocopier and library. Robin Young of *The Times*; food and restaurant consultant Alan Crompton-Batt; Jeremy Round who writes so well about food in *The Independent*; my greengrocer Naki Adamous of Adamous and Sons in Chiswick; my mother Jean Bareham; Elizabeth David; Jane Grigson; Elisabeth Lambert Ortiz; the late Captain Donald Maclean; Hugo Dunn-Meynell of The International Wine and Food Society; Lesley Scott who until recently cooked at her delightful Walberswick restaurant The Potter's Wheel; Heidi Lascelles of Books For Cooks; Tom Jackson; Jenny Dereham and Richenda Todd all contributed greatly to this book in one way or another.

Most particularly I would like to thank my friend Andrew Payne who expanded his waistline to accommodate almost the entire contents of this book and my children Zachary and Henry who can still look a potato in the eye and eat it.

To Elizabeth David,
who unwittingly inspired this book.

1.

Introduction

'These [potatoes] are very usual in foreign parts, and are planted in several places of this country to a very good advantage . . . I do not hear that it hath been as yet assayed whether they may not be propagated in great quantities for food for swine or other cattle.'

John Worlidge, *Systema Agriculturae*, 1669

I wonder what John Worlidge would have to say if he knew just how ubiquitous the potato has become today. For 15 years I wrote a weekly column about the restaurants of London and one of the legacies of those years is a great affection and respect for the potato and its seemingly endless versatility.

Going back over my cuttings it came as no surprise to see how frequently potato dishes are a major feature of many memorable meals: a Bombay *aloo* made with nine spices in Knightsbridge; Hungarian dumplings in Bayswater; perfect chips in Leicester Square; Irish boxty in Islington; Swedish anchovy and potato bake in Stoke Newington; roast new potatoes stuffed with caviare in Belgravia; Spanish omelette in Vauxhall; and *gnocchi di patate* by the Thames in Hammersmith. As an enthusiastic amateur cook with a large and discerning family to feed, I've attempted to reproduce with varying degrees of fidelity many of these dishes at home. Additionally, one of the bonuses of my work as a critic has been the opportunity to review new cookery books. As a result my potato repertoire has been increased to include some unusual variations on old favourite dishes, exotic new ideas and recipes from countries not especially associated with the potato.

For a long time I've wanted to put all these recipes together as a personal paean to the potato. This book, then, is the result of an on-going love affair and I hope my selection of recipes will give you, your friends and family as much pleasure as they've given me and mine.

LINDSEY BAREHAM
LONDON, SEPTEMBER 1988

2.

The History of the Potato

'Though the potato is an excellent root, deserving to be brought into general use, yet it seems not likely that the use of it should ever be normal in the country.'

David Davies, *The Case of the Labourers in Husbandry*, 1795.

The potato originates from South America and there is evidence of its cultivation and domestic use in Peru by 3000 BC. Before they started eating *Solanum tuberosum esculentum* (its official Latin name as chosen by the eminent Swiss botanist, Gaspard Bauhin), the Peruvians probably worshipped it. Pottery in the shape of potatoes has been found dating from the second century AD.

The first European encounter with the potato is difficult to pinpoint largely because there is historical confusion about whether the discovered tuber was the sweet potato (*batata*) or a distant strain of the plump potato of today. The earliest claim seems to be the Spanish explorer Gonzalo Jiménez de Quesada in 1536. Equally uncertain is how the potato, originally cultivated long before the discovery of America, came to be called the Virginia potato. This is a theory developed by the American food writer Waverley Root. In 1586 Sir Walter Raleigh's cousin Sir Richard Grenville sailed to do battle with the Spaniards in the Caribbean, and the story goes that he was asked to drop off some provisions in Virginia for premature colonists. One of Raleigh's men, Thomas Hariot, went along for the ride as far as Virginia and on arrival they discovered the colonists wanted out. Around that time Sir Francis Drake was about to set sail for England after a successful series of battles against the Spaniards in the Caribbean. Drake stocked up with provisions for the return journey at Cartagena, Colombia, and included some potatoes. Next stop was Virginia to pick up the colonists. They returned via Ireland and Raleigh is supposed to have planted some of the tubers in his property at Youghal, near Cork in Ireland. But by the time the ship arrived in England the potato and the Virginian settlers had become inextricably intertwined and the potatoes became known as Virginia potatoes.

After its first recorded mention in John Gerard's herbal in 1597, the potato spread all over the world and by 1650 had become the staple food of Ireland. The potato has been blamed for the over-population of Ireland which had an estimated nine million people by 1840. In 1845 and 1846 the successive failure of the potato crop devastated the country, leading to over a million fatalities and mass emigration to America and Britain.

In France the potato was publicly reviled yet privately cultivated and eaten on a small scale until the pharmacist Antoine-Auguste Parmentier recommended the potato as a solution to the country's widespread and recurring famine. There is an amusing story that shows Parmentier as something of an exponent of lateral thought. Early in the 1770s Parmentier is supposed to have persuaded Louis XVI to let him plant a field of potatoes just outside Paris. Parmentier posted ostentatious 'guards' to protect the crop. The curiosity of the Parisians was aroused and the field was lavishly plundered with the result that it became chic to grow potatoes. Parmentier compounded the potato's new reputation by giving a court dinner at which every course included potatoes. He even persuaded Marie Antoinette to wear potato flowers in her hair, and so the potato 'arrived' in France. Parmentier's highly developed marketing skills mean that now many classic French dishes are prefixed by his name and if you see *Parmentier* on a menu it means potato.

Today the potato is recognised as the third most important crop in the world, both for human and animal consumption, and is firmly established in some form in societies throughout the world. Russia, Poland and West Germany lead in potato consumption (262 lb/119 kg per capita per year and rising) followed by Holland and Cyprus, closely followed by Ireland, Belgium, Denmark and Spain. But the potato hasn't had an easy ride establishing itself. It has been ridiculed, feared and ostracised. The fact that it was the first cultivated crop that was not grown from seed and reached maturity underground was regarded as devil's work. It has been blamed for all manner of ills ranging from leprosy, syphilis and consumption to hermaphroditism, wind and aphrodisiacal qualities.

All the critics have had their say and they've all been proved wrong. I think American writers John and Karen Hess have got it right: 'The potato is one of nature's best-designed products; it is born in a sturdy package, with wonderful shelf life. Yet we haul it from field to factory, peel and slice it by machine, cook it in hot grease, dose it with additives, wrap it in a petroleum or natural-gas derivative, freeze it, store it in a frozen warehouse, haul it across the country in a diesel refrigerated truck, store it in another freezer warehouse, deliver it to a supermarket freezer, move it to a kitchen freezer, and, eventually, we reheat it. Then we eat it.'

3.

The Nutritional and Calorific Content of the Potato

*'Our own people [of the city of Basle] sometimes roast
them under embers in the manner of tubers [truffles]
and having taken off the cuticle eat them with pepper:
others having roasted them and cleaned them cut them
up into slices and pour fat sauce with pepper and eat
them for exciting Venus, increasing semen: others regard
them as useful for invalids since they believe them to be
good nourishment.'*

Gaspard Bauhin, *The Podromos*, 1619

We eat an average 242 lb (110 kg) a head per year of potatoes and potato consumption is on the increase, say the Potato Marketing Board. Despite the fact that the potato is almost 80% water, it also contains a number of vitamins and minerals that are important to a nutritious and healthy diet.

The potato is not the fattening vegetable that its reputation supposes. In fact an 8 oz (225 g) serving of boiled, steamed or baked potatoes without butter averages 160 calories. That represents just a twentieth of the daily energy needs. When the potatoes are mashed with milk and butter the calories creep up to 280, roast averages 360 calories, and were you to eat the equivalent amount of crisps, the figure is closer to 500. It is what we put on our potatoes and what we cook them in that tots up the calories, not the potato itself. Bad cooking also contributes more calories. Roast, sauté and deep-fried potatoes should always be put into hot fat, as this seals the outside and prevents saturation. When you eat soggy chips, you are eating chips soaked through with fat.

Most of the minerals and vitamins are stored in or just below the skin of the potato, which is why it is important to cook potatoes in their skin or to peel them as lightly as possible. Many people even advocate using the potato water for soup or for cooking some other vegetable. The potato's actual composition is something like this: 81% water, 16% starch, 1% minerals and trace elements, 0.7% vitamins, 0.6% fibre, 0.35% protein, 0.27% sugar and 0.08% fat. Of that 0.7% vitamins and 1% minerals and trace elements the greatest quantity is vitamin C and iron. A medium-sized potato supplies an average 33 mg of vitamin C, or approximately the amount contained in a glass of tomato juice, and 1.5 mg of iron, the same amount as in an egg. During the winter the potato is often the main source of vitamin C and it is stored cumulatively in the body. Vitamin C is easily destroyed and in the case of the potato it is most often lost because of bad and prolonged storage and lengthy soaking in cold water. Salt also draws out nutrients and when nutritive value is lost so too is flavour. That means we should really only salt our vegetables when they have finished cooking.

Aside from vitamin C and iron, that seemingly small percentage of nutrients in the potato also accounts for approximately 4% of our total intake of iron, 10% thiamin, 3% riboflavin and 9% nicotinic acid. It also contributes significant amounts of potassium, which counters the effects of salt which contributes to high blood pressure and heart disease. These amounts are based on the average British daily intake of 6 oz (175 g) of potatoes.

There is no doubt that the potato has a vital role in providing a healthy, balanced diet. Incidentally, Audrey Eyton's bestseller, *The Complete F-Plan Diet*, devotes an entire chapter to the benefits of eating baked potatoes.

BAD POTATOES

As a result of the rigorous grading and standardisation required by the Potato Marketing Board, it is becoming less common to find more than the occasional mouldy potato. Bad potatoes smell and demand to be noticed. Small pockets of disease can be cut out with no detriment to the rest of the potato.

Discolouration of a peeled potato is not dangerous and is caused by a chemical reaction between tyrosine, present in all potatoes, and oxygen in the air. The reaction creates melanin which is harmless though unattractive. Blackening during or after cooking is caused by a high level of iron either in the potato or the water and a reaction with chlorogenic acid in the potato. This is also harmless but unsightly. It can be eliminated by adding some lemon juice or vinegar to the cooking water.

Green-skinned potatoes should be chucked. The green is the result of bad storage either on the farm, in the shop or at home. When potatoes are exposed to any form of light they turn green. All potatoes contain solanine and when exposed to light the solanine level soars and results in the green. Too much solanine is poisonous and a potato is deemed unfit for human consumption if it is found to have more than 0.1% of solanine. Small patches can be cut out but may cause the potato to taste a little bitter. Bin is Best for green potatoes.

4.

Buying and Storage Advice

Potatoes intended for storage are left in the ground until fully matured. As the tuber matures underground, the plants wither and the potatoes can be left in the ground for up to 6 weeks after that. Ideal storage conditions are humid, cool but frost-free and in the dark at a temperature between 45°F/7°C to 50°F/10°C. Storing them at temperatures below 40°F/5°C causes some of the potato's starch to turn to sugar which spoils its flavour. This can be reversed by keeping the potatoes at room temperature for several days. Potatoes do not freeze well. Raw potatoes soften when frozen and cooked potatoes become grainy and mushy. Part-cooked chips and other fried potatoes can be successfully frozen and should be finished off in the oven. Properly stored, potatoes can be kept for months. On a national level there is absolutely no excuse for dying and discarding (as happens regularly) one season's crop to make way for the next.

Unlikely though it seems, potatoes bruise easily and should be handled as little as possible. These bruises manifest themselves as black cooked potatoes. Potatoes go mouldy and rotten if they are kept in the damp. If you buy potatoes in polythene bags, they should be decanted as soon as you get home. Rotting and sprouting will happen if they are kept in the bag. They will also sprout if they are stored in a warm place. Light turns them green and this can be poisonous. Potatoes must not be stored anywhere near strong smelling foodstuffs or chemicals. They are best stored in a vegetable rack so that air can circulate around them.

5.

Guide to Potato Varieties

---

*'For the thousandth time, why, why, why I ask, do we,
the English, the pioneers of European-potato cultivation,
now grow such uninteresting potatoes . . .'*

Elizabeth David, *An Omelette and a Glass of Wine*, 1984.

Since Elizabeth David's oft-echoed lament for the commercial sale of
potatoes other than 'our own all-purpose collapsible English spuds', there
has been some improvement. The efforts of Donald Maclean who, until
his premature death in 1988, cultivated over 400 varieties of potato
collected over 25 years, have had an effect. Despite a sceptical yet realistic
view of why there are only 15 potato varieties generally available, Captain
Maclean kept up a constant campaign to make more potato varieties
available. While potato consumption rises, the number of producers is
reducing (in 1969 there were 70,000 producers, in 1988 only 21,000) and
that is because 97% of potato plantings are of the 15 maincrop varieties
that have a proven record of high yield and pest resistance. Companies
such as chip giant McCains spend thousands of pounds developing the
best variety for their needs (Pentland Dell is one) but thank goodness not
everyone is interested in high yield as opposed to high flavour. In the
years before his death, Captain Maclean advised Marks and Spencer,
Waitrose and Sainsburys about long-forgotten old English potato varieties
and it is probably because of him that the Pink Fir Apple (pre-1900) is
gracing the shelves of all these food stores. Because the Pink Fir Apple
isn't cultivated on a mass commercial level it is necessarily far more
expensive than the common varieties. Perhaps to justify pricing this and
the other 'designer' potatoes at the same level as luxury vegetables, the
supermarkets have taken to almost gift packaging a pound of potatoes.
The concept of the designer or gourmet potato is part of a grand hype
masterminded to make it 'easier' for the consumer to part with four times
the price of English reds or whites for these newly introduced old English

varieties such as the Pink Fir Apple, Charlotte and Carlingford, and the French varieties Belle de Fontenay, sometimes called Cornichon and La Ratte.

Since it was made law in 1983 to display the variety at the point of sale, we have as a nation become variety aware. Much potato packaging now gives cooking guidelines and there is no longer any excuse to settle for un-named whites or reds and expect them to make equally good chips, mash, dauphinois and baked.

POTATO VARIETIES AND THEIR USES

There are over 400 varieties of potato but less than 30 are commercially cultivated and even fewer generally available in the shops. Waxy Dutch, Cyprus and Egyptian varieties are available at some enterprising and usually Cypriot-run greengrocers, but as a general rule the choice is refined to 15 varieties: 8 earlies and 7 maincrops.

British potatoes are either Earlies or Maincrop. Earlies are widely available at the end of May and throughout the summer, and maincrops begin in mid-September. Some of the finest, tastiest new potatoes are grown in Cornwall and Jersey. Both appear at the very beginning of the season and are very highly priced. Jerseys continue throughout the summer and their price drops in direct relation to their increased size. The most commonly available earlies are:

Jersey Royal, these delectable little potatoes with their flaky skins first appear in this country in May. They are packaged in distinctive 15-lb wooden barrels (rather similar to oyster crates) packed with dark sand. The season continues until October but it's at its height in August and September. The little kidney-shaped potatoes were originally called International Kidney, the flesh is yellow and firm and the flavour distinctive. They are not to be confused with ordinary Jersey whites which are maris pipers grown in Jersey.

Home Guard, usually the first new potato and with a floury texture. Best at the beginning of the season, thereafter often collapses during cooking and has a tendency to blacken after cooking.

Arran Comet, grown mainly in Kent, with a characteristic white skin and creamy flesh. Bland flavour.

Ulster Sceptre, oval shaped with shiny white skin and pale flesh. One of the first earlies and with a soft, waxy texture. Good all-rounder and suitable for boiling, mashing, salads, baking, roasting and chipping.

Maris Bard, oval shaped, good for boiling but unspectacular flavour.

Maris Peer, flesh is dry and floury yet it has a waxy texture too, rarely disintegrates when cooked. Best at the beginning of the season.

Pentland Javelin, the most widely grown early potato which, like all potatoes with the Pentland prefix, is grown in Scotland. Moderately waxy all-rounder.

Second earlies, available from mid-August:

Wilja, pale yellow-flesh and oval shape, introduced from Holland. Good all-rounder but especially good for boiling and dishes that require parboiled potatoes.

Estima, similar to Wilja with yellow flesh, boils well and is a good all-rounder.

The most commonly available maincrops are:

Desiree, pink skinned, pale yellow soft textured flesh and originally from Holland (1962). Good for baking, boiling, chipping and roasting. Not so good for mashing.

Maris Piper, now the most popular maincrop variety. Creamy white flesh, dry floury texture. Good for baking, chipping, roasting and mashing.

Cara, distinctive pale skin with pink eyes and introduced as an alternative to King Edward because of its high yield. Good for baking.

Pentland Crown, creamy flesh, best for baking otherwise unexceptional.

King Edward, excellent mashed, roasted and chipped. Disintegrates when boiled so hopeless for boiling.

Pentland Squire, white skin and flesh, excellent baked, otherwise unremarkable.

Pentland Dell, long oval-shaped potato with a soft moderately dry texture. It tends to disintegrate during cooking and is therefore good for roast potatoes that look messy and uneven but crisp up beautifully.

Romano, similar in look and style to Desiree.

Other varieties:

Pink Fir Apple, old English variety most similar to the smooth-skinned French varieties. Pink nobbly skin that turns brown when cooked. Dense firm flesh, good for salads, boiling and sautéeing.

Charlotte, recently relaunched old English variety, also similar to the dense-fleshed French varieties. Same uses as Pink Fir Apple.

La Ratte, Cornichon, Belle de Fontenay, French smooth-skinned varieties. Waxy, yellow, firm flesh. Good for salads, boiling, dauphinois and any dish that requires a potato that won't disintegrate.

Linzer Delikatess, looks like a long Jersey Royal with smooth skin. Flavour lacking despite dense flesh. *The Sunday Times* recently conducted a designer-potato tasting and voted the Linzer a disappointment.

Salad Red, Purple Congo, Salad Blue, all dense fleshed and similar to the Pink Fir Apple. Very rare and available in seed from Mrs P. Maclean, Dornock Farm, Crieff, Perthshire, PR7 3QN.

Black Potatoes, also called *négresses* or *pommes de Madagascar*. This is not listed in Maclean's exhaustive list of potato varieties. According to Larousse it is remarkable only for its colour, which after cooking is not really black but a dark purple. They are most often used for their novelty value and in hors d'oeuvre.

Sweet Potato, native to tropical America, the West Indies and the Pacific but widely available in Asian and West Indian shops and markets and most supermarkets. The skin is generally pink, the shape long and nobbly and the flesh either white, yellow or bright orange. It can be cooked in exactly the same way as the potato but is most successful baked and served with butter, mashed and in a variety of desserts.

6.

Conversion Tables

This is a chart of the metric and imperial measures used throughout this book. All these are approximate conversions, which have either been rounded up or down. Never mix metric and imperial measures in one recipe; stick to one system or the other.

Weights		Volume	
½oz	15g	1fl oz	25ml
1oz	25g	2fl oz	50ml
2oz	50g	3fl oz	75ml
3oz	75g	5fl oz (¼ pt)	150ml
4oz	110g	10fl oz (½ pt)	275ml
5oz	150g	15fl oz (¾ pt)	400ml
6oz	175g	1pt	570ml
7oz	200g	1¼pts	700ml
8oz	225g	1½pts	900ml
9oz	250g	1¾pts	1l
10oz	275g	2pts	1.1l
11oz	310g	2¼pts	1.3l
12oz	350g	2½pts	1.4l
13oz	375g	3pts	1.75l
14oz	400g	3¼pts	2.1l
15oz	425g	3½pts	2l
1lb	450g	3¾pts	2.1l
1¼lb	550g	4pts	2.3l
1½lb	700g	5pts	2.8l
2lb	900g	6pts	3.4l
3lb	1.4kg	7pts	4.0l
4lb	1.8kg	8pts (1 gal)	4.5l
5lb	2.3kg		

Measurements	
¼in	0.5cm
½in	1.0cm
1in	2.5cm
2ins	5.0cm
3ins	7.5cm
4ins	10.0cm
6ins	15.0cm
7ins	18.0cm
8ins	20.5cm
9ins	23.0cm
10ins	25.5cm
11ins	28.0cm
12ins (1 ft)	30.5cm

Oven Temperatures		
275°F	140°C	Gas Mark 1
300°F	150°C	Gas Mark 2
325°F	170°C	Gas Mark 3
350°F	180°C	Gas Mark 4
375°F	190°C	Gas Mark 5
400°F	200°C	Gas Mark 6
425°F	220°C	Gas Mark 7
450°F	230°C	Gas Mark 8
475°F	240°C	Gas Mark 9

Methods of Cooking

7.

Boil and Steam

'One of the greatest luxuries . . . in dining is to be able to command plenty of good vegetables, well served up. Excellent potatoes, smoking hot, and accompanied by melted butter of the first quality, would alone stamp merit on any dinner: but they are as rare on state occasions, so served, as if they were of the cost of pearls.'

Thomas Walker, *The Original*, 1835

BOILING

A couple of years ago Chris Searle presented a programme on Radio 4 extolling the virtues and recording the history of the potato. One of his guests was the 2-Michelin-starred chef Nico Ladenis. Nico is widely regarded as one of this country's most dedicated chefs and one who goes to enormous trouble to get the very finest ingredients for his complex cooking with its density of flavours. Food at both Chez Nico and Very Simply Nico is always memorable and never 'simple'. Nico was invited to prepare his favourite potato dish and I suspect was chosen for this task because of his reputation for doing something special with the most modest ingredient. True to his controversial reputation Nico came up with a dish of plainly boiled (in their skins) new Jersey Royals, tossed with butter and chopped parsley. That to him was perfection.

Jersey Royals are one of the few varieties of potato that have got most of the cards stacked in their favour. Most importantly, they taste how our memory thinks potatoes ought to taste. They have a distinctive, earthy flavour and the dense but not overly waxy flesh means this variety doesn't disintegrate when boiled. The availability of Jersey Royals is limited to the summer season. Initially they are fiendishly expensive and it's only towards the end of the summer when they are far larger and somehow less appealing that their price drops to somewhere near the national average.

So just how can you get the most flavour out of boiled potatoes? Potatoes are rich in nutrients and nutrients mean flavour. Nutrients, though, dissolve in water and this is why what little flavour there may be in your boiled spud can be saved by following a few little tips. Don't soak the potatoes; instead, scrub them under running water. Don't peel them because most of the potato's nutrients are just under the skin. If the potatoes are new and relatively fresh the skin is quite edible. If the skin is old peel it away while holding the hot potato in a dishcloth.

Merely cover the potatoes with water, add a generous pinch of salt, bring the water to the boil and then simmer gently for 15–20 minutes, depending on the size of the potatoes. Remember that the more potatoes there are in the pot the longer the cooking will take. I always partially cover potatoes but this is personal preference; it doesn't seem to affect either flavour or length of cooking. New potatoes should be put into boiling water, old potatoes brought to the boil in the water. As André Simon says in his *Concise Encyclopedia of Gastronomy*: 'Old, warty potatoes, should you have no other, must be peeled and soaked in cold water for an hour, then put into boiling water and boiled fast for 30 minutes. They are then drained, and the best thing to do with them is to mash them.'

Old potatoes are prone to discolour after cooking, but this can be avoided by adding lemon peel to the cooking water: that keeps them white. All boiled potatoes should be drained carefully. If they need to be kept waiting, cover them with a clean teacloth instead of the lid of the serving dish. This absorbs the moisture and results in dry and floury, instead of sodden, potatoes.

Try cooking in stock rather than water, it will enrich the potatoes' flavour. Or in milk: nutrients dissolve less readily in milk than they do in water and the potatoes will taste milder and sweeter than normal. Unless the potatoes are very new, peel thinly first. The milk won't scorch or curdle if it is kept at a simmer; it can be used to make a cream sauce or soup.

STEAMING

These days the pressure cooker is rarely an essential part of the *batterie de cuisine*. Potatoes cooked in a pressure cooker take 5–6 minutes but precision cooking is vital, otherwise the results are a slop. Specific directions are given with each cooker but as a general rule only a few tablespoons of water are needed and it should be brought to the boil before the potatoes are put in the pot. Once the cooking time has finished, the cooker must be cooled immediately. From the point of view of nutrient value, pressure cooking of potatoes is not recommended unless the cooking liquor is served with the potatoes. Best results are had by leaving the potatoes unpeeled. During steaming, moisture continually condenses on the surface of the vegetables and sugars, minerals, vitamin C and the B vitamins can dissolve in the moisture.

Steaming without pressure takes a little longer than boiling but the results are lighter and the flavour seems to intensify. But, because the potatoes take 10–15 minutes longer to cook there is a greater loss of vitamins (especially C) than when potatoes are boiled.

The cheapest steamers come from Japan and China. The Japanese version is a collapsible metal basket with short legs that fits into any saucepan. Chinese steamers are rustic bamboo baskets, available in various sizes, with a separate metal stand.

BEST VARIETIES FOR BOILING AND STEAMING

Jersey Royal, Belle de Fontenay (La Ratte, Cornichon), Bintje, Kipfler, Pink Fir Apple, Charlotte and any Cyprus, Egyptian, Dutch or Belgian variety or any freshly dug potato.

An 8 oz (225 g) serving of boiled potatoes without butter averages 160 calories.

BOILED POTATOES/POTATOES À L'ANGLAISE

Take care to cook even-sized potatoes, and boil them in their skin unless you wish to 'turn' them to give a uniform shape. Allow between 15 and 30 minutes depending on the size of the potato before you check if they are ready. Quantities over 2 lb (900 g) in one pan will take longer.

Put new potatoes into boiling salted water, old into cold. Simmer gently. Drain carefully, peel if necessary and toss in butter; garnish with parsley or mint and serve. If you see *Pommes de Terre Persillées* on a French menu, it means potatoes boiled and sprinkled with parsley and melted butter. Occasionally bacon is included.

BOILED PINK FIR APPLES

This old English variety with its pink skin, nobbles and distinctive tuber shape is the closest this country has to the dense-skinned waxy varieties

of France. It lends itself especially well to salads but simply boiled it is
good enough to serve alone or as an accompaniment to any dish what-
soever. The skin is firm and tough but peels away very easily after boiling.
Proceed as if you were boiling new potatoes à l'anglaise (page 19).

POTATOES DUG FROM THE GARDEN   Serves 4–6

Nothing can beat the pleasure of cooking your own home-grown potatoes
freshly dug from the garden. They will be sublime treated simply as in the
standard recipe (page 18), but this recipe is for a special treat.

> 2 lb (900 g) new potatoes
> sprig of mint
> 2 oz (50 g) unsalted butter
> ¼ pt (150 ml) single cream
> salt, pepper
> 1 heaped tbs parsley, chopped

Wash the potatoes, boil with the mint in salted water. Drain. Melt the
butter in the potato saucepan; when melted add the potatoes and roll
around until all are coated. Pour on the cream, season with plenty of black
pepper, add most of the parsley and stir as the cream bubbles. Pour into a
warmed serving dish, sprinkle on the remaining parsley and serve.

THE LANCASHIRE WAY TO BOIL POTATOES   Serves 4–6

This time-honoured method breaks all the rules but the results are
delicious, marred only by the thought of dealing with the saucepan!

> 2 lb (900 g) potatoes
> 4 oz (110 g) butter
> plenty of salt or sea water

Thinly peel the potatoes, cut into even-sized pieces and soak in very salty
cold water for a couple of hours. Drain and put the potatoes into fresh,
well-salted water. Boil and when nearly done add a little cold water to
lower the temperature and make the potatoes floury. Drain and return to
the pan, cover with a folded cloth and complete the cooking over a low
heat. Lumps of potato will stick to the pan: scrape these off and mix in
with the rest of the potatoes. The scorched flavour is essential. Serve with
plenty of butter.

STEAMED POTATOES/POMMES VAPEUR   Serves 2–4

    1 lb (450 g) potatoes
    2 oz (50 g) unsalted butter

Bring 2 ins (5 cm) water to the boil. Insert the steamer and the washed or, if necessary, peeled potatoes. Do not season. Cover with a tight-fitting lid and check if they're done after 30 minutes if the potatoes are an average medium size, less if they are small and new. Serve with the butter.

THE THOMAS OR POTATO POT/EN DIABLE   Serves 4

This is an unglazed lidded clay pot in which potatoes are cooked without water or fat. The pottery absorbs much of the moisture out of the potatoes and gives them back an earthy flavour. Potatoes should be of an even size, washed and dried (not peeled). The potatoes will look and taste as if they've been cooked in the embers of a bonfire.

    1 lb (450 g) potatoes
    Thomas pot (stocked by John Lewis chain, Habitat and other kitchen
        shops)

Wash and dry the potatoes, pack into the Thomas pot (this incidentally should never be washed), and put on a low gas/electric ring or place in a pre-heated moderate oven (350°F/180°C/gas mark 4) for 40 minutes–1 hour, depending on the size and number of potatoes. Shake the pot a couple of times during cooking if the pot is over direct heat. The pot will crack if put on a cold surface directly after use.

RISSOLE POTATOES   Serves 2

    1 lb (450 g) small new potatoes
    4 oz (110 g) butter
    salt, pepper
    1 tbs chervil, chopped

Wash and boil the potatoes for half the normal cooking time. Drain. Melt the butter in a heavy frying pan, add the potatoes and cook them, shaking the pan periodically, over a low heat. When they are browned all over drain on absorbent paper, season and serve sprinkled with chervil. This is also good with fresh mint or dill.

NEW POTATOES WITH BACON AND MINT　　　　　Serves 4

> 1 ½ lb (700 g) new potatoes
> 8 oz (225 g) smoked, streaky bacon
> 4 oz (110 g) unsalted butter
> salt, pepper
> 4 tbs fresh mint, chopped

Choose small, even-sized potatoes and boil them in their skins in very lightly salted water for 10 minutes. Drain and spike each potato in a couple of places with the prongs of a fork.

Meanwhile, cut the bacon into ½-in (1-cm) dice and fry in a non-stick pan to release some of the fat. As they begin to splutter add half the butter and continue cooking over a moderate flame turning frequently. Add the almost cooked potatoes and finish cooking with the bacon to absorb the fat and flavours.

Transfer to a serving dish, dot with the remaining butter, season generously with pepper and sprinkle with the mint.

SAVOURY POTATOES　　　　　　　　　　　　Serves 6

> 2 lb (900 g) potatoes, boiled in their skins
> 3 oz (75 g) smoked, streaky bacon
> 1 tbs plain flour
> 1 tbs sugar
> ½ pt (275 ml) stock
> 4 tbs wine vinegar
> pepper

Skin and dice the potatoes. Dice bacon and fry in a large non-stick pan. When the bacon begins to crisp mix in the flour and sugar and brown well. Pour in the stock, allow to bubble and then add the potatoes. Add the wine vinegar and pepper. Cook for 5 minutes, rest for 5 minutes and serve. This dish has a decidedly sour-sweet taste and only works if the potatoes have a dense flesh.

NEW POTATOES IN MUSTARD DRESSING   Serves 4

This idea comes from *The Home Gardener's Cookbook* and is particularly good with grilled or baked gammon.

 1½ lb (700 g) small new potatoes

 For the dressing:

 2 tbs plain flour
 1 tbs each caster sugar, made English mustard
 ½ pt (275 ml) milk
 1 dsp olive oil
 1 egg, beaten
 4 tbs vinegar
 1 tsp salt, pepper

Scrub and boil the potatoes. Drain and keep warm while you mix the flour, sugar, salt, mustard and pepper in a saucepan. Stir in the milk, then the oil and the beaten egg. Slowly bring to the boil, stirring constantly, and cook for a couple of minutes. Remove from the heat and gradually beat in the vinegar.

Transfer the potatoes to a warmed serving dish and pour the sauce over.

NEW POTATOES WITH SOUR CREAM   Serves 6

This is a Russian dish that is very good with lamb kebabs.

 2 lb (900 g) new potatoes
 ¼ pt (150 ml) sour cream
 4 spring onions, finely sliced or 1 small onion, diced and 1 tbs
 ⸱ chives.
 salt, pepper
 1 tbs fresh dill, chopped

Boil the potatoes in salted water. Drain and if necessary peel. Put into a serving dish and pour over the sour cream and spring onions (or onion and chives), season with plenty of pepper and mix thoroughly. Sprinkle with dill and serve.

SPANISH STEAMED POTATOES WITH CHILLI SAUCE Serves 2–4

This dish is fiery hot.

> 1 lb (450 g) new potatoes
> 2 dried red chilli peppers
> ½ tsp cumin seeds
> 1 tbs paprika
> 3 cloves garlic, crushed
> 2 tbs red wine vinegar
> ¼ pt (150 ml) olive oil
> salt

Steam the potatoes in the skins while you prepare the sauce. Work the chillis, paprika and cumin to a paste (either in a mortar or blender), add the garlic and salt and gradually first the vinegar and then the olive oil. Serve the potatoes and sauce separately.

INDIAN STEAMED POTATOES/ALOO DAM   Serves 2–4

> 1 lb (450 g) potatoes
> 1 onion, chopped
> 1 in (2.5 cm) piece fresh ginger, peeled
> 1 tsp coriander seeds
> 1 in (2.5 cm) piece cinnamon
> 2 tbs chilli powder
> ghee
> 2 bay leaves
> ½ tsp turmeric
> 4 fl oz (110 ml) yoghurt
> salt
> garam masala and 1 tbs fresh coriander, chopped

Peel the potatoes, prick with a fork and leave to soak in water for at least an hour.

Make a paste with the onion, ginger, coriander seed and cinnamon and reserve while you drain the potatoes and rub them with the chilli powder. Fry the potatoes until golden in the ghee, remove and fry the paste. Add the salt, bay leaves, turmeric and yoghurt. Cook through, then return the potatoes together with a little water. Cover and let the potatoes steam in the yoghurt mixture until cooked; about 15–20 minutes.

Serve sprinkled with garam masala and fresh coriander.

8.

Mash

'The purée potatoes, which he would have called
mashed, were like no mashed potatoes he had ever
sampled . . . if angels ever ate mashed potatoes they
would call on Pellew's chef to prepare them.'

C.S. Forester, *Hornblower and the Hotspur*, 1962

Forester didn't go on to give a recipe for his angel mash but the
description brings to mind a steaming dish of fluffy clouds. To arrive at
such a sublime-sounding mash at every cooking is beyond the hope of
any cook. Still, while there are many things that affect the quality of the
mash it takes a very special skill to produce a dish of mashed potatoes *at
home* that isn't edible. But, to be purist about mashed potato and to
pursue the very smoothest, lightest, fluffiest, creamiest and tastiest
mashed potato possible, there are few points worth considering.

The fluffiest mash is made from floury, mealy varieties but these
potatoes are the ones that tend to explode in the cooking and invariably
have bullet-like insides. Best results come from cooking even-sized
potatoes in cold water that is brought to the boil, the pan partially covered
and then the water allowed to boil lightly until the potatoes are cooked.
Albert and Michel Roux, the only chefs in this country to hold the much
coveted 3 Michelin stars, recommend putting a quarter of a lemon in the
cooking water to prevent the potatoes breaking up.

As the potato is almost 80% water, potatoes that are to be mashed
should be cooked in their skins to prevent them getting waterlogged. Once
cooked and drained leave the potatoes to cool slighly before beginning the
slimy task of removing the skins. This is best done by holding the potato
in a cloth and using a small pointed vegetable knife to tear away the skin.
This tiresome chore can be speeded up if you remove a ¼-in of skin
round the centre of the potato before boiling. When done, the skins can be
slipped off with one pull at either end. Leave the potatoes to steam dry

under a clean cloth for 5–10 minutes before you begin mashing. When flaky dry, return the potatoes to their cooking pan and dry-mash with a knob of butter. A Mouli légume takes the fag out of this part of the procedure but best results are had by separating the mashing from the whisking (the part that most people don't bother with) and regarding it as a two-tier job.

A firm mash needs at least 2 oz (50 g) of butter and somewhere between ¼- and ½-pint (150–275 ml) of milk for every 2 lb (900 g) of potatoes. It is actually easier to incorporate warm milk than cold and there is the advantage that the mash won't be tepid. Always add the milk gradually so that you can gauge the consistency. The *ideal* consistency of the mash will be ruled by what the potatoes are to be eaten with and whether they are to be incorporated into another dish. For instance, a French-style runny purée wouldn't do for bangers and mash or to top shepherd's pie.

The final beating or whisking of the potato is a vital part of creating a light mash. It doesn't matter what implement you use for this job so long as you work fast and evenly to incorporate air into the mixture. The 'K' beater of the Kenwood Chef is the only machine that does the job effectively (Simon Hopkinson, the chef of Bibendum, Terence Conran's restaurant, keeps one in his kitchen for that purpose exclusively) and opinion is divided between the wire whisk (Elizabeth David) and wooden spoon (Michel and Albert Roux, Fredy Giradet and Anton Mosimann), while almost every Irish recipe for mashed potatoes specifies the use of a fork.

Should you need to keep mashed potatoes warm before serving, cover the surface with melted butter and the pan with foil. Just before serving whisk the butter into the mash.

VARYING THE MASH

Basic mashed potatoes can be changed quite dramatically with a few additional ingredients and it can be tailored exactly to fit its many roles. With no liquid it is used in soufflés, as a proving agent for bread, in cakes, doughnuts and sticky puddings. It forms the basic ingredient for many stuffings, sauces, bakes and gratins and combined with meat juices, cream, yoghurt, cheese, eggs, fresh herbs and aromatic spices, other puréed vegetables and fruits or fruit juices its origins are almost unrecognisable. It turns up, too, in sweet as well as savoury potato cakes, balls, gnocchi, in potato wine and even in Christmas pudding.

Good mashed potato is one of the great luxuries of life and I don't blame Elvis for eating it every night for the last year of his life. What follows are some of the finest mashed potato recipes known to man; some classic, some involving unexpected additional ingredients but all delicious.

Recipes that incorporate mashed potato as part of a separate cooking method or as an ingredient of a recipe appear in most other sections within the book. These dishes are all indexed at the end of the book.

BEST VARIETIES FOR MASHING

The whole point of mashing potatoes or creating a *pommes purée* is to incorporate liquid, fat or oil and air into the potato. Dense-fleshed waxy varieties don't make good mash. I don't consider that Joel Rebuchon or Fredy Giradet's *pommes purée* made with new potatoes, cream and olive oil (page 31) is comparable to the sort of mash or purée that most people expect of a dish by that name.

Fluffy mash is made with varieties such as Golden Wonder, King Edward, Wilja and Maris Piper.

There are approximately 140 calories in a portion of mashed potato with milk and butter.

PERFECT MASHED POTATO   Serves 4

> 2 lb (900g) floury-variety potatoes
> 4 oz (110 g) butter
> ¼–½ pt (150–275 ml) hot milk
> salt, pepper

Choose even-sized potatoes and cook them at a simmer in enough salted water to cover. Drain, skin and, using a masher, Mouli légume or sieve, mash the potatoes with the butter to get rid of all the lumps. Adjust the seasoning, pour in about half the milk and, using a wire whisk, wooden spoon or fork, beat the potatoes for as long as your arm can stand. Rest and do it again. Adjust the consistency by adding more milk. The results will be light and lump-free and the beginning of the end of leftover mashed potato.

POTATO PURÉE WITH MEAT JUICE/POMMES MOUSSELINE FAÇON PROVENÇALE

A delicious embellishment to a supper of mashed potatoes and a chop is to dribble the meat juices over the potatoes, prepared according to the recipe for Perfect Mashed Potato (page 27). In *French Provincial Cooking* Elizabeth David mentions the French predilection for pouring some of the juice from a garlic and herb-flavoured roast of pork or veal around the purée and eating it first, as a separate course. I agree with her that it's preferable to eat both dishes at the same time.

PLAIN ENGLISH MASH   Serves 2

I came across this recipe in a cookbook entitled *Hand Book of Plain Cookery*, published in 1892; the 10p it cost was a snip for this recipe alone. It is delicious but radically improved if you include a little jelly with the dripping; it's also a good way of using up leftover potatoes but can obviously be made with freshly boiled.

    4 or 5 cold cooked potatoes
    1 oz (25 g) dripping
    5 fl oz (150 ml) milk
    salt to taste

Mash the potatoes finely with a fork and then a masher. In a saucepan, melt the dripping and add the milk. When very hot stir in the potatoes, mix thoroughly until heated through. Season and serve.

MICHEL AND ALBERT ROUX'S CREAMED POTATOES

The Roux brothers' reputation for perfection in their cooking is extended to their *pommes purée*. Potatoes are first baked in a moderate oven (to remove moisture as well as giving a distinctive flavour to the purée), the flesh then scooped out and pushed through a fine sieve or Mouli légume. Butter and hot milk is then beaten into the potatoes with a wooden spoon to the consistency of your taste. Finally the purée is seasoned with salt, freshly grated black pepper and a little nutmeg. Other favourite finishes are finely chopped parsley and the zest of a lemon.

SWEET POTATO PURÉE   <u>Serves 6</u>

This goes well with game but is quite addictive on its own!

>   2 lb (900 g) sweet potatoes
>   2 large white potatoes
>   4 oz (110 g) salted butter
>   salt, pepper

Bake all the potatoes in a hot oven; the flesh should be soft after about an hour. Cut in half and scoop out the flesh. Press through a sieve or Mouli légumé and warm through in a saucepan. Season and add the butter. Stir briskly, incorporating the butter as it melts. Serve with an extra knob of butter.

MASHED POTATOES WITH EGGS

Add the yolk of an egg to a *pommes purée*/mash (page 27) and the result is a firmer, richer version of what went before. The egg, whisked in at the end, gives 'body' and can thus transform a mash made with unexceptional potatoes. However, mashed potatoes made with an egg are generally used for something else. The most important dish is that of *pommes duchesse* (page 251) but the combination makes wonderful gratins and enables mash to be piped and maintain its form.

MASHED POTATOES WITH CREAM

PATATE ALLA PANNA   <u>Serves 6</u>

>   2 lb (900 g) potatoes
>   4 oz (110 g) butter
>   1 tsp flour
>   ½ medium-sized onion, sliced
>   ½ pt (275 ml) cream
>   salt, pepper, nutmeg, parsley

Boil the potatoes in salted water and when cool remove their skins. Chop into small pieces. Soften the onion in some butter, then put with the rest of the butter, flour, parsley, salt, pepper and nutmeg in a saucepan, heat through and let it bubble up before adding the cream. Stirring constantly, bring back to the boil and add the potatoes. Stir thoroughly, cover and leave for five minutes. Give a final stir and serve.

HUNGARIAN CREAMED POTATOES/BURGONYAHAB   Serves 4

1¼ lb (550 g) potatoes
1 oz (25 g) bacon dripping
¼ pt (150 ml) milk
2 tbs sour cream
salt, pepper

Boil and mash the potatoes and then stir in the melted fat. Bring the milk to the boil and whisk into the potatoes gradually. Season with salt and pepper and mix in the sour cream.

JOHN TOVEY'S MASHED NUT POTATOES   Serves 6

This is inspired by potatoes eaten at John Tovey's restaurant, Miller Howe, in the Lake District.

2 lb (900 g) potatoes, peeled and evenly cut
1 egg, lightly beaten
4 tbs double cream
2 oz (50 g) butter
7 oz (200 g) broken walnuts
pinch sea salt

Cover the potatoes with water, add the sea salt and bring to the boil. Reduce heat and simmer until soft. Strain well and dry over a low heat. Mash thoroughly and add the egg, double cream and butter. Cream well and fold in the nuts. This is extremely rich.

FREDY GIRADET'S PURÉE OF NEW POTATOES WITH OLIVE OIL/PURÉE DE POMMES NOUVELLES À L'HUILE D'OLIVE   Serves 4

When this recipe (from one of the most highly regarded chefs alive today) was published in this country in 1985 it caused something of a sensation. A variation on the recipe is invariably on the menu at Terence Conran's restaurant Bibendum and along with Joel Rebuchon's recipe for *pommes purée* has achieved cult status. This, my adaptation, is not a dish for the fainthearted.

>   10 oz (275 g) new potatoes, peeled and scraped
>   ¼ pt (150 ml) double cream
>   ¼ pt (150 ml) fruity olive oil
>   salt, pepper, cayenne

Cook the potatoes in boiling salted water. Drain and either push through a sieve or mash with a Mouli légume. Add the warmed cream and, using a wooden spoon, beat until the cream is absorbed into the potato. Now beat in the olive oil and continue beating after all the oil has been absorbed. Season with salt, pepper and cayenne and turn into a serving dish.

CREAMED YAM OR SWEET POTATOES   Serves 4

>   1½ lb (700 g) yams or sweet potatoes
>   4 oz (110 g) butter
>   1 medium-sized onion, grated
>   4 fl oz (110 ml) cream
>   black pepper
>   ½ tsp nutmeg, freshly grated

Cook the potatoes unpeeled in boiling salted water; meanwhile melt the butter and stir fry the onion over a very low flame for 5 minutes until transparent. Remove the potatoes' skins and mash thoroughly with your chosen implement. Pour the onion and melted butter into the potatoes, add the cream and amalgamate with a wooden spoon. Adjust the seasoning, warm through and serve piping hot with a dusting of nutmeg.

MASHED POTATO WITH YOGHURT   Serves 4

The addition of yoghurt instead of cream gives mashed potatoes a pungent flavour. It is also lighter and less fattening.

>   2 lb (900 g) potatoes, boiled in their skins
>   2 oz (50 g) butter
>   2 oz (50 g) yoghurt
>   salt, pepper, chopped mint

Peel the potatoes, mash with the butter and whip in the yoghurt. Check seasoning and serve with chopped mint if liked.

MASHED POTATOES WITH CHEESE

Cheese works very well with potatoes, particularly in gratins and as a topping for baked potatoes. The next two recipes though are exceptional.

PURÉED POTATOES WITH GARLIC AND TOMME
DE CANTAL   Serves 4

This dish is a speciality of the Auvergne and only really works with Tomme de Cantal cheese which goes stringy when cooked. The only acceptable alternative is Mozzarella.

>   2 lb (900 g) potatoes, boiled and mashed
>   2 oz (50 g) butter
>   8 cloves garlic, crushed (you may prefer to moderate the quantity)
>   10 oz (275 g) Tomme de Cantal cheese, grated
>   salt, pepper

Melt the butter in a saucepan large enough to accommodate all the ingredients. Add the garlic, let it sizzle for a moment before you add the potatoes, cheese, salt and pepper. Mix well over a low heat. The moment the cheese goes stringy, the dish is ready. Good on its own, with simply grilled lamb chops or with poached eggs.

ITALIAN MASHED POTATOES WITH PARMESAN/PURÈ DI PATATE   Serves 4

In the foreword to this recipe in her book *The Classic Italian Cookbook* Marcella Hazan ranks this along with gnocchi as the only two nice things the Italians do with potatoes. Perhaps to compensate, this recipe is written with enormous attention to detail and the results are perfection. Corners can be cut, which this adaptation of the recipe shows. It makes the perfect side dish to *fegato alla Veneziana* (liver and onions); Ms Hazan's preference is with *fegatini di pollo alla salvia* (chicken livers with sage).

> 1 lb (450 g) potatoes, boiled in their skins
> 8 tbs milk
> 1½ oz (40 g) butter
> 1 oz (25 g) Parmesan, freshly grated
> salt to taste

When cooked, peel the potatoes and purée through a Mouli légume into the top deck of a double boiler. In a separate pan bring the milk to the verge of boiling. Start beating the potatoes with a whisk, adding half the butter and 2 or 3 tbs milk at a time. When you have added half the milk, beat in the grated cheese. When the cheese has been well incorporated into the potatoes resume adding the milk and the rest of the butter without ceasing to beat, except to rest your arm for an occasional few seconds.

The potatoes should become a very soft, fluffy mass, a state that requires a great deal of beating and as much milk as the potatoes will absorb without becoming too thin and runny. As you finish adding the milk, taste and check the salt.

MASHED POTATOES WITH OTHER VEGETABLES

CHAMP, STELK OR CHAPPIT TATTIES   Serves 4

Champ or stelk are the Irish names for this simple but luxurious dish of mashed potatoes. In Scotland the same dish is called Chappit Tatties; in London I have seen it billed on fashionable menus as *Pommes Purée* with Green Onions. Champ should be served in individual mounds or dishes as everyone needs to have their own pool of butter.

6–8 mealy potatoes
8 fl oz (225 ml) milk
bunch of spring onions, chopped including the green part
4 oz (110 g) butter, chopped into small pieces
salt, pepper

Boil the potatoes in their skins and simmer the onion in the milk. When cooked remove the skins of the potatoes and mash. Using a wooden spoon, beat in the onion and milk until the purée is light and fluffy. Divide between four dishes and make a well in the centre of each. To each well add the chopped butter which will melt in the heat. Eat with a fork taking potato from the outside and dipping it into the butter.

COLCANNON   Serves 4–6

Another traditional Irish dish, but this one is always eaten at Halloween when it forms part of the tradition of fortune telling. A button, silver coin, ring, thimble and horseshoe are dropped into the mixture. Whoever is served the ring will marry within the year, the coin indicates wealth to come and horseshoe good fortune, the button a bachelor and the thimble an old maid. Cooked without the onion, this dish is called Kailkenny in Scotland and Rumbledethumps on the Border.

1½ lb (700 g) hot mashed potatoes
1 lb (450 g) green cabbage or kale, finely shredded
2 tbs grated onion or 3 spring onions, finely chopped
2 fl oz (50 ml) cream or milk
2 oz (50 g) butter
salt, pepper

Cook the cabbage until tender but still crisp either by steaming or in a little water in a covered pan. Cook the onions in the cream or milk until soft and mix in with the mashed potatoes. Fold in the cabbage and turn into a serving dish or individual bowls. Make several holes and fill with butter.

Colcannon is also very delicious when fried in butter and finished under the grill.

MASHED POTATOES WITH CABBAGE   Serves 6–8

This is a variation on Colcannon adapted from a book called *Edible Ornamental Garden*, by John Bryan and Coralie Castle.

1½ lb (700 g) hot mashed potatoes
4 oz (110 g) onion, celery stalks and leaves, finely chopped
4 oz (110 g) butter
8 oz (225 g) cabbage, finely shredded
4 juniper berries, lightly crushed
4 tbs rich beef stock
salt, pepper, cayenne

Sauté the onion and celery in the butter until soft. Add the cabbage, juniper berries and stock and cook until tender. Add the potatoes, season and stir thoroughly. Serve dusted with cayenne.

PUNCH-NEP   Serves 4

This can be made for any number of people using equal quantities of potato and white turnip. Here's the recipe for 4.

1 lb (450 g) old potatoes
1 lb (450 g) turnips
4 oz (110 g) butter
2 fl oz (50 ml) cream
salt, pepper

Boil the potato and turnip separately. Mash both with butter and then beat the two together, season well and smooth into a serving dish. Make several deep wells and fill each with cream.

In *Food In England* Dorothy Hartley aptly describes this surprisingly delicious dish as looking like hot alabaster.

CELERIAC AND POTATO PURÉE   Serves 4

This is the most widely regarded of all the combination root vegetable purées and is a good dish to remember when the potatoes seem especially lacking in flavour. It makes a lovely accompaniment to simply grilled meats, and teams well with poultry and sausages.

8 oz (225 g) or half the celeriac's weight of potatoes
1 celeriac weighing around 1 lb (450 g)
3 fat cloves garlic, peeled
3 tbs cream
2 oz (50 g) butter
salt, pepper

Peel and roughly chop the celeriac and potato in similar sized chunks.
Simmer the vegetables and garlic in a pan of salted water until tender.
Drain, mash carefully (the bulk is somewhat unwieldy) and then season
before beating in the cream and butter. Continue beating until you have
created a light, fluffy purée. Serve dotted with butter.

PARSNIP AND POTATO PURÉE   Serves 4

      12 oz (350 g) potatoes
      1 lb (450 g) young parsnips
      1 tbs butter
      ¼–½ pt (150–275 ml) milk
      salt, pepper
      1 tbs chopped parsley and grated nutmeg to garnish

Cook the peeled and chopped vegetables separately in salted water. Mash
and then cream with the butter and milk until the purée is light and
creamy. Reheat and serve garnished with grated nutmeg and parsley.

   This is also very good if the dish is latticed with thin slices of smoked
streaky bacon and put in a hot oven for 10 minutes; in which case omit
the parsley until serving.

PURÉE OF POTATOES FLORENTINE   Serves 4

Marcel Boulestin gives this recipe in his book *101 Ways of Cooking
Potatoes* published in 1932. Boulestin made his purée by 'boiling some
floury potatoes; when cooked drain and put them back into the saucepan.
Dry them a while over the fire, mash them and add butter, salt and pepper. Then little by little add some warm milk and whip the potatoes with a
whip. Do all this over a moderate fire, taking care that the purée does not
catch. Go on whipping and adding milk until you have a purée the
consistency of a very thick cream; the drier the potatoes are when you begin, the more milk they will absorb and the more creamy the purée will be.'

      1½ (700 g) potatoes
      ½ pt (275 ml) milk
      4 oz (110 g) butter
      1 lb (450 g) spinach
      2 oz (50 g) cream
      salt, pepper

Cook the potatoes and mash with the milk. Meanwhile melt the butter and add the spinach. Cover and cook until it has softened and collapsed. Mash the cream into the spinach and boil off any excess liquid. Mix the spinach into the potatoes and serve with croûtons.

ANTON MOSIMANN'S YOUNG NETTLE AND
POTATO PURÉE   Serves 2

This summer purée can be made with spinach if there are no nettles to hand. The recipe is adapted from *Cuisine Naturelle*, a book devoted to *haute cuisine* without *hautes* calories.

> 1 small potato, peeled and diced
> 8 oz (225 g) young nettle tops
> ¾ pt (400 ml) vegetable stock
> 4 oz (110 g) fromage blanc
> salt, pepper, freshly grated nutmeg

Wash the nettle tops in salted water and drain. Place the nettles, potato and stock in a pan, cover and simmer for 20 minutes. Pour off any excess liquid and purée the potato mixture in a liquidiser. Season well and stir in the fromage blanc.

MASHED POTATOES WITH HERBS, SPICES AND FLAVOURINGS

GREEN PURÉE

Prepare the mashed potatoes as for any of the basic recipes (pages 27–28) and whisk in a further knob of butter and 4 oz (110 g) of very finely chopped parsley, chives or mint. The parsley version is especially good with fish but a chive or mint purée is good with lamb.

CREAMED SPICED POTATOES   Serves 4

This recipe, adapted from Ranse Leembruggen's book *Easy Eastern Cooking*, is an unusual accompaniment to barbecued meat and dry curries.

8 oz (225 g) floury-variety potatoes
2 oz (50 g) onions, diced
large handful fresh mint leaves, finely chopped
1 oz (25 g) butter
½ tsp lemon juice
grated rind of ½ lemon
salt, chilli powder

Cook the potatoes and allow to drain thoroughly before mashing. Mix in
the onions, mint and butter, the juice and rind of the lemon and salt. When
thoroughly mixed shape into large or small patties, dust with chilli powder
and serve hot or cold.

POTATO BHURTA   Serves 4–6

The distinctiveness of this recipe comes from the mustard oil so a
substitute oil won't do. You can make your own by frying some black
mustard seeds in hot oil, being carefuly not to burn them. It is particularly
good with curries but is worth making when you fancy something fiery
hot.

2 lb (900 g) potatoes, boiled and mashed
juice of 1 lemon or lime
2 green chillis, finely chopped
1 medium onion, finely chopped
1 tsp mustard oil
salt

Squeeze the lemon or lime over the chillis and onion; after 5 minutes mix
in the mustard oil. Season and beat this mixture into the potatoes. Mix
very thoroughly and serve hot or cold.

MASALA POTATOES   Serves 4

1 lb (450 g) potatoes, cubed and boiled
1 large onion, finely chopped
1 medium-sized green pepper, finely chopped
2 tbs mustard oil
juice of 1 lemon
¼ tsp each coriander powder and turmeric
½ tsp salt

Cook the onion and pepper in the mustard oil over a low flame until both are soft. Stir in the coriander, turmeric and salt. Stir in the potatoes thoroughly and if the mixture is too dry add 1 or 2 tbs of water.

The potatoes will by now be roughly mashed, either leave them in this state or beat them until they make a purée. Stir in the lemon juice, cover and leave to stand for 5 minutes before serving.

ORANGE MASHED POTATOES   Serves 6

This goes very well with duck. A richer oven-baked version appears in *Side Dishes* where it is called *Pommes Siciliennes* (page 252).

    2 lb (900 g) mashed potatoes
    2 medium-sized onions, finely chopped
    4 tbs butter
    4 fl oz (100 ml) crème fraîche
    6 fl oz (175 ml) freshly squeezed orange juice
    finely grated peel from 1 orange

Cook the onions in the butter over a low flame until soft but not coloured. Mix the cooked onions and butter into the potatoes. With the wire whisk carefully beat the cream and orange juice into the potatoes until they are light and fluffy. Mix in half the orange peel and scatter the rest over the potatoes before serving.

GARLIC MASHED POTATOES/PURÉE DE POMMES DE TERRE
À L'AIL   Serves 4–6

This is a wonderful dish that ranks very high as the ultimate mashed potato recipe. Don't be alarmed by the extraordinary amount of garlic the recipe requires, the long cooking removes all the heat and leaves a pungent flavour. Serve with roast lamb.

    2 lb (900 g) floury-variety potatoes, thoroughly drained and mashed
        with 2 oz (50 g) of butter
    2 heads garlic (20–30 cloves)
    4 oz (110 g) butter
    1 oz (25 g) flour
    ½ pt (275 ml) boiling milk
    4 tbs cream
    4 tbs chopped parsley
    ¼ tsp salt

Separate the garlic cloves and drop into boiling water. Drain after 2 minutes and peel. Melt half the butter in a heavy-bottomed lidded pan and add the garlic. Cook gently for 20 minutes until the garlic is soft. Stir in the sifted flour and add the boiling milk and salt. Boil, stirring for 1 minute, liquidise and then cook for a further couple of minutes.

Add this liquor to the hot mash (if you need to reheat the mash, do so in a double burner, mixing continuously) and, when this is incorporated, beat in the cream a little at a time. Finally mix in the parsley and serve.

SAFF MASH   Serves 4

This delicious and stunning recipe for bright yellow mashed potatoes was devised by Simon Hopkinson, the talented young chef at Terence Conran's restaurant Bibendum. The first version of saff mash was created with fish in mind, so it is the fish version that I am giving. Use also as a topping for a fish pie. To serve saff mash with meat, cook the potatoes in chicken stock or water.

  2 lb (900 g) floury-variety potatoes
  Large pan of prepared fish stock
  Generous tsp saffron threads
  1 clove garlic
  ½ pt (275 ml) best quality extra virgin olive oil
  ½ pt (275 ml) thin cream or gold-top milk
  salt, pepper to taste

Lightly peel the potatoes and cut into even-sized pieces. Drop into the fish stock and add the saffron and garlic. Bring slowly to the boil and simmer until the potatoes are cooked, bearing in mind that the slower the cooking the more yellow the potatoes will be.

When cooked strain off the liquid and retain the saffron threads and clove of garlic with the potatoes. Add a tbs or two of the hot liquor to the potatoes and pass through a Mouli légume, sieve or use a masher. If you possess a Kenwood chef use the 'K' beater on speed 2 and gradually add the olive oil and cream until the mixture is light and fluffy. Manual beating is best done carefully and with a wooden spoon. Adjust seasoning and serve. The saffron threads will bleed slightly into the mash giving a pretty effect.

Simon's favourite accompaniment to saff mash is individual portions of cod cooked thus: heat a dessert spoon of olive oil in a thick Le Creuset-type frying pan. Dust the cod with seasoned flour and cook for one minute on each side. Transfer to a very hot oven for five minutes and serve with wedges of lemon and a big bunch of watercress.

Incidentally, the fish stock, now thickened by the potatoes, can be served as a soup. Merely season with salt and pepper and fold in some chopped fresh coriander for an oriental flavour.

MASHED POTATOES WITH PINE NUTS   Serves 6

The addition of spices and fried nuts transform mashed potatoes into an exotic dish. This recipe is adapted from Claudia Roden's *A Book of Middle Eastern Food*.

>   2 lb (900 g) potatoes
>   1 large onion, coarsely chopped
>   2 tbs oil
>   3 oz (75 g) butter
>   3 fl oz (75 ml) milk
>   3 tbs pine nuts
>   1 tsp cinnamon
>   1 tbs parsley, finely chopped
>   a good pinch nutmeg and chilli pepper
>   salt, pepper

Wash and boil the potatoes. Fry the onion in oil till golden, add the pine nuts and let them brown. Peel and mash the potatoes, beat in butter and milk and season with salt, pepper and spices. Serve with the onion and pine nuts on top and a sprinkling of parsley.

9.

Roast

Peter Pirbright in his wacky, post-war antidote to Mrs
Beeton, *Off The Beeton Track*, 1946

Roast potatoes in particular should never be taken for granted. It is no
good just to peel and bung any old potatoes round the roast and expect
them to turn deliciously crispy without any attention.

I always parboil potatoes for roasting for at least 10 minutes, sometimes longer. The advantages are numerous. The cooking is faster, the
potatoes are crisper (they tend to be hard and leathery if they aren't
parboiled) and they seem to accept readily the flavouring of the cooking
fat and any herbs or onions that you might add.

Always parboil potatoes in their skins and, when peeled, cut them to
similar sized pieces. If you like really crunchy roast potatoes, let the
potatoes boil until they are virtually collapsed. Alternatively score each
potato with a fork to get the furrowed field effect or rough-handle them a
bit in the colander.

Always put the potatoes into hot fat. They will absorb less, require less,
won't be so greasy and will crisp up better and faster. If you coat the
potatoes with the oil or fat there is no real need for basting. Always turn
the potatoes at least twice during the cooking so that they roast evenly.
Allow at least 1 hour in a hot oven (425°F/220°C/gas mark 7) to cook
enough regular-sized, decently crisped potatoes to feed 6. Though many
recipes here specify far longer, cooking time can of course be speeded up
if the potatoes are cut into small pieces.

The type of fat or oil used in the roasting pan affects the flavour of the
final product greatly. Dripping or lard, rendered chicken, duck or goose fat,
olive oil, groundnut and sunflower oil are all suitable whatever the
potatoes are to accompany.

BEST VARIETIES FOR ROASTING

Any potato is suitable for roasting but floury varieties such as Cara, Desiree, King Edward, Maris Piper and Pentland Dell are best for roast potatoes with crispy edges.

An 8 oz (225 g) portion of roast potatoes averages 360 calories.

ALASTAIR LITTLE'S CLASSIC ROAST POTATOES   Serves 6

2 lb (900 g) big Jersey Royal, Belle de Fontenay or La Ratte potatoes
olive oil or duck fat (or even foie-gras fat)
coarse sea salt

Peel and parboil the potatoes for 5–10 minutes. Pre-heat the oven to 450°F/230°C/gas mark 8 and heat a very heavy baking tray with sea salt and oil. Meanwhile cut the potatoes in half horizontally, lay on the hot tray and bake for 45 minutes before turning and cooking for a further 30 minutes. Serve with bits of salt clinging to the potatoes.

VERY CRISP ROAST POTATOES   Serves 6

2 lb (900 g) floury-variety potatoes, parboiled in their skins
2 oz (50 g) lard or dripping
salt

Pre-heat the oven to 400°F/200°C/gas mark 6. Peel the potatoes and cut into even-sized pieces. Drag a fork all over the potatoes making ridges; if you can't be bothered with this then rough-handle them in the colander.

Put the lard in a baking tray, heat through and then add the potatoes. Turn them so they are evenly coated with fat, sprinkle with salt and roast for 30 minutes. Turn, salt again and check if they are ready after 20 minutes.

VERY, VERY CRISP ROAST POTATOES   Serves 6

It is essential to make at least twice as many of these as you think you might need. They are quite irresistible.

3 lb (1.4 kg) potatoes, variety is immaterial
6–8 oz (175–225 g) flour
½ pt (275 ml) olive or sunflower oil
salt, pepper

Parboil the potatoes in their skins for 15 minutes. Cool and peel. Cut the potatoes into even sized pieces, the smaller the better. Sieve and then season the flour and roll the potatoes in the mixture.

Meanwhile, pre-heat the oven to 400°F/200°C/gas mark 6 and heat 1 or 2 baking trays with the fat; the fat should be ¼ in (0.5 cm) deep so adjust accordingly. Carefully place your floured potatoes in the hot fat, turn frequently and cook for a minimum of 2 hours. The result will be wonderfully almost-all-crisp potatoes. Scrapings from the dish are an additional perk. Season with salt and pepper and serve.

POTATOES AROUND THE JOINT/POMMES BOULANGÈRES

Potatoes with the Sunday roast were always cooked around the joint in my childhood. I never really found it satisfactory because those potatoes tucked under the meat tended to be soggy and those around the edge were only partially crisped. A great improvement on this method of cooking is to put the joint on a rack above the potatoes so that the fat and juices can run into the potato dish. The amount can be monitored and excess fat drained off and kept for another occasion. Incidentally, potatoes roasted this way can be enhanced by adding a chopped onion.

POTATOES TO ACCOMPANY ROAST CHICKEN

Proceed as for the recipe for Very Crisp Roast Potatoes (page 43) but 10 minutes before the end of cooking, add 4 oz (110 g) finely chopped, thinly sliced bacon and omit the second seasoning of salt. If you follow the method above, with the chicken in a rack above the potatoes, remember to drain the fat regularly or the potatoes will go soggy.

ROAST POTATOES WITH THYME OR ROSEMARY   Serves 4

This is very good with lamb.

    1½ lb (700 g) potatoes
    6 oz (175 g) Spanish onions
    ¼ pt (150 ml) olive oil
    1 sprig rosemary or thyme
    salt, pepper

Pre-heat oven to 400°F/200°C/gas mark 6. Slice onions and cut the potatoes into ½-in (1-cm) thick slices. Mix the two together and season.

Heat a baking tray or large shallow dish and add the oil. Stir in the potatoes and scatter with the chosen herb. Place in the oven and bake for 20 minutes.

Remove and stir around, season again and replace for a further 30–40 minutes. It is done when a crisp layer has formed on the top.

JOHN TOVEY'S FURROWED-FIELD-EFFECT ROAST POTATOES   Serves 6

Ringing the changes with your roast potatoes needs no more than to cut them into different shapes and sizes. The following is John Tovey's lavish version of the furrowed field effect.

> 2 lb (900 g) potatoes
> 4 oz (110 g) beef dripping
> salt

Pre-heat the oven to 375°F/190°C/gas mark 5 and when ready heat up a roasting tray and the dripping. Parboil the potatoes for 5 minutes, peel and cut them into approximately the same sized domes. Using a small paring knife, cut lines from the top to the bottom of the potato halves so they resemble a cock's comb. Paint each potato with hot fat and 'plant' on the baking tray. Sprinkle with salt and roast for 1½ hours. During cooking the edges fan out and are deliciously crisp.

STOCK-ROASTED POTATOES   Serves 4–6

This is a delicious weight-watchers' recipe that uses no fat at all, just hot stock. The end result is a crispy half and a moist soggy half.

> 2 lb (900 g) potatoes, parboiled and peeled
> 1 pt (570 ml) hot stock
> salt
> parsley to garnish

Cut the potatoes into even-sized pieces and put in a large baking tin. Half fill the tin with the hot stock, sprinkle with salt and put in a pre-heated (400°F/200°C/gas mark 6) oven. Cook for 50 minutes until the top is brown and most of the stock has been absorbed. Serve garnished with parsley.

ALASTAIR LITTLE'S IRRESISTIBLE
ROAST POTATOES   Serves 4-6

Alastair Little is obsessive about potatoes and is always trying out new dishes at his eponymously named restaurant. Of this recipe he says there are never any leftovers *however* much you make.

3 lb (1.4 kg) potatoes
4 Knorr chicken stock cubes
8 oz (225 g) butter
4 pts (2.3 l) water
pepper

Dissolve the stock cubes and melt half the butter in the heated water while you parboil the potatoes for 10 minutes. Pre-heat the oven to 400°F/200°C/gas mark 6. Cut the potatoes in half lengthways and then lay each half flat side down and slice in ½-in (1-cm) rounds. Butter a heavy baking dish copiously and strew with the potatoes. Season liberally with pepper. Pour over the stock so that potatoes peek through. Cook until all the liquid has evaporated, about 1 hour.

PAPRIKA ROAST POTATOES   Serves 4

This is a variation on the famous Hungarian Paprika Potatoes (see page 255) cooked fondante-style. They make a good alternative to baked potatoes with cold meat.

2 large potatoes, boiled and peeled
1½ oz (40 g) butter
2 oz (50 g) plain flour
1 oz (25 g) paprika
2 oz (50 g) onion, finely chopped
hot milk and hot water as required
salt, pepper

Pre-heat the oven to 350°F/180°C/gas mark 4, butter a shallow dish and cut the potatoes horizontally into ½-in (1-cm) thick slices. Make a layer of potatoes, sprinkle on half the sifted flour, season with salt, pepper and half the paprika and then with half the onions. Repeat and finish with potatoes. Season and pour on enough milk and water (in equal quantities) almost to cover. Dot with butter, cover with foil in which you've punched a few holes. Bake for 1 hour, remove the foil and bake for a further 30 minutes.

SPICED ROAST POTATOES   Serves 6–8

This is an adaptation of an exotic roast potato recipe given by Colin Spencer in his book *Cordon Vert*.

>   6–8 large potatoes
>   2 tsp sunflower oil
>   5 bay leaves, crushed
>   1 tsp each turmeric, garam masala and chilli powder
>   1 tsp muscovado sugar
>   4 cloves garlic, crushed
>   1 pt (570 ml) natural yoghurt
>   salt, pepper
>   2 oz (5 g) coriander leaves, chopped

Heat the oil and fry the bay leaves and spices for a few minutes, then stir in the sugar and garlic. Season with salt and pepper and mix into the yoghurt.

Pre-heat the oven to 400°F/200°C/gas mark 6 while you parboil the potatoes for 10 minutes. Drain, peel and prick each potato all over. Place the potatoes in a large shallow ovenproof dish and pour over the yoghurt mixture, mix around and bake for 30–40 minutes. Serve sprinkled with coriander.

10.

Sauté

The closest translation of this generic term is 'to jump', and the precise way to sauté is to heat some oil or clarified butter in a wide shallow pan (called a *sauteuse*) and to quick fry small pieces of food while giving the pan the occasional shake. While some dishes lend themselves to this *à la minute* treatment, many sauté or pan-fried dishes require long, slow cooking after the initial stage of cooking at a high temperature to seal. Potatoes should either be parboiled or rinsed and dried.

Any frying pan is suitable for sauté dishes but there is less chance of food burning if the pan is thick and heavy, and many recipes require that the pan is covered. An asbestos mat gives an even distribution of heat. Heating the pan before adding the oil helps prevent food sticking to the pan.

FATS AND OILS

Ordinary butter is not suitable for sauté dishes because it burns at a low temperature, turns brown, smokes and ruins the food. Mixed with a little oil (2–4 tsp of oil to 2 oz/50 g butter) butter can reach a higher temperature without burning. When heated the mixture will begin to foam and that is the right moment to start cooking. Salt burns easily in the sauté pan so always use salt-free butter and don't season the food. If a recipe demands butter, it should be clarified. This is a simple and worthwhile chore but clarified butter is widely available in Indian and Middle Eastern food shops, where it's called ghee. To clarify butter, melt it in a frying pan over a low heat. When the whole surface is bubbling, remove from the heat and allow to cool slightly before you pour it through muslin, cheesecloth or a coffee filter paper into a storage jar. The impurities that make butter go rancid are now removed and the ghee will keep indefinitely.

Rendered bacon fat also burns at a low temperature but, like butter, is 'saved' when mixed with a little oil. Bake or fry streaky bacon or thick fatty rinds until the fat begins to run. This takes 10–15 minutes. Strain through muslin and store.

Duck, goose and foie-gras fat are the ultimate for roasting and sautéeing potatoes. The fat can be collected during the cooking, poured into a jar and stored. In France goose fat is bottled and tinned and widely available. In this country the only retail outlet is Harrods, who import it from France. It costs about half the price of the bird! Game butchers can be persuaded to sell goose fat pulled from inside the bird, in which case it should be rendered before use. Chop the fat into ½-inch pieces and simmer for 20 minutes in a covered saucepan with ½ pint water (275 ml) to draw the fat out of the tissues. Uncover the pan and boil slowly to evaporate the water. When the spluttering is finished you will end up with a pale yellow liquor dotted with globules. Strain and reserve.

Olive oil, beef dripping, lard (pork fat), groundnut (peanut), sunflower and corn oil are all suitable for sauté dishes.

BEST VARIETIES FOR SAUTÉEING

Any potato can be sautéed but firm-fleshed varieties are most suitable. Any Dutch, Egyptian or Cyprus variety, Pink Fir Apple, Charlotte, Cornichon, La Ratte, Kipfler or Belle de Fontenay.

SAUTÉ POTATOES/POMMES DE TERRE RISSOLÉES   Serves 6

> 2 lb (900 g) waxy-variety potatoes
> olive oil, clarified butter, beef dripping or lard
> salt

Bring the potatoes to the boil and cook for 10 minutes. Drain, peel and cut up into even-sized pieces.

Heat up enough fat to fill a large sauté pan to a depth of ¼ inch (0.5 cm). Add sufficient potatoes to cover the bottom of the pan. Turn down the heat and, if you are cooking over gas, use an asbestos mat to distribute the heat evenly. Cook for 10 minutes, turn and repeat or shake the pan every couple of minutes. The potatoes should have crispy brown skins and be 'melt-in-the-mouth' inside. Sprinkle with salt before serving.

SAUTÉ POTATOES WITH ONIONS/POMMES DE TERRE LYONNAISES

Follow the recipe for sauté potatoes (page 49) and in a separate pan sauté 8 oz (225 g) finely sliced onions. A couple of minutes before you are ready to serve the dish, stir the onions into the potatoes.

SAUTÉ NEW POTATOES/POMMES FONDANTES   Serves 6

> 2 lb (900 g) small new potatoes, scrubbed and dried
> 2 oz (50 g) clarified butter
> salt

Heat up the butter and, when bubbling, add sufficient potatoes to cover the pan. Turn down to a low heat and leave the potatoes to cook for 15 minutes. Give the pan the odd shake and if necessary turn them over.

Cook for a further 10 minutes or until they are browned all over. Sprinkle with salt before serving.

SAUTÉ NEW POTATOES WITH GARLIC/POMMES FONDANTES À L'AIL

Follow the recipe for sauté new potatoes above but throw in half a dozen cloves of garlic, unpeeled. When the potatoes are cooked either squeeze out the soft flesh of the garlic and spread over the potatoes or leave the cloves whole. Sprinkle the potatoes with salt before serving.

TURNED POTATOES   Serves 4–6

This is a wasteful but professional-looking way to present sauté potatoes.

> 2 lb (900 g) potatoes
> 4 oz (110 g) clarified butter or butter and oil

Cut the potatoes in half and then quarters. Square off the rounded end and trim all curves to make an oblong. Trim the length of the potato to make a hexagonal barrel. Blanch in boiling water for 2 minutes, drain and proceed as for sauté potatoes (page 49), browning evenly on all sides.

If your potatoes end up looking more like large olives than hexagonal barrels, call them Chateau Potatoes/*Pommes de Terre Château*. These are the traditional accompaniment to a Chateaubriand steak.

SAUTÉ POTATO BALLS/POMMES DE TERRE PARISIENNES

Use a melon baller to scoop out balls from large, peeled potatoes. Rinse in cold water, drain, pat dry and proceed as for sauté potatoes (page 49). They take slightly less time.

DICED POTATOES SAUTÉED IN BUTTER/POMMES DE TERRE SAUTÉES EN DÉS

Dice the potatoes, put into cold water, drain, pat dry and proceed as for sauté potatoes (page 49).

When diced potatoes are cooked in goose fat and sprinkled with chopped parsley towards the end of cooking, they are a traditional accompaniment to preserved goose.

DICED POTATOES SAUTÉED WITH GARLIC AND PARSLEY/POMMES DE TERRE PAYSANNES

Cook the washed, diced potatoes as in preceding recipe but in goose or pork fat, and a few minutes before serving add 3 cloves of minced garlic. Stir into the potatoes and just before serving sprinkle with salt and chopped flat-leaf parsley.

SPICED SAUTÉED POTATOES   Serves 6

This is a 200-year-old recipe adapted from Ranse Leembruggen's book *Easy Eastern Cooking*.

        2 lb (900 g) small new potatoes, scrubbed
        4 tbs ghee
        2 cloves garlic, crushed
        2 tsp turmeric
        4 tsp each coriander, black cumin seeds
        4 tsp sugar
        salt, pepper
        chives and flat-leaf parsley, chopped

Parboil the potatoes for 5 minutes and then drain. Heat the ghee and when it begins to bubble sauté the spices and garlic for 1 minute. Add the potatoes, stirring them around to get an even coating of spices and sprinkle on the sugar, a little salt and pepper.

Bake for 30 minutes in a moderate oven (350°F/180°C/gas mark 4), turning them twice. Serve sprinkled with the parsley and chives.

POMMES DE TERRE MAÎTRE D'HÔTEL   Serves 4

1 lb (450 g) firm-variety potatoes
4 oz clarified butter or butter and oil
salt, pepper
3 oz parsley, finely chopped

Boil the potatoes for 10 minutes, drain and peel. Cut into ¼-in (0.5-cm) slices. Heat the butter and when hot add the potatoes. Turn down the temperature immediately and sauté gently for 5 minutes on each side. They should be golden and crispy but not browned.

Sprinkle with the parsley, salt and plenty of black pepper before serving.

SAUTÉ PANCAKES

RÖSTI   Serves 4–6

2 lb (900 g) potatoes
1 tbs olive oil
1 oz (25 g) unsalted butter
salt, pepper

Parboil the potatoes for 10 minutes and allow to cool in their skins. Peel and grate with a coarse grater. (The potatoes are easier to grate if they are chilled.) Use a 9-in (23-cm), heavy, non-stick frying pan and heat up the oil and butter. When the oil is very hot spread the potato evenly into the pan. Turn down the heat and cook for 10 minutes. To turn the pancake over put a plate that fits snugly inside the pan, flip it over and slip the pancake back into the hot pan. It might not sound like it, but it makes the operation slightly easier if you put a bread board on top of the plate.

Cook for a further 10 minutes. If the pan seems rather dry, add more butter and oil. Season well, slip on to a plate and serve.

SALLY CLARKE'S STRAW POTATO PANCAKES   Serves 4

These have to be made to order but are very quick to make. They are compulsive on their own, very good with simply prepared meats and game but are a personal favourite served under pan-fried liver with a wild mushroom and red wine sauce.

> 4 medium-sized Maris Piper potatoes
> 1 dsp each clarified butter and peanut oil for each pancake
> salt, pepper

Peel 1 potato, grate on the julienne slicer of a mandoline and heat the oil in a non-stick pan. When it's smoking pile in the unrinsed potato and pat down. Cook for 45 seconds, flip it over and turn down the heat. Season the cooked side and removed to draining paper. The finished pancakes can be stacked in a warm oven; they will keep well enough for 4–5 minutes.

LARGE POTATO STRAW CAKE/PAILLASSON DE POMMES DE TERRE Serves 4

A *paillasson* is a thin straw mat which is what this dish should resemble. If the mat is too thick it will be raw in the middle and burnt on the outside; it should be cooked as swiftly as possible. Better to make 2 paillassons than 1 thick one.

> 8 medium-sized floury-variety potatoes
> 4 oz (110 g) clarified butter or butter and oil
> salt, pepper

Grate the potatoes on a coarse grater or mandoline and rinse twice in cold water. Depending on the size of your pan/s (10–12 in/25–30.5 cm would be ideal to make one paillasson) take out all or half the potatoes, drain and wrap them up tightly in a tea towel to get rid of all moisture.

Heat up most of the fat and when it's smoking press down the potatoes to make a ½-in (1-cm) layer. Adjust the heat so it is still very hot but doesn't burn the potatoes and, as soon as the mat is crisp underneath (about 10 minutes), turn the pancake. Quickly slip the rest of the fat in the pan before you cook the other side.

Cook for a further 5 minutes, slip out of the pan on to a serving plate, sprinkle with salt and pepper and serve.

ANTON MOSIMANN'S POTATOES HOME-STYLE Serves 4

For his paillasson Anton Mosimann uses melted chicken fat.

14 oz (400 g) julienne of potato, washed and dried
1¼ oz (30 g) chicken fat, melted
1¼ oz (30 g) butter
salt, pepper

Proceed as for the paillasson (page 53).

POMMES DE TERRE LIMOUSINE

Proceed as for the paillasson (page 53) but add a few finely chopped pieces of bacon amongst the potatoes. The addition of finely chopped garlic is also very good.

GALETTE DE POMMES DE TERRE   Serves 4

This is a pan-cooked version of *Pommes Anna* (page 80) and is served cut in wedges like a cake. It has a rich butter flavour, the outside layer is crisp while the inside is soft. Individual galettes can be cooked in small gratin dishes.

1½ lb (700 g) waxy-variety potatoes
1½ oz (40 g) butter
1½ fl oz (40 ml) oil
salt, pepper, grated nutmeg

Peel and slice the potatoes very thinly and evenly (a mandoline takes the fag out of this) and rinse in plenty of cold water.

Heat the butter and oil and spread the drained and dried potato slices into the pan. Turn the heat down, cover the pan and leave to cook for 15 minutes. Carefully turn the pancake over and let the underside brown for 5 minutes.

Season with nutmeg, salt and pepper and serve slices cut from the pan or turned out whole on a flat dish.

LA TRUFFADO

I have Elizabeth David to thank for the recipe for this very delicious variation on the potato galette. As she explains in *French Country Cooking* this peasant dish from the Auvergne relies on the local Cantal cheese. It is available over here but a real (not processed) Cheshire is the closest equivalent.

Proceed exactly as for the preceding galette recipe (page 54) but add a few dice of bacon and a finely chopped clove of garlic between the potato slices. When the potatoes are almost cooked add the cheese, about 2 oz (50 g), chopped into very small pieces. Cover the pan and leave the cheese to melt for 5 minutes before serving.

PATATE ALLA BORGHESE   Serves 6

  2 lb (900 g) potatoes
  4 oz (110 g) clarified butter
  juice of 2 lemons
  salt, pepper, chopped parsley

Boil the potatoes in their skins until they are completely cooked. Peel and slice into ¼-in (0.5-cm) rounds.

Melt the clarified butter and when bubbling, arrange a layer of potatoes in the pan, season and pour over some lemon juice and continue making layers until all the potatoes are finished. Pour any remaining lemon juice into the pan and cook covered over a low heat for 15 minutes. Cook for a further 10 minutes uncovered. The potatoes will have formed a crisp bottom layer and the top potatoes will be saturated with butter and lemon juice.

Don't worry if you fail to lift the 'pancake' out cleanly, it tastes so good that it doesn't matter if the dish looks a bit of a mess. Sprinkle with parsley, season with pepper and serve.

POMMES DE TERRE GASTRONOME/POMMES DE TERRE CUSSY

'Take big yellow potatoes, cut off the two ends, and cut them with a special cutter (called in French a colonne) into cork-shaped chunks, about 2½ cm (1 in) in diameter. Cut them into slices 5 mm (¼ in) thick, putting them into water as you cut them. Dry on a cloth to absorb all water. Put them into a big pan with 225 g (8 oz) hot clarified butter, so that they cook gently, colouring without sticking to the pan or drying up. In the meantime, slice 6 or 8 truffles, toss them in butter with 1 tablespoon of Madeira and a piece of chicken jelly the size of a walnut. When the potatoes are cooked and acquire a fine golden colour, remove them from the fire, add the truffles and the juice of ½ a lemon and serve piping hot.

'We owe this side dish [!] to the late Monsieur de Cussy, a fine gourmet and former administrator of Napoleon's palace.'

11.

Deep Fry

'I have to declare my interest in the matter of deep-fried potatoes. They are most unsuitable for making in the ordinary family kitchen. The telephone rings, a child crawls round your feet, the cat demands his supper with a paw, and your attention is diverted. I once set a pan of oil on fire in this sort of way. The horror was appalling, out of all proportion to the black ceiling.'

Jane Grigson, *Jane Grigson's Vegetable Book*, 1983

And so I begin this important chapter with a list of safety rules for deep frying:

1. Never leave a deep-fat frying pan unattended when cooking.
2. Always ensure that the handle is turned towards the side of the cooker to prevent it being knocked over.
3. If the fat starts to smoke thick acrid fumes, turn the heat off immediately. This means it is near to flash point when the whole lot will go up in flames.

If the fat does catch fire:

1. Turn off the heat immediately.
2. Do not attempt to carry the pan anywhere.
3. Do not attempt to put out the fire with water.
4. Smother the fire with the lid (this may not be practicable) and/or with a thick damp towel. Anything will do.
5. Do not touch the pan until the fat has cooled down.

CORRECT DEEP FRYING

The most sophisticated deep fryers have an inbuilt thermometer which indicates by colour the heat of the fat in the pan. It is also likely to be marked with lines for the minimum and maximum safe levels if oil (normally about 4 pts/2.3 l) and fitted with a deodorising filter in the lid. This is made of charcoal and should be removed after 20–30 fry-ups.

It is important that the oil is checked, before use, for leftovers from previous use. This can be done by dragging the oil with absorbent kitchen paper but the most effective way is to strain the oil through muslin or a coffee filter paper. Impurities left in the oil decompose at high temperatures and will cause unpleasant smells and off flavours. It is also wise to wash out the chip pan and basket regularly and to scrape off the inevitable gunk that accumulates. This is not a pleasant task but a sensible one. Always dry the pan and basket very thoroughly: moisture in the fat affects its longevity and also causes splattering. Change the oil regularly and never mix oils.

Always heat the oil up gently to the required temperature. If you don't own a food thermometer you can do a simple test with a chip. If the chip sinks to the bottom of the pan and there is no movement of the fat it is not sufficiently hot. If the fat bubbles immediately around the chip and the chip stays on top of the fat, then the temperature is correct.

This is another method: 'It is possible to test the heat of the fat by adding a drop of water to it or by dipping any substance into it other than purified fat. If the sound of sizzling is deep and low, the fat is boiling, if it is sharp and high, the fat is frying or crying out that it is hot enough. This is the moment at which to put into it whatever is to be fried.' (Reculet in *Le Cuisinier Practicien*, 1859.)

Don't be mean with the oil and don't attempt to cook too many chips (or whatever) at any one time. The success of good deep frying depends on the clean oil being at the right temperature. The moment the food hits the hot oil it is sealed and doesn't absorb the fat. Food put into fat that isn't hot enough absorbs the fat. It also takes an inordinately long time to cook.

The correct temperature for deep frying chips is 300°F/150°C for the initial plunge and 360°F/185°C for the second cooking. Remember that when the food is immersed in the fat it lowers the temperature immediately.

Always rinse the potatoes in cold water after they have been cut into their appropriate size. This removes the starch that makes them stick together. Soaking the cut potatoes in salty water helps make the chips extra crispy. Pat dry in a tea towel.

I leave the last word to Brillat-Savarin: 'The whole virtue of good frying lies in the element of surprise. The boiling liquid, with its capacity to brown or char, carries out a surprise attack on the surface of foodstuffs plunged into it, at the very moment of immersion.'

FATS AND OILS

Rendered fat from a duck, goose, foie gras, ox kidney or bacon, ghee (clarified butter) and olive oil produce delicious fried potatoes but, with the exception of suet (ox kidney) which is commercially packed, it isn't really practicable to deep fry in any of these fats except for special occasions. Furthermore all these fats actually contribute a flavour to the potatoes and that isn't always appropriate. Lard, groundnut and sunflower oil are highly suitable, cheaper, widely available and provided they are kept free of impurities, won't radically affect the flavour of the food.

BEST VARIETIES FOR DEEP FRYING

Arran Comet, Maris Peer, Ulster Sceptre, Desiree, King Edward, Maris Piper and Pentland Dell.

Leaving aside the temperature of the oil, the size of the chip determines how much fat it absorbs and therefore the number of calories. Thin cuts have a greater surface area so are more fattening than the good old English chip. Crinkle cuts are also more fattening than straight cuts. An 8 oz portion (around 225 g) has approximately 500 calories.

BASIC CHIP RECIPE/POMMES FRITES PONT NEUF   Serves 4

My idea of perfect chips are served at Manzi's, the Italian fish restaurant in Leicester Square.

> 4 large floury-variety potatoes
> minimum 4 pts (2.3 l) groundnut oil
> salt, pepper

Put the oil on to heat at a low temperature. Peel the potatoes, rinse and put into a bowl of cold water. Cut the potato in strips that are approximately ½ in (1 cm) wide and 2 ins (5 cm) long. Alternatively use a special chip cutter that can deal with one potato at a time. Put the chips into a fresh bowl of water until the oil has reached 300°F/150°C.

For best results cook the chips in batches so they don't all lump together. Dry off the first batch, put into the chip basket and lower into the fat. Cook for 5–6 minutes or until they get flabby-looking, are soft but not browned. Shake the basket a couple of times to ensure even cooking. Lift the basket and drain. At this point the cooking can be arrested indefinitely. When you are ready to continue, bring the oil to 360°F/185°C and plunge the chips into the hot fat to brown. This takes only 2–3 minutes. Drain, put on a hot serving dish and keep warm in the oven (275°F/140°C/gas mark 1).

When all the chips are ready sprinkle with salt and serve with tomato ketchup, vinegar, lemon or whatever is your fancy.

CRINKLE-CUT CHIPS

To make crinkle-cut chips you will need a special crinkle-cut chopper. Its blade is slightly angled and the peeled potatoes are cut first into grooved slices, then cut into wavy-edged chips. Proceed as for basic chip recipe (page 58).

CHIPS WITH SKINS

Proceed as for the basic chip recipe (page 58) but instead of peeling the potatoes, scrub them thoroughly before slicing. At Bob Payton's American restaurants (Chicago Rib Shack, Henry J. Beans and Chicago Pizza Pie Factory) they call chips with their skins on 'strips'.

THE CHIP BUTTY

To celebrate the 150th anniversary of the Royal College of Art, a lavish *Artists' Cookbook* was produced with an introduction by Henry Moore. Alf Dunn gave his recipe for chip butties under a wonderful pen and ink drawing.

Proceed as for the basic chip recipe (page 58) but when the chips are done sprinkle with garlic salt. 'While the chips are cooking, cut slices of granary bread and spread thickly with butter. Drain the chips and fill the sandwiches, sprinkling them with salt and vinegar. A good sandwich should be more chips than bread and should ooze butter when bitten. Serve with a glass of beer.'

FRIED POTATO PEEL   Serves 4

In Birmingham, I am reliably informed, chips are coated in a thin batter to give an even golden colour. More interesting, I think, is this recipe, to be made when you need peeled potatoes for something else.

    3 large floury-variety potatoes
    oil for deep frying
    4 oz (110 g) plain flour
    2–3 tbs water
  · salt, pepper

Put the oil on to heat (to 375°F/190°C) and make a stiff batter by mixing the sifted flour with salt, pepper and a little water. Scrub the potatoes and peel. When the oil is ready, dip the peel in the batter and deep fry in batches until crisp. Children love these.

FRITES À LA CRÈME   Serves 6–8

This Burgundian dish is one to remember when there is a mushroom glut or you are lucky enough to have a successful mushroom hunt. It is best made with wild mushrooms.

    2 lb (900 g) potatoes
    2 lb (900 g) mushrooms, cleaned and sliced
    3 tbs butter
    1 tbs vegetable oil
    2 eggs
    1 tbs wine vinegar
    3 tbs cream
    2 cloves garlic, crushed
    salt, pepper

Prepare the *frites*, following the basic chip recipe (page 58) and keep warm. Sauté the cleaned mushrooms in the butter and oil while you whisk together the eggs, vinegar, cream, salt and pepper and garlic. Put the *frites* in a large hot serving dish, stir in the mushrooms and mix in the egg mixture. It is important that everything is very hot, so that the egg vinaigrette is very slightly cooked.

CHIP CURRY 1 Serves 4–6

    1½ lb (700 g) waxy-variety potatoes
    1 tsp each poppy seeds, paprika and cumin seeds
    1 tbs coriander seeds
    5 green cardamoms
    6 cloves
    6 black peppercorns
    10 almonds
    4 cloves garlic
    1 in (2.5 cm) piece of fresh ginger
    2 onions, finely chopped
    ghee and oil for frying
    ½ tsp each turmeric powder and garam masala
    2 tsp salt
    8 fl oz (275 ml) yoghurt

Peel the potatoes, cut them in thick chips and prick them all over with a fork. Leave to soak in cold water while you prepare the spices.

Grind the poppy seeds, cumin, coriander, cardamoms, cloves, peppercorns, almonds, garlic and ginger in a little water to make a paste. Fry the onion in a small amount of ghee and when soft add the paprika, turmeric, salt and paste. Cook gently for 5 minutes and stir in the yoghurt.

Remove from the heat while you cook the chips (see page 58) until golden. Drain the chips and mix with the yoghurt mixture, stir in the garam masala and cook for a further 5 minutes in the frying pan. Serve with puris for an Indian chip butty.

CHIP CURRY 2 Serves 4–6

    1½ lb (700 g) waxy-variety potatoes
    1 oz (25 g) each ground coriander, turmeric, ground ginger and fenugreek seed
    1 large onion, finely chopped
    1 tsp each salt and chilli powder
    8 oz (225 g) fresh tomatoes
    8 cloves garlic
    ghee and oil for frying

Sauté the fenugreek seed in the ghee and add the onion. When the onion is limp add the salt and all the spices, cook for a minute while you quarter the tomatoes and mash the garlic. Add these to the pan, cook for a couple of minutes and then stir in the yoghurt and a little water.

Take off the heat and cook the chips (page 58). Drain and add the chips to the yoghurt mixture, simmer gently for 10 minutes and add a little more water if it gets too dry.

MATCHES/STICKS/POMMES ALLUMETTES

Cut the potatoes (allowing one large potato per person) into ¼-in (0.5-cm) wide and 2½-in (6-cm) long strips. Rinse, pat dry and drop into very hot fat (360°F/185°C) for 5–10 minutes until golden brown. Drain on absorbent kitchen paper and serve sprinkled with salt.

SPICY MATCHSTICKS/ALOO KA TALA HUA LACCHA   Serves 4–6

        1 lb (450 g) potatoes
        4 oz (110 g) onion, chopped
        2 cloves garlic, peeled
        1 dried red chilli
        1 tsp ground cumin
        ½ tsp ground coriander seeds
        oil for frying
        salt

Using a food processor blend the onion, garlic and chilli into a paste and stir in the cumin and coriander. Prepare the potatoes as for the preceding recipe, cooking them in batches until very crisp. Drain each batch on absorbent kitchen paper and set aside to cool in a serving dish while you cook the chilli mixture.

Heat a little oil in a frying pan and gently sauté the spices until they are brown and dry. Remove from the heat, cool and scrape out the spices. In a small bowl mix the spices with the salt and sprinkle over the sticks, mix thoroughly and serve with drinks.

STRAW POTATOES/POMMES PAILLE/KARTOFFEL SOLOMKOI

Cut the potatoes (allowing one large potato per person) in long, thin julienne or use a mandoline. Rinse in plenty of cold water, dry thoroughly and plunge into very hot fat (360°F/185°C) for 2–3 minutes until golden brown.

JONATHAN WAXMAN'S SHOE-STRING POTATOES

Scrub some waxy-variety potatoes (allowing one large potato per person) and grate them on a mandoline with their skins on. Cover with water, rinse and spin dry in a lettuce spinner. Plunge in batches into very hot fat (360°F/185°C) and cook for 2 minutes. Drain, sprinkle with salt. Alternatively, toss with a mixture of finely chopped thyme flowers and rosemary, salt and pepper.

Jonathan Waxman is the chef/proprietor of Jams in New York and London.

STRAW NESTS/NIDS POUR LE DRESSAGE DES POMMES DE TERRE FRITES

You will need potato nest baskets for this recipe. They look like two wire ladles, one fits inside the other and they are clipped together.

Cut the potatoes as for making straw potatoes (page 62) but don't rinse them in water; the starch helps to hold them together. Overlap the straws inside the large 'basket' and clip the smaller basket into position. Plunge into very hot fat (360°F/185°C) and cook for 4 or 5 minutes until golden brown. Drain and remove from the mould. Serve filled with savoury titbits; traditionally they are filled with peas and served as an accompaniment to chicken kiev.

DEEP FRIED NEW POTATOES

Peel, thinly slice (¼ in /0.5 cm) and rinse the new potatoes in plenty of cold water. Deep fry in batches in very hot oil (360°F/185°C) for 5–10 minutes until golden brown.

FRIED POTATO BALLS/POMMES DE TERRE PARISIENNES

Use a melon baller to scoop out balls from large, peeled floury-variety potatoes. Rinse in cold water, drain, deep fry at 360°F/185°C for 5 minutes.

MOCK ROAST POTATOES   Serves 4

2 lb (900 g) floury-variety potatoes
oil for frying
salt

Choose even-sized potatoes and boil them in their skins until almost done. Pre-heat the chip pan to 300°F/150°C. When the potatoes have cooled slightly, peel and cut into appropriate sizes. Deep fry in 3 batches for 8 minutes or until the potatoes are golden and look as if they've roasted. Keep warm and sprinkle with salt before serving.

CRISPS   <u>Serves 4</u>

'Thirty-nine-year-old Willie Newgent of Armagh holds the Guinness Book of Records for crisp consumption. He can eat 30 bags of crisps without a drink in 24 minutes, 33.6 seconds. That's two bags every 1½ minutes. It's a 20-year-old record.'

The UK crisp and snack market is worth £1 billion a year and crisp sales continue to rise at 7% a year. Last year, according to the Snack, Nut and Crisp Federation, we crunched our way through five million six hundred packets. That means we average around 30 lb (13 kg) per head a year.

It may help you to resist the enormous choice of crisp styles and flavours now on sale when I tell you that the wholesale and retail profit on a packet of crisps is approximately half the packet price. Also interesting is the fact that the Chancellor of the Exchequer considers crisps a luxury item so they are VAT rated. There is no VAT on smoked salmon and caviare.

If you make your own crisps it will cost you 2p to make the equivalent number of crisps in a 30 g packet.

There are nearly 550 calories in a 4 oz (110 g) portion of crisps; that's more than double the calories in the same quantity of chips.

Home-made crisps are also called game chips and are a traditional accompaniment to game; in which case their French name is *en liard*, in America they are chips.

> 2 medium-sized floury potatoes
> oil for frying
> salt

Peel the potatoes and, using a sharp knife or mandoline, cut the potatoes into wafer-thin slices. Put immediately into a big bowl of cold water. Swirl around to get all the starch out and dry in a cloth.

Cook in small batches in very hot oil (375°F/190°C) for 2 minutes. Drain and serve on a doily sprinkled with salt. Uneaten crisps can be kept in an air-tight tin.

CRISPS WITH SKINS

Scrub the potatoes instead of peeling and proceed as for the preceding crisp recipe above.

SOUFFLÉ POTATOES   <u>Serves 4</u>

These are similar to crisps but more impressive. The potato slices should be cut marginally thicker than for crisps and they are not washed. Like chips they are cooked twice and on the second cooking they puff up like balloons.

In a traditional French kitchen crisps and soufflé potatoes are made in a large oval cast iron pot called a *négresse*. In the case of soufflés, two *négresses* are on the go at the same time and it falls to the most junior trainee-chef to learn this very hazardous skill. The *négresse* has to be manually rotated with a very fast action to get the air circulating in the oil. This has to be done with one hand while the other is cooking the potatoes and scooping them out with a special slotted spoon called a spider. Fortunately, on a domestic level soufflé potatoes can be prepared very easily in a chip pan.

> 3 medium-sized floury-variety potatoes
> oil for frying
> salt

Peel the potatoes and cut into ⅛-in (0.25-cm) slices. Do not put into water, but wipe dry.

Pre-heat the oil to 300°F/150°C and cook the potatoes in small batches (they will have a tendency to stick together because of the starch). Put the slices in the oil and gently shake the pan while they begin to blow. This takes a couple of minutes. Drain on greaseproof or absorbent paper while you cook the rest. The soufflés will deflate and can be left in this state indefinitely.

When required, bring the oil up to 360°F/185°C and throw in the baggy crisps, cooking a handful at a time. They will puff and brown. Drain and serve sprinkled with salt.

Like many good things, this method of cooking was discovered by accident. On the inaugural train journey into the station at Saint-Germain-en-Laye in 1837 the train had great difficulty getting up the final slope into the new station. When the party of dignitaries arrived several hours late for their celebratory lunch, the restaurant chef was taken completely by surprise. In his haste to provide some food immediately, he threw cold fried potatoes into hot fat. He was amazed to see them all puff up. An analytical chemist called Chevreul looked into the phenomenon and explained that when the potatoes are plunged into boiling fat for the second time, the surface of the slices is transformed into a waterproof skin, which swells as a result of the volatilisation of the water contained inside.

12.

Bake

One of the most enticing and evocative kitchen smells is that of the baked potato. Its association with childhood and most particularly with Bonfire Night keeps it forever as something of a treat. It remains too a comfort food but one that can be transformed daily with a different stuffing.

The jacket potato is The Great Standby and The Complete Meal. Treated simply with a pinch of salt and a generous dollop of butter it's a pauper's supper fit for a king. With a liberal grating of mature Cheddar cheese it's even better. After Christmas it really comes into its own. When served with pickles, a couple of crunchy baked potatoes make the prospect of unlimited cold turkey almost seem attractive.

In France they call the jacket potato *pommes de terre au four* – *au four* for short – or most often *robe de chambre*, a corruption of the original *robe des champs* (of the fields), meaning in their skins as they were grown. Many French chefs use the flesh of baked potatoes for making *pommes purée* because the steam-cooking makes for dry potato flesh. It also breaks down the flesh of their waxy potato varieties.

Perhaps because the French don't go in for the mealy variety of potato which is best suited to baking, their baked potatoes tend to be elaborately stuffed. These baked potatoes are usually called *pommes de terre farcies*. They are prepared by partial baking then the flesh is scooped out, mixed with the stuffing and returned for a final baking. The potato becomes a vehicle for very fanciful combinations and is a very different animal from the potato baked in the embers of the dying bonfire.

The secret of perfect baked potatoes is to put the potatoes into a very hot oven; from 400–425°F/200–220°C/gas mark 7) and to cook them for a minimum of 1 hour. The exact length of time depends on the size of the potato and the number of potatoes being cooked – they will take longer the more there are. Any variety of potato will taste good baked but mealy varieties are best. The starch expands under the intense heat and the potato becomes fluffy on the inside and with a nice crisp skin: the combination that makes the baked potato such a delight. Some people rub salt or oil into the washed skin to make it crispy but I rather like the nutty flavour that is most prevalent if the skin is merely washed. Also good is the burnt flesh edge of halved potatoes. If you favour a soft skin, wrap the potato in foil.

To allow the steam to escape cut the potato with a cross or prick it a few times with a fork. Baked potatoes can be partially cooked in advance and finished to order, this is especially useful to remember when providing baked potatoes for a party. In fact in his delightful *Cooking In Ten Minutes* Edouard de Pomiane recommends keeping a stock of baked potatoes for making instant meals.

BEST VARIETIES FOR BAKING

With the exception of Marks and Spencer's baking potatoes, avoid those over-sized polythene and expanded polystyrene-wrapped baking potatoes now on every supermarket shelf. The following floury varieties are the best: Cara, Desiree, Maris Piper, Pentland Squire, Pentland Crown and Pentland Dell, Wilja, Romano, King Edward and Golden Wonder.

A 7 oz (200 g) baked potato served with a modest amount of butter or sunflower margarine has approximately 170 calories. Contrary to popular belief, baked potatoes are not overly fattening; it's the topping or the filling that's the culprit!

BASIC BAKED POTATO RECIPE   Serves 6

> 6 large floury-variety potatoes
> At least 2 oz (50 g) butter per potato
> salt, pepper

Pre-heat oven to 425°F/220°C/gas mark 7. Scrub the potatoes and pierce with a fork or make some sort of slit to allow the steam to escape. Place in the middle of the oven and cook for between 1 and 1½ hours. Serve instantly with plenty of butter, salt and pepper.

If you like garlic, make an incision at either end of the potato and slip in half a clove of garlic before baking.

THE KARATE CHOP METHOD

Rosemary Stark, the former cookery editor of *Options*, believes that the
best baked potatoes are cooked entirely in their own steam. Potatoes are
scrubbed but not pierced, rubbed with salt while still wet and put into a
pre-heated oven. The ideal temperature would be 400°F/200°C/gas mark
6 for 1½ hours but temperature is immaterial to the final effect.

When the potato flesh feels soft to the touch (on no account pierce the
skin) remove and place on a wooden board. Cover the potato with a
folded cloth and crack it open with a swift karate-style chop with the side
of your hand. This alarming method lets the steam out quickly and the
potato is wonderfully floury.

One word of warning; on no account raise the temperature of the oven
suddenly, this could result in a horrible mess and no supper!

BAKED SWEET POTATOES

Sweet Potatoes are delicious baked; proceed exactly the same as for
ordinary potatoes (page 67). Their distinctive flavour is less receptive to
fillings than the normal potato and they are best served with plenty of
butter, salt and black pepper.

BARBECUED BAKED POTATOES

Wash and spike the potatoes, brush with oil and lay directly on to the grill.
Turn frequently. Alternatively they can be put directly into the hot embers.
They are less messy (but not so good) if you wrap them in foil. Either way
the potatoes will take a minimum of 1½ hours.

TOPPINGS FOR BAKED POTATOES

Here are some excellent toppings for baked potatoes. Please note,
however, that the quantities are only guidelines since it all depends on the
size of the potato and personal preference.

GRATED CHEDDAR AND CHOPPED PARSLEY

Serve in quantity for guests to help themselves. Plenty of butter is
essential.

POACHED OR FRIED EGG

Allow one egg for each potato and serve with plenty of butter and perhaps grated cheese. The addition of baked beans turns this into one of the most delicious pig-outs possible.

SOUR CREAM AND CHIVES

Instead of butter mix together a generous dollop of soured cream and chopped chives. Spoon into potatoes, season with plenty of black pepper and serve with an additional bowl of the soured cream mixture for replenishments.

ANCHOVY BUTTER   For 4 potatoes

Rinse 6 anchovies under running water to remove excess salt and stiff bones. Pound to form a paste with 2–4 oz (50–110 g) butter and season with cayenne, black pepper, chopped parsley and a generous squeeze of lemon juice. Pack into a pot and store in the fridge until ready to use.

ANCHOVY AND GARLIC/NIÇOISE   For 2 potatoes

Mash together 1 anchovy, 1 crushed clove of garlic, 1 tbs chopped parsley (flat-leaf is preferable), 2 oz (50 g) butter, a little of the oil from the anchovies and plenty of freshly ground pepper. Spoon into the potatoes immediately they come out of the oven.

SOUR CREAM AND CAVIARE

This unbelievably scrumptious combination is worth the investment in a pot of caviare. A far cheaper and quite acceptable version is with Danish black lumpfish roe. Serve 1–2 fl oz (25–50 ml) sour cream and ½–1 oz (15–25 g) caviare per potato for guests to help themselves (it is of course 'easier' to be generous if using lumpfish!); a small jug of melted butter and black pepper are also vital.

BACON

While the potatoes are in their final stage of cooking, chop up 2–4 rashers per potato of good smoked streaky bacon. Fry gently so they cook in their own fat and if liked add some chopped onion. Stir continuously and share, juice and all, equally between the potatoes. You will still need butter.

CAPERS

For 6–8 potatoes you will need ½ pt (275 ml) soured cream and 4 oz (110 g) capers, salt and pepper. Mix the cream, capers and seasoning together just before you serve the potatoes.

MUSTARD

For 4 large potatoes you will need 3 oz (75 g) butter, 1 tbs double cream, 1 tbs made-up English mustard, 1 tsp Dijon mustard, salt and pepper. Cream the butter, mustards and cream to form a thick butter. Season, pot and chill. Serve in place of butter.

STUFFED BAKED POTATOES/POMMES DE TERRE FARCIES/ FOURRÉES

Stuffed potatoes are almost completely baked, a 'lid' is cut off or the potato is halved horizontally, most of the flesh scooped out, mashed and then mixed with the filling. The filling is then returned to the shell and the potato is baked again either with or without the lid.

Always take care not to puncture the skin and try to do the scooping and filling quickly so that the skin doesn't have a chance to go baggy.

Stuffed baked potatoes are marvellously versatile and can be served as an appetiser, as a complementary side dish, as a complete light meal or with a crisp salad. They are exceptionally useful vehicles for using up leftovers. A meal composed of 4 or 5 potato skins stuffed with different fillings is particularly popular with children.

To cook the potatoes follow the basic baked potato recipe already given (page 67). Only instructions that relate to the stuffing are given in the following recipes.

WITH EGGS   To fill 4 potatoes

      1 oz (25 g) butter
      2 tbs single cream
      4 eggs
      2–4 oz (50–110 g) grated cheese
      salt, pepper

Cut a lid off the cooked potatoes, scoop out the flesh and mash with the butter and cream. Season and half fill the potatoes with the mixture. Make a depression in the mixture with the back of a spoon and crack an egg into each well. Season and if liked pipe the rest of the potato mixture round the top. Return to the oven for 10 minutes, sprinkle with the cheese and brown under the grill.

MIDDLE EASTERN   <u>To fill 4 potatoes</u>

> 4 oz (110 g) feta cheese
> 4 tbs chopped black olives
> 4 pickled chilli peppers, sliced
> 4 oz (110 g) sour cream
> salt, pepper
> 1 tbs flat-leaf parsley or fresh coriander, chopped

When the potatoes are almost done, cut off a lid and scoop out most of the flesh, leaving a layer of approximately ¼ in (0.5 cm). Lower the oven temperature to 400°F/200°C/gas mark 6. Crumble the cheese and mix with the olives, pepper, half the cream and the potato flesh. Return to the oven and cook for a further 15 minutes and serve with the remaining cream divided between the potatoes and sprinkled with parsley or coriander. Cook the lid separately, it will be delicious frazzled.

WITH FISH AND HERBS   <u>To fill 4 potatoes</u>

This is really a glorified fishcake and is a delicious way of using up leftover scraps of cooked fish.

> 8 oz (225 g) butter
> 1 tbs each parsley, tarragon and chervil, finely chopped
> 4–8 oz (110–225 g) cooked fish, flaked (salmon or smoked
>   haddock would be favourite choices)
> salt, pepper

5 minutes before the potatoes are ready take them out of the oven and cut them in half. Pre-heat the grill to its highest temperature and scoop out the potato flesh. Mash with half the butter, fold in the herbs and then fish. Pile into the potato halves, season with pepper and top with butter. Flash the potatoes under the grill until the butter has melted and serve.

WITH TUNA OR SARDINES/À LA PROVENÇALE   <u>To fill 4 potatoes</u>

> 8 oz (225 g) tuna fish or sardines in oil
> yolks of 2 lightly boiled eggs
> 3 tbs tomato purée (not ketchup!)
> 2 tbs flat-leaf parsley, chopped
> salt, pepper

10 minutes before the potatoes are ready remove them from the oven and slice in half to make 2 boats. Scoop out the flesh and dry mash it to a purée. Incorporate the other ingredients and spoon back into the shells. Return to a slightly lower oven (350°F/180°C/gas mark 4) for 15 minutes.

WITH MUSHROOMS, SHALLOTS AND GARLIC/MAINTENON

To fill 4 potatoes

> 2 shallots, finely chopped
> 2 oz (50 g) butter
> 4 oz (110 g) mushrooms, finely chopped
> 2 cloves garlic, crushed
> 2 oz (50 g) mild hard cheese, grated
> salt, pepper

20 minutes before the potatoes are ready gently sauté the onion in the butter. When softened add the mushrooms, garlic and seasoning. Stir around and cook for 5 minutes until everything is softened. Remove the potatoes from the oven, cut them in half and scoop out the flesh. Dry mash the flesh and mix with the mushrooms, return to the skins and top with grated cheese – use mild Cheddar or Parmesan. Cook for a further 10 minutes until the cheese has melted.

WITH FRESH HERBS/AUX FINES HERBES

To fill 4 potatoes

> 4 oz (110 g) cream cheese
> 4 oz (110 g) mixed fresh herbs such as parsley, thyme, dill,
>   marjoram, chives, rosemary and basil
> salt, pepper

20 minutes before the potatoes are ready mix the herbs into the cream cheese and season well. Cut the potatoes in half, scoop out the flesh and mix thoroughly with the cream cheese. Stuff the skins and return them to the oven for 15 minutes. They will be oozing and aromatic.

WITH CURED HAM

To fill 4 potatoes

Ordinary ham can't be substituted for this simple but moreish dish.

> 4 oz (110 g) butter
> ¼ pt (150 ml) hot milk
> 4 oz (110 g) piece of cured ham, finely diced
> 2 tbs home-made bread crumbs
> salt, pepper

15 minutes before the potatoes are cooked remove them from the oven and slice off an oval lid. Scoop out the flesh and beat in 3 oz (75 g) of the butter and enough of the milk to make a good mash. Season well and stir in the ham. Spoon into the potato shells, sprinkle with breadcrumbs and dot with butter. Return to the oven for 10 more minutes.

SOUFFLÉ   To fill 4 potatoes

      2 oz (50 g) butter
      2 tbs cream
      1 large or 2 small eggs, separated
      salt, pepper
      fresh parsley or chives, chopped

When the potatoes are cooked cut them in half lengthways and scoop the flesh into a bowl. Mash with the butter and cream, season and then beat in the egg yolk. Whisk the egg white stiff and carefully fold into the mixture. Put the potato skins on a suitable serving dish and divide the mixture between them. Return to the oven for 10 minutes, serve immediately sprinkled with parsley or chives.
    This recipe can be varied by including grated cheese, chopped ham or by incorporating fresh herbs into the mixture.

SORREL OR SPINACH CHIFFONNADE   To fill 4 potatoes

Chiffonnade is a culinary term for a purée; in this case, sorrel and spinach will become a chiffonnade with a little extra help when sweated in a small amount of water or with butter. When making a chiffonnade remove all stalks and don't use any salt.

      2 oz (50 g) butter
      ¼ pt (150 ml) hot milk
      6 oz (175 g) sorrel or spinach chiffonnade
      Parmesan or Gruyère, freshly grated
      salt, pepper

Cut the cooked potatoes in half lengthways, scoop out the flesh and quickly mash with the butter and milk, beat with a wooden spoon for a minute or two and mix in the chiffonnade. Season to taste, refill the shells and sprinkle liberally with the cheese. Flash under the grill until the cheese has melted, bubbled and browned. This is good served with fish.

WITH CHILLI   To fill 4 potatoes

    8 oz (225 g) red kidney beans, soaked overnight
    1 onion, chopped
    2 fresh chilli peppers, seeded and chopped
    4 ripe tomatoes, skinned and chopped
    1 tbs fresh coriander, chopped
    oil for frying
    salt, pepper

While the potatoes are cooking bring the soaked beans to the boil and simmer for 45 minutes until soft. Salt the water and cook for a further 5 minutes. Drain. Meanwhile, gently sauté the onion and chillies. When the onions are limp, add the tomatoes and cook until they form a pulp. Stir in the beans, coriander and seasoning. This can be kept warm until the potatoes are ready. Cut a deep cross in the top of each potato, squeeze the sides and spoon over the mixture.

KIDNEYS EN PYJAMA 1   To fill 4 potatoes

    4 lamb's kidneys encased in their own fat
    Dijon mustard
    salt, pepper

Place the encased kidneys on a baking tray and bake alongside the potatoes. After 1 hour, remove the kidneys and trim off any remaining fat. Remove the potatoes and cut off a lid. Scoop out the flesh, mix with 1 tbs mustard per potato, season and pile back into the potato. Press a kidney into each potato, add a dribble of the delicious kidney fat, pepper and serve. This is remarkably rich and filling.

KIDNEYS EN PYJAMA 2   To fill 4 potatoes

    4 lamb's kidneys, with fat and core removed
    butter
    salt, pepper, mustard

Cut the uncooked potatoes in half lengthways. The idea is to encase the kidney totally in the potato, so scoop out an appropriate sized cavity. Season the cavity and the kidney, fit everything together and secure with a piece of string. Bake as normal but use a baking tray; the kidney oozes into the potato during the cooking. Serve with mustard – Dijon for mild flavour, English for hot – butter and supply scissors!

BEEF, ONION AND BREADCRUMBS   <u>To fill 4 potatoes</u>

This is a glamorous way of using up a small amount of beef stew or
trimmings from a steak dinner; it's not worth cooking up some meat
specially.

    1 onion, finely chopped
    2 oz (50 g) butter
    leftover meat, finely chopped
    1 egg, lightly beaten
    2 tbs home made breadcrumbs
    ¼ pt (150 ml) stock
    salt, pepper

Sauté the onions in the butter over a gentle flame while you attend to the
potatoes. Peel and cut them in half horizontally, cut off a slice so they
don't wobble about and carefully scoop out most of the raw flesh. Add the
bits of potato to the onion and cook, turning frequently, until the potatoes
are browned and the onion soft.

Transfer to a mixing bowl and stir in the leftover meat, egg, breadcrumbs and seasoning. Divide the stuffing between the potatoes and put
them in a suitable ovenproof dish. Pour round the stock and bake at
375°F/190°C/gas mark 5 for 1 hour, basting a couple of times after the first
20 minutes' cooking.

BAKED POTATOES FOR A PARTY

The theory behind these baked potatoes is that all the work is done for
your guests, they don't have to do anything to the potato themselves
except eat it. The potatoes can be baked well in advance of the party (the
day before if you have the space to keep them), the stuffing prepared and
stuffed so all that is required is to pop them into a hot oven in batches.

Allow 1 potato half per person if there is other food.

Bake the potatoes in the usual way (page 67) and when they are ready
(don't forget that if you have an oven full of potatoes, they will take ½–1
hour longer to cook) cut all the potatoes in half. Scoop out the flesh and
mash with plenty of butter (allow at least 2 oz/50˙g per potato) and
enough warmed milk to make a firm purée. Season to taste and fill the
potato halves. Top with a grating of cheese. Return to the oven for 30
minutes. Any of the preceding stuffing recipes (pp 70–75) can be easily
adapted for larger quantities.

STUFFED SWEET POTATOES   Serves 4

This recipe originates from John Parkinson, the great botanist, gardener
and royal apothecary writing in 1629. Jane Grigson brought the recipe up
to date for her *Vegetable Book* and I've adapted it to suit 4 average-sized
sweet potatoes.

    4 similarly sized sweet potatoes
    4 oz (110 g) butter
    4 tbs cream
    1 tsp Angostura bitters
    salt, pepper

Bake the potatoes as usual (page 67) and when ready cut them in half
horizontally. Scoop out the flesh, season the shells and beat the butter,
cream and bitters into the flesh. Divide between the shells and return to
the oven for 10 minutes. As Jane Grigson says, the bitters give a
deliciously spicy flavour.

RICHARD OLNEY'S STUFFED BAKED POTATOES/POMMES DE TERRE FARCIES AU FOUR

This and the next recipe (like the Beef, Onion and Breadcrumbs stuffing)
require the raw potato to be hollowed before cooking. It is incredibly fiddly
and the best tool is a vegetable ball-cutting spoon. Failing that, use a
small, sharp paring knife.

    For each potato:

    1 clove garlic, finely chopped
    1 tbs flat-leaf parsley, chopped
    olive oil
    salt, pepper

Choose even-sized floury-variety potatoes and cut slices from the pointed
end of the potato to form a flat base and top. Carefully hollow out the
potato. Chop the slices and the inside flesh and mix with the garlic,
parsley, salt and pepper and a few drops of olive oil. Wipe the potato
cases dry, rub them with oil and pack them full of the stuffing.
    Arrange the potatoes in a lightly oiled casserole, dribble a little more oil
over the surfaces, cover and bake at 400°F/200°C/gas mark 6 for 45
minutes. Baste several times after the first 20 minutes.

AUVERGNE STUFFED POTATOES   <u>Serves 4</u>

These potatoes are peeled before they are stuffed and baked. When they come out of the oven, the skins are blistered and scorched brown. Choose even-sized, medium potatoes.

> 8 potatoes, peeled
> 3 tbs oil
> 4 oz (110 g) smoked streaky bacon, diced
> 1 oz (25 g) butter
> 1 onion, finely chopped
> 4 cloves garlic, finely chopped
> 1 tbs flat-leaf parsley, chopped
> 1 egg
> 3 tbs potato flour
> 3 tbs flour
> dash of milk
> salt, pepper

Remove a 'lid' the length of the potato and carefully scoop out the flesh to leave a ¼-in (0.5-cm) shell. In a little of the oil, sauté the potato on all sides and set aside. Put the potato bits in a bowl of cold water.

Sauté the bacon over a low heat and when the fat has started to run add a little of the butter and the onion. Stir continuously and when the onion is almost cooked, add the garlic. Cook for a further minute and transfer to a mixing bowl. Add the parsley, seasoning and egg. Gradually mix in the sifted flour and then the milk. Form into a firm dough. Stuff the dough into the potatoes, drain and pat dry the lids and put in position.

Salt the potatoes and place them in an appropriate lightly greased ovenproof dish. Bake at 325°F/170°C/gas mark 3 for 1 hour.

13.

The Gratin

There is something immensely satisfying about a gratin, a dish that has been baked at a very high temperature or grilled to acquire a crisp golden-brown crust but is soft and creamy inside. A gratin may be made with raw or cooked food and its crust is generally helped along by a topping of breadcrumbs or grated cheese, Parmesan in particular, and moistened with melted butter.

Gratins are meant to be served in the dishes in which they are cooked. Really these dishes should be made of materials that can be used under the grill as well as the oven: copper, porcelain, earthenware or cast iron. Above all else a gratin dish must be shallow so that every serving has plenty of the crusty top – many gratin dishes have sloped sides for this very reason. Some gratin dishes can be used over direct heat which is useful for initial stages in the preparation of certain recipes. Sizes range from dishes suitable for individual servings up to those able to hold large joints of meat.

TO RINSE OR NOT TO RINSE

The potato gratin is a versatile feast that can seem so different just by the cut of the potato. Wafer-thin to ½-inch thick slices, shreds, julienne and dice of varying thickness: all give different textured results. The versatility of a potato gratin knows no bounds and it can range from a modest dish cooked in water to the ultimate luxury of the Dauphinois which is cooked in butter and double cream.

The potato's ability to absorb flavours makes the gratin the perfect vehicle for making a little of something luxurious or hard to come by go a long way. For example, a few wild mushrooms or a slice of truffle 'multiply' in a potato gratin.

A vexed question, though, about the potato gratin is whether or not to rinse the raw potatoes of surface starch. Top chefs appear to be divided, some favour unrinsed floury potatoes when the starch acts as a binding agent while others favour the lighter texture of rinsed waxy potatoes.

GRATIN DAUPHINOIS

There are numerous 'definitive' recipes for this, the ultimate potato gratin. Escoffier and Austin de Croze cooked theirs with cheese and eggs, de Pomiane denies the use of either but is controversial in using 4 cloves of garlic. Scalded milk as opposed to cream is another contentious point: Elizabeth David suggests that the correct measure is ½ pint (275 ml) of thick cream to 1½ lb (700 g) potatoes but that the proportion of cream may be slightly diminished as the quantity of potatoes is increased. It is also important only to fill the dish to approximately ¾ in (1.5 cm) from the top. A mandoline is the best implement for cutting the consistently wafer-thin slices necessary for a Dauphinois.

Quantities given for these recipes are approximate; it is a dish that brings out the greed in the most reticent eater. It also depends whether the Dauphinois is to be served as an hors d'oeuvre (Elizabeth David's favourite way to eat the dish), with a salad as a 'light' meal or as an accompaniment to roast meat. It is very rich and filling.

EDOUARD DE POMIANE'S GRATIN DAUPHINOIS   Serves 4–6

1½ lb (700 g) potatoes
1 oz (25 g) butter
4 cloves garlic, finely chopped
1 tsp flour, sifted
7 fl oz (200 ml) double cream
¾ pt (400 ml) milk, boiled
salt, pepper

Butter a gratin dish, rub with garlic and then make layers of finely sliced potatoes seasoned with garlic, salt and pepper. Mix the sifted flour into the cream (this stops it separating during cooking) and then mix with the milk and pour over the gratin.

Pre-heat the oven to 400°F/200°C/gas mark 6 and cook for 50 minutes, then raise the temperature for 10 minutes.

ELIZABETH DAVID'S GRATIN DAUPHINOIS   Serves 2–4

1 lb (450 g) Pink Fir Apple or other waxy/yellow potatoes
1 clove garlic
2 oz (50 g) butter
½ pt (275 ml) double cream
salt, pepper

Rinse the potatoes thoroughly in cold water, shake them dry in a cloth.
Rub a shallow earthenware dish with garlic, grease it well with butter and
make layers of thinly sliced potatoes, seasoning each layer.

Pour over the cream and cook for 1½ hours at 325°F/175°C/gas mark
3. During the last 10 minutes turn the oven up fairly high to get a fine
golden crust on the potatoes.

NICO LADENIS'S GRATIN DAUPHINOIS   Serves 2–6

4 medium-sized potatoes
3 fl oz (75 ml) milk
3 fl oz (75 ml) double cream
1 clove garlic
1 tbs clarified butter
salt, pinch nutmeg

Peel the potatoes and slice very finely on a mandoline. Soak in cold water.
Boil together the milk and cream, season with salt and nutmeg. Rub a 6 ×
12 in (15 × 30.5 cm) roasting pan with garlic and brush with clarified
butter. Drain the potatoes and dry thoroughly on absorbent kitchen paper.
Spread the potatoes in thin, closely packed layers adding a little creamy
liquid between each layer. The mixture should be no more than ¾ in (2
cm) thick. Pour the rest of the liquid on top and bake at 350°F/180°C/gas
mark 4 for 30–45 minutes or until nicely browned on top.

POMMES ANNA   Serves 4

This delicious dish is a variation on gratin Dauphinois. It is entirely cooked
with butter and is a matter of preference whether you rinse out the starch
or not. Either way the potatoes must be dry. They will hold together
because of the butter.

2 lb (900 g) waxy-variety potatoes
8 oz (225 g) butter
salt, pepper

Peel the potatoes and slice wafer thin. Butter a round fireproof dish well (a heavy cast-iron frying pan is ideal) and neatly pack in the potatoes, seasoning and brushing each layer with melted butter. When the dish is nearly full pour more melted butter over the top.

Bake for 1 hour at 425°F/220°C/gas mark 7. Remove from the oven and put the serving plate over the cooking dish, turn upside down and serve. The top (that was the bottom) will be browned and the potatoes will be soaked with butter.

POMMES DE TERRE VOISIN

These are prepared in exactly the same way as the preceding recipe, Pommes Anna, except that between each layer of potatoes there is a thin layer of grated cheese.

MICHAEL QUINN'S POTATO GRATIN   Serves 4

When he was chef at the Ritz, Michael Quinn devised this version of the Dauphinois using fromage blanc rather than cream.

1½ lb (700 g) waxy-variety potatoes
oil
3 cloves garlic
5 oz (150 g) fromage blanc
3 oz (75 ml) skimmed milk
salt, pepper, grated nutmeg

Brush the gratin dish with oil and pre-heat the oven to 375°F/190°C/gas mark 5. Slice the potatoes and garlic into wafer-thin slices and make alternative layers starting and ending with potatoes. Season each layer and pour over the fromage blanc mixed with the milk and a grating or two of nutmeg. Bake for 1 hour.

GRATIN SAVOYARD   Serves 4–6

The difference between a Dauphinois and a Savoyard is that a Savoyard is

cooked in stock as opposed to cream. It is normally topped with cheese
too.

2 lb (900 g) potatoes
1 clove garlic, finely chopped
melted butter
¾ pt (400 ml) stock or water
4 oz (110 g) Gruyère, Emmental or Parmesan cheese, grated
salt, pepper

Rub the gratin dish with the garlic and butter liberally. Slice the potatoes
very thinly, rinse and dry in a tea towel. Make layers of potato seasoned
with garlic, salt and pepper. Cover with the water or stock and top with
cheese.

Bake for 50 minutes at 400°F/200°C/gas mark 6 then raise the heat for
the last 10 minutes.

SAVOYARD CUISINE NATURELLE   Serves 4

This is Anton Mosimann's gourmet slimmers' potato gratin.

14 oz (400 g) potatoes, peeled and washed
1 small clove garlic, peeled and cut in half
7 fl oz (200 ml) vegetable stock
3¼ oz (80 g) soft goat's cheese, crumbled
salt, pepper

Rub the gratin dish with the garlic and pre-heat the oven to 375°F/190°C/
gas mark 5. Slice the potatoes wafer thin and arrange in the dish,
seasoning each layer.

Cover with the stock and bake for 30 minutes. Sprinkle with the cheese
and bake until the top turns a golden brown.

MICHEL AND ALBERT ROUX'S GRATIN SAVOYARD   Serves 4

1 lb 6 oz (625 g) medium-sized potatoes
1 pt (570 ml) double cream
4 tbs milk
½ clove garlic
salt, white pepper, freshly grated nutmeg

Wash the potatoes and slice them ¹⁄₁₀ in (3 mm) thick on a mandoline. Spread them on a table and sprinkle lavishly with salt. Rub the slices together then heap them up in a pile and leave for 5–10 minutes. The salt will extract the water and soften the potatoes.

Combine the cream and milk in a saucepan large enough to take the potatoes later. Salt very lightly, add 2 turns of the pepper mill and grate in a little nutmeg. Set over a high heat and bring to the boil. Simmer for several minutes.

Rub a medium gratin dish, preferably made of fine metal, with half the garlic dipped in salt. Press the potatoes lightly between your hands to squeeze out the excess water. Add the potatoes to the boiling cream and bring the mixture back to the boil. Remove from the heat and, using a large spoon, spread the mixture evenly in the prepared dish. The gratin should be about 2 ins (5 cm) thick. Bake at 250°F/120°C/gas mark 1 for about 45 minutes.

POTATO GRATIN WITH MUSHROOMS   Serves 4

Wild mushrooms would be my first choice for this dish, large flat cultivated mushrooms would be second and dried and reconstituted ceps would be third.

> 1 lb (450 g) waxy-variety potatoes
> 1 oz (25 g) butter
> 1 clove garlic, finely chopped
> 8 oz (225 g) mushrooms
> ¼ pt (150 ml) each double and single cream
> 2 fl oz (50 ml) water
> 4 oz Parmesan, grated
> salt, pepper

Butter a large gratin dish and pre-heat the oven to 350°F/180°C/gas mark 4. Slice the potatoes very finely and rinse in cold water. Drain, pat dry and pack half of them into the dish. Sprinkle with the garlic, cover with the sliced mushrooms and top with the rest of the potatoes. Season each layer and pour over the whisked cream and water. Sprinkle the cheese on top, dot with butter and bake for 1½ hours.

GRATIN WITH A TRUFFLE   Serves 1 (or 4!)

Or how to make the most of truffle trimmings.

1 lb (450 g) waxy-variety potatoes
1 oz (25 g) butter
½ clove garlic
trimmings, half or a whole truffle
½ pt (275 ml) double cream
1 tbs water
salt, pepper

Rub the garlic around the gratin dish and butter it liberally. Slice the potatoes and truffle very finely. Depending on the quantity of truffle you have make alternate layers starting and ending with the potato. Season each layer well. A tiny bit of truffle has a phenomenal effect as Jeremy Round discovered when he made a version of this with just a hint of truffle. Mix the water into the cream and pour over the gratin. Dot with butter and bake at 350°F/180°C/gas mark 4 for 1 hour.

POTATO GRATIN WITH PESTO   Serves 4

2 lb (900 g) waxy-variety potatoes
1 oz (25 g) butter
2 oz (50 g) pesto
½ pt (275 ml) vegetable or chicken stock
salt, pepper

Proceed as for the mushroom gratin (page 83) but spread pesto between the sandwich of potatoes.

POTATO GRATIN WITH LEEKS   Serves 4

1 lb (450 g) waxy-variety potatoes
butter
1 lb (450 g) leeks, washed and thinly sliced
3 tbs parsley, chopped
½ pt (275 ml) chicken stock or water
salt, pepper

Slice the potatoes very finely, wash, drain and dry in a tea towel. Butter the gratin dish and make alternate layers of potato and leek sprinkling each layer with parsley and seasoning. Finish with the potatoes, pour over the stock, dot with butter and bake at 350°F/180°C/gas mark 4 for 1 hour. This is also good with a topping of grated Parmesan.

GRATIN OF POTATOES AND JERUSALEM ARTICHOKES

1½ lb (700 g) waxy variety potatoes
½ clove garlic
butter
8 oz (225 g) artichokes
13 fl oz (340 ml) double cream
salt, pepper

Rub the gratin dish with garlic and grease it with butter. Peel and finely slice the potatoes and artichokes. Make circular layers of alternating slices of the two vegetables, season and pour over the cream. Bake for 1¼ hours at 375°F/190°C/gas mark 5.

GRATIN OF POTATOES AND FENNEL   Serves 6

2 lb (900 g) waxy-variety potatoes
5–6 fennel bulbs with green shoots
butter
1 clove garlic
1 sprig fresh thyme
3 tbs Gruyère, grated
salt, pepper

Boil the potatoes in their skins for 10 minutes. Cool, peel and slice ¼ in (0.5 cm) thick. Slice the fennel and gently sauté in 2 tbs butter to soften but not brown. Rub the gratin dish with garlic, grease with butter and sandwich the fennel and thyme between 2 layers of potato. Season and dot the top generously with bits of butter.

Bake at 350°F/180°C/gas mark 4 for 35 minutes, basting at least twice (tip the dish sideways and scoop out the buttery juice). Remove from the oven, sprinkle on the cheese and flash under a hot grill to brown the top. This is good with fish.

HARENGS GRATINÉS/SILLGRATANG   Serves 4–6

This is a very pretty dish that comes from the Café Restaurant Cattelin, the Langan's Brasserie of Stockholm.

1½ lb (700 g) waxy-variety potatoes
butter
2 large onions, finely sliced
4 salted Icelandic herrings, skinned and filleted
½ pt (275 ml) cream
breadcrumbs
salt, pepper

Parboil the potatoes in their skins, cool, peel and slice about ¼ in (0.5 cm) thick. Butter the gratin dish, put in a layer of potatoes and then onions, season. Arrange the top layer with diagonal strips of fish, onion and potatoes, pour over the cream, season and bake at 325°F/170°C/gas mark 3 for 30 minutes.

Remove from the oven and sprinkle with a thin layer of breadcrumbs, return for a further 10 minutes until the top is crisp.

GRATIN OF SALT COD   Serves 4–6

2 lb (900 g) waxy-variety potatoes, boiled and sliced
2 lb (900 g) salt cod, soaked in several changes of water for a
     minimum 12 hours
3 oz (75 g) butter
6 small onions, sliced
1 bayleaf
1 sprig thyme
¾ pt (400 ml) Béchamel sauce made with 2 oz (50 g) butter and
     2 oz (50 g) flour
4 oz Gruyére cheese, grated
pepper

Give the cod a final rinse and cut into big chunks. Poach in about ½ pt (275 ml) water with the bay leaf, thyme and one of the onions. Gently sweat the other onions in 2 oz (50 g) of the butter and use the rest to grease a large gratin dish. After 5 minutes of cooking remove the fish and remove any bones.

Cover the bottom of the dish with potatoes, pile on the onions and then fish, season with pepper and top with the rest of the potatoes, then pour on the white sauce. Sprinkle on the cheese and bake at 375°F/190°C/gas mark 5 for about 40 minutes until nicely golden.

The Recipes

14.

Appetisers and Hors D'Oeuvre

In the eighties the potato has become a victim of fashion. Newly discovered varieties are hyped to extraordinary lengths – as witness the hundreds of column inches devoted to the calculated 'launch' in this country of the French variety La Ratte. Sainsburys have used an 'art' shot of a single Pink Fir Apple (see the back cover of this book!) to advertise their extensive stock of varieties and Alastair Little, arguably London's most fashionable chef, was hired for a chic advertising campaign to cook a dish of chips that was photographed and used as a symbol of ultimate style. However, an intense PR hype does have its advantages. The spotlight of interest on potatoes has given the green light to chefs, professional and amateur cooks to treat the potato as an item worthy of the attention it most certainly deserves. People are beginning to talk varieties and notice that different types of potatoes lend themselves to different styles of cooking. After a decade of the potato being regarded as almost single-handedly responsible for a nation of fatties and the all-pervading British view that potatoes are like bread and only good for filling you up, it's now fashionable to be doing witty things with potatoes. Some of the most interesting, novel new ideas are for starters.

LITTLE ROAST POTATOES

A dish of small, very crispy and well seasoned roast potatoes (pages 43–4) never fails to please as an appetiser with pre-dinner drinks. Serve on a doily garnished with parsley and a squeeze of lemon.

ALASTAIR LITTLE'S FRIED POTATO SALAD   Serves 4

Serve as an appetiser, as a snack with a few cold beers or as an informal shared starter.

1½ lb (700 g) floury-variety potatoes, peeled and sliced into 1 mm
   thick rounds
vegetable oil for deep frying
lemon juice
olive oil
salt, pepper
chopped parsley to garnish

Pre-heat oil to 375°F/190°C while you rinse and pat dry the potatoes. Drop
the potatoes into the oil and cook for a couple of minutes until golden.
Don't allow the potatoes to stick together and keep the first batch warm
while you cook the rest.

   Put all the crisps in a serving dish, sprinkle with lemon juice, olive oil,
salt, black pepper and dress with chopped parsley. Serve at once.

NEW POTATOES WITH CAVIARE   Serves 4

During an interview about his favourite restaurants, chef Simon Hopkinson remembered being served a dish of tiny new potatoes that had been
split in half and stuffed with sour cream and caviare. They had been
served as a *bonne bouche* at London's only 3-Michelin-star restaurant, Le
Gavroche. That was in 1980 and since then variations on that idea have
become very popular.

1 lb (450 g) small Jersey Royals or other small, waxy potatoes that
   you know are full of flavour
4 fl oz (110 ml) sour cream, unstirred
2–4 oz (50–110 g) jar caviare; salmon roe is equally good but the
   widely available dyed black cod's roe is an adequate pauper's
   alternative
black pepper
watercress to garnish

Scrub the potatoes and drop into boiling, salted water and cook until just
tender. Drain and split in half and divide the potatoes between 4 serving
plates. Allow to cool to room temperature, spoon a dollop of cream into
each potato and divide the caviare equally between the potatoes. Season
with freshly ground pepper. Garnish with watercress or stand in a bed of
rock salt and serve immediately.

ANOTHER VERSION

Instead of boiling the new potatoes, bake them on a lightly greased baking tray at 400°F/200°C/gas mark 6 for ½ an hour. The skins will be slightly crunchy and are particularly good with salmon eggs.

SALLY CLARKE'S POTATOES WITH CAVIARE   Serves 4

    4 medium-sized King Edwards or similar floury-variety potatoes
    peanut or vegetable oil for deep frying
    4 fl oz (110 ml) sour cream, unstirred
    4 oz (110 g) jar salmon eggs or smoked or marinated salmon cut
        into curls or crisply fried duck livers or curls of prosciutto ham
        sprinkled with lemon juice
    several leaves of seasonal lettuce to garnish

Pre-heat oven to 400°F/200°C/gas mark 6. Wash and prick the potatoes and bake until ⅞ths cooked when the skin is crisp but not crackling crisp. Leave to cool and the skin will soften. Split horizontally to get flat sides, scoop out the flesh leaving ¼ in (0.5 cm) potato around the side. Drop the skin into pre-heated (375°F/190°C) oil and cook for 2–2½ minutes or until golden brown. Drain well, salt and fill with sour cream and chosen filling. Serve on a bed of seasonal lettuce like a little nest.

MASHED POTATO BALLS WITH CAVIARE FILLING   Serves 4

When Mark Chayette was in charge of the kitchens of the fashionable American restaurant the Quilted Giraffe he was in the enviable position of having 2 kilos of caviare to use up. He came up with this idea that also uses leftover mashed potato.

    1 lb (450 g) leftover mashed potato, made with butter not milk
    2 oz (50 g) jar caviare
    4 oz (110 g) flour
    1 egg, beaten
    2 tbs dried breadcumbs
    oil for deep frying
    4 fl oz (110 ml) sour cream
    salt, pepper
    1 ripe avocado, 3 or 4 radishes, 1 finely chopped red onion to
        garnish

Season the mash with pepper and a little salt. Working with the mash at room temperature divide it into eight 2-oz (50-g) pieces. Roll into balls and cut in half with a sharp knife. Make a depression in one half with your thumb and fill up with caviare. Press the two halves back together and softly rework into a ball. Roll in flour, dust off the excess, roll in beaten egg and then breadcrumbs.

Meanwhile pre-heat the chip pan to 375°F/190°C and deep fry the balls for between 45 and 60 seconds until they are golden brown. Drain and serve two per person; slice one ball in half to reveal the secret. Arrange with a spoonful of sour cream, 4 thin slices of avocado, a few thin slices of radish and onion.

TROISGROS STEAMED POTATOES AND TRUFFLES/DUO DE TRUFFES À LA VAPEUR   Serves 4

9 oz (250 g) waxy-variety potatoes
6 oz (175 g) raw truffles
unsalted butter
salt, coarse and fine, pepper

Brush the truffles clean under running water. Cut the potatoes into the same number of pieces as there are truffles and carve them into the same shape. Lightly season the truffles and potatoes and place them in the steamer. Cover the pan, bring to the boil, turn down the heat to simmer and leave to cook for 25 minutes.

When done slice the truffles and potatoes equally between the 4 plates. Scatter a few grains of coarse salt over the top and put the butter in the middle of the table so guests can help themselves.

RAYMOND BLANC'S MILLE-FEUILLE OF POTATOES, TURNIPS AND FOIE GRAS WITH WILD MUSHROOMS/MILLE-FEUILLE DE POMMES DE TERRE ET NAVETS AU FOIE GRAS AVEC GIROLLES   Serves 4

Raymond Blanc, who cooks exquisite food at his 2-star restaurant Le Manoir aux Quat' Saisons, prepared this dish for the BBC television series *Take Six Cooks*. He experimented for some time before he came up with his final *mille-feuille* combination. These can be served on their own, with a few mushrooms cooked in butter and a little garlic or as a side dish when they are particularly good with pan-fried liver. This recipe is well worth the effort.

1 lb (450 g) waxy-variety potatoes
4½ oz (125 g) turnips
3 oz (75 g) unsalted butter
7 oz (200 g) foie gras, calf or chicken liver
salt, pepper

For the sauce:

4½ oz (125 g) mushrooms, finely sliced
1 tbs sunflower or groundnut oil
15 shallots
½ oz (15 g) butter
2 fl oz (50 ml) sherry vinegar
2 fl oz (50 ml) each ruby port and dry Madeira
¼ pt (150 ml) veal stock
1 sprig thyme
pinch of powder of dried cepes
1 tbs old sherry
salt, pepper
¼ truffle or 1 tbsp double cream (optional)

For the garnish:

4 oz (110 g) wild mushrooms, cepes or morilles but button
    mushrooms will do
¼ oz (10 g) butter
pinch salt, squeeze lemon juice, 4 or 5 tarragon leaves and a few
    sprigs chervil

Peel and finely grate the potatoes, wash under cold running water, drain
and pat dry. Peel the turnips, grate finely and add to potatoes with 3
pinches each salt and pepper. Melt 2½ oz (65 g) of the butter, pour over
the mixture and stir thoroughly. Butter the bottom of a large non-stick
frying pan with remaining butter and line with a thin layer of turnip and
potato. Press down with a fork and crisp gently over a medium heat for
3–4 minutes, turn and crisp again. Remove from the pan and drain on
kitchen paper to absorb excess fat. Dry in a cool oven (275°F/140°C/gas
mark 1) for 5 minutes. Keep warm.
    To make the sauce, sauté the mushrooms in very hot oil to colour them
slightly. Finely chop 3 of the shallots and sauté in 1 tsp butter until well
coloured. Add the sherry vinegar and heat until evaporated, then add the
port, Madeira and mushrooms and reduce the liquid by two-thirds. Pour
in the veal stock, add the thyme and powdered cepes, bring to the boil,

skimming any impurities. Add 2 fl oz (50 ml) cold water and the sherry and pass through a fine sieve; you should have 4 fl oz (110 ml) liquid. Taste and season.

Peel and chop the remaining 12 shallots and place in a roasting pan with the remaining butter, 6 tbs water and a pinch of salt. Cook in oven at 350°F/180°C/gas mark 4 for 20 minutes. When the shallots are soft, reduce their juices over a strong heat until the shallots colour and caramelise.

To prepare the garnish, wipe the mushrooms clean and cut them down to an average size. Sauté them in a pan with the butter and salt for 1 minute. Add the lemon juice and chopped tarragon, check seasoning.

If using foie gras, divide into 4 pieces. Season. Heat a thick-bottomed pan and cook the foie gras for 10 seconds on each side. Keep warm. Similarly, seal the calf or chicken liver but use a small amount of oil. Divide the liver into 4 slivers per portion. Cut the pancake into 12 portions. Take 4 plates, place a piece of pancake in the middle of each plate and top with 2 slivers of liver, then another slice of pancake and the remaining 2 slivers of liver. Finish with a third layer of pancake.

Pour the sauce over the caramelised shallots and bring to the boil. If it lacks sharpness, add a dash more sherry vinegar and the truffle. If it's too sharp, add the cream. Pour round the *mille-feuille* and garnish with the mushrooms and sprigs of chervil.

THE POTATO AS PART OF THE MEZE, TAPAS OR MULTI-COURSE STARTER

GARLIC POTATO PÂTÉ/PATATES EZMEZI   Serves 6–8

In Turkey and Greece cold mashed potato cooked with garlic is a favourite appetiser. It should be regarded as one of the Great Standbys for Unexpected Guests. Here is a simple version.

> 1 lb (450 g) floury-variety potatoes
> 4–6 cloves garlic, peeled
> 6 tbs olive oil
> 1 tbs white wine or cider vinegar
> ½ tsp salt, plenty of black pepper
> chives, flat-leaf parsley or coriander, black olives and olive oil to
>   garnish

Pop the garlic in with the unpeeled potatoes and boil in salted water until cooked. Drain and peel the potatoes and mash with the garlic. Mix in the olive oil and vinegar and check for seasoning.

Turn on to a plate and garnish with a swirl of olive oil, the chopped parsley, coriander or chives and dot with olives. Serve with hot pitta bread and more olives.

COMPLEX VERSION

    1 lb (450 g) floury-variety potatoes
    2 egg yolks
    2 oz (50 g) butter
    1 lemon
    2 cloves garlic, chopped
    1 small onion, chopped
    1 oz (25 g) chopped flat-leaf parsley or coriander
    2 fl oz (50 ml) natural yoghurt
    salt, pepper
    black olives to garnish

Boil the potatoes in salted water, mash. Beat the egg yolks and mix them and the butter into the mash. Stir constantly over a low flame for a few minutes and mix in the juice of the lemon.

Meanwhile, grate half the lemon skin on a fine grater and mix it with the garlic, onion, herbs and yoghurt; if you have a food processor, purée it in that. Mix the yoghurt mixture in with the potato purée and check the seasoning.

Divide into individual ramekins or spread on an appropriate serving dish. Dot with olives and serve with hot pitta bread and more olives.

POTATO, GARLIC AND SMOKED HADDOCK PÂTÉ   Serves 4

    8 oz (225 g) floury-variety potatoes
    1 small onion, finely chopped
    6 cloves garlic, peeled and crushed
    2 tbs sunflower oil
    1 tbs lemon juice
    1 egg, beaten
    4–8 oz (110–225 g) smoked haddock, chopped and flaked
    salt, black pepper

Boil the potatoes in salted water, peel and mash. Lightly cook the onion and garlic in the oil and liquidise with the lemon juice before mixing in with the potatoes and beaten egg. Finally mix in the haddock and check the seasoning.

Serve chilled in individual ramekins or as a dip with hot pitta bread.

TARAMASALATA   Serves 4

Using a combination of mashed potato and bread creates a very light, fluffy version of this famous Greek dish.

   1 large floury-variety potato, boiled and mashed
   4 oz (110 g) smoked cod or grey mullet roe
   1 medium onion, finely chopped
   1 thick slice stale white bread
   ½–¾ pt (275–400 ml) olive oil
   juice of 1 or 2 lemons, according to taste
   salt, pepper

Cut the skin off the roe and pound it with the onion. Cream with the dry mashed potato. Next cut the crusts off the bread, dip in water, squeeze dry and work that into the mixture. Gradually beat in the olive oil and lemon juice and when finished check for seasoning. (This whole operation can be done in a jiff in a food processor.)

Serve with hot pitta bread and black olives.

POTATO AND CARROT APPETISER/AJLOUKE
DE CAROTTES   Serves 6

I first encountered this surprisingly delicious dish when I worked in Tunisia many years ago.

   1 lb (450 g) potatoes
   1½ lb (700 g) carrots
   2 cloves garlic, chopped
   4 tsp cumin
   3 tbs olive oil
   2 tbs wine vinegar
   salt, large pinch of cayenne
   coriander leaves to garnish

Peel the vegetables and cut them into pieces. Put them in a pan with the salt, garlic and water to cover then boil until soft. Drain and mash, then stir in the rest of the ingredients. Garnish with coriander leaves, and serve cold with hot pitta bread.

CRACKED NEW POTATOES/PATATES ANTINAKTES   <u>Serves 4–6</u>

This Cypriot dish is generally served as part of a meze. The recipe was given to me by a therapist friend called Carol Grace who lived for many years in Cyprus; she tells me the dish is devised from the Greek Cypriot word *antinasso* which means 'toss'!

> 2 lb (900 g) new potatoes
> 1 cup vegetable oil
> ½ cup dry red wine
> ¼ cup crushed coriander roots
> salt, pepper
> flat-leaf parsley or coriander leaves to garnish

Wash the potatoes and dry with a cloth. Hit each one with an implement to break slightly.

Heat the oil until hot in a frying pan and stir fry the potatoes until evenly browned. Drain off most of the oil, reheat and add the wine, salt, pepper and coriander. Reduce the heat and simmer gently with the lid on for 15–20 minutes.

Turn into a serving dish, allow to cool to room temperature and serve garnished with parsley or coriander.

PEPPERY POTATOES/PATATAS BRAVAS   <u>Serves 4–6</u>

Claudia Roden gives the recipe for this simple Spanish peasant dish in her book of *Mediterranean Cookery*. It is commonly served as part of a tapas.

> 2 lb (900 g) new potatoes
> olive oil for frying
> salt

<u>For the sauce:</u>

> 5 tbs olive oil
> 1 tbs tomato paste
> 1 tbs wine vinegar
> 1 tsp paprika
> pinch cayenne or a few drops of Tabasco

Boil the potatoes in their skin until almost tender. Drain and, when they are cool enough to handle, peel and cut into quarters or into bite-sized pieces. Shallow-fry them in hot oil until crisp and golden all over.

Transfer to a serving dish, mix all the other ingredients for the sauce together and pour over the potatoes. Serve hot or warm.

SPANISH OMELETTE/TORTILLA ESPAÑOLA   Serves 4–6

2¼ lb (1 kg) waxy-variety potatoes, peeled and cut into thin slices or diced
oil for frying
2 large onions, peeled and finely chopped
6 large eggs, beaten
salt, pepper

Heat some of the oil in a heavy, flat, non-stick frying pan. Gently sauté the onions and when they are transparent add the potatoes and season lightly with salt. Continue cooking until the potatoes are soft but not browned, then add the vegetables to the beaten egg and season generously with pepper.

Wash out the pan, add some fresh oil and heat until the oil begins to smoke. Gently pour in the omelette mixture, turn down the heat and cook for a few minutes. To cook the other side, either pop the pan under a moderate grill for a few minutes or cover the omelette with a plate, slip it out of the pan and turn it over to sauté the other side.

Alternatively the entire cooking can be done in a moderate oven (300°F/150°C/gas mark 2) for 10–15 minutes. The omelette should be firm; crisp on the outside and slightly runny on the inside. Slice up like a cake and eat warm or cold.

This recipe can be varied by cutting the quantity of onions in half and replacing it with a red pepper finely sliced.

TIMBALES OF BLUE POTATOES WITH TOMATO AND DILL SAUCE   Serves 6

Cookery writer Alice Wooledge Salmon devised this recipe using the somewhat obscure Salad Blue potato variety after an inspirational trip round two old English kitchen gardens.

Salad Blue and other exotic potato varieties can be ordered from Mrs

Donald MacLean, Dornock Farm, Crieff, Perthshire, PR7 3QN. Pink Fir
Apples or other waxy varieties may be substituted.

  6 floury-variety potatoes, 5 oz (150 g) each
  2 fl oz (50 ml) Jersey cream
  1 egg and 1 extra egg yolk
  2 medium-sized Salad Blue potatoes, 3–4 oz (75–110 g) each
  1 oz (25 g) butter
  salt, pepper

  For the sauce:

  2 lb (900 g) sweet red tomatoes
  1 oz (25 g) butter
  3 tbs tomato purée
  3 fl oz (75 ml) dry white wine
  handful of chopped dill
  salt, pepper
  fronds of dill to garnish

Bake the floury potatoes until done. Scoop out the flesh, mash, add the
warmed cream, egg and extra egg yolk and season.

Scrub the blue potatoes, cube and simmer for 4–5 minutes until
cooked. Drain and mix in with the purée. Butter ramekins and divide the
mixture between them. Bake in a bain-marie at 375°F/190°C/gas mark 5
for 20 minutes and leave to rest for 5 minutes before unmoulding.

Meanwhile, make the sauce by roughly chopping the tomatoes and
bringing them to the boil with the butter, salt and pepper. Add the tomato
purée, wine and chopped dill and simmer uncovered for 15 minutes.
Sieve, check seasoning and pour a little round each of the timbales,
garnish with fronds of dill.

COMPOSED SALADS

QUAILS' EGGS AND POTATO SALAD   Serves 4

Combining named varieties of potato with other fashionable ingredients
has become a common feature on fashionable restaurant menus or cook

books written by chefs. This one is typical and I found it on the menu of a
Soho juice bar called Presse.

> 1 lb (450 g) Pink Fir Apple or other waxy-variety potatoes, boiled in
>   their skins
> ¼ pt (150 ml) vinaigrette
> 24 quails' eggs
> 8 oz (225 g) French stick beans, cooked briefly so still crunchy
> 2 tins anchovies, rinsed under running water
> pepper
> fresh chervil to garnish

Peel the potatoes while still warm and slice into a warmed salad bowl;
pour over the vinaigrette while you cook the quails' eggs. It is preferable to
have soft quails' eggs for this recipe but peeling 24 soft eggs is a labour of
love. For soft eggs: place in cold, salted water and bring to the boil. Boil for
1 minute, drain and tap each egg immediately to crack the skin and break
the strong membrane. Leave in cold water while you begin peeling. For
hard eggs, cook for 2–3 minutes. Dry carefully and combine with the
potatoes.

Snap the beans in half, cut or tear the anchovy fillets into pieces and mix
everything in the salad bowl. Season with plenty of pepper and garnish
with chervil.

POTATO AND ARTICHOKE HEART SALAD   Serves 4

> 1 lb (450 g) waxy-variety potatoes boiled in their skins
> 4 tbs olive oil
> 1 dsp lemon juice
> parsley, finely chopped
> 11 oz (310 g) tin artichoke bottoms
> 2 oz (50 g) fresh walnuts, roughly chopped
> salt, pepper

Peel and slice the potatoes while still hot in thick slices into a salad bowl.
Whisk the olive oil, lemon juice, salt, pepper and parsley thoroughly and
pour over the potatoes. When the potatoes have cooled add the sliced
artichoke bottoms and walnuts. Season, mix thoroughly and serve.

POTATO AND APPLE SALAD Serves 4

1 lb (450 g) even-sized Pink Fir Apple potatoes, boiled in their skins
2 tbs each vinaigrette and mayonnaise
2 hard Cox's apples
juice of ½ lemon
½ clove garlic, crushed
salt, pepper

Peel the potatoes while still hot and slice into thick rounds into the well-seasoned vinaigrette. Mix and leave to cool.

Meanwhile, core and chop the apple and sprinkle immediately with lemon juice to prevent discolouring. When the potatoes have cooled add the apples. Whisk the garlic into the mayonnaise and carefully fold into the salad.

POTATOES AND BEANS WITH CUCUMBER/FRICOT D'PAIS
ET D'PATATES AVEC CONCOMBRE À LA JERRIASE Serves 4

This recipe from Jersey doesn't use the famous Royals but instead a floury variety. It is adapted from Sophie Grigson's excellent column in the London *Evening Standard*.

1 lb (450 g) floury-variety potatoes boiled in salted water with 8 oz
(225 g) French beans
1 cucumber
2 tbs wine vinegar
2 oz (50 g) lard or dripping
1 onion, finely chopped
2 tsp salt, pepper

A couple of hours in advance of cooking the vegetables, thinly slice the cucumber, sprinkle with salt and leave for half an hour. Pat dry and marinate in the vinegar for at least an hour.

While the vegetables are cooking, gently fry the onion in the lard and when it is transparent, turn up the heat to brown. Add the onion and its cooking juices to the drained vegetables and mash thoroughly with plenty of salt and pepper.

Serve a dollop of potato with a pile of cucumber; the combination is perfection.

ROWLEY LEIGH'S POTATO SALAD WITH TRUFFLES   Serves 4

During the truffle season (mid-December to mid-February) this dish is on
the menu at Kensington Place, a fashionable French restaurant in
London's Notting Hill Gate.

> 1 lb (450 g) Belle de Fontenay potatoes
> virgin olive oil
> 3–4 truffles, depending on size
> salt, pepper
> chopped chives to garnish

Boil the potatoes in their skins; while still hot slice horizontally and fan out
on the plate. Dress with a thick dribble of olive oil. With an Italian truffle
shaver, shave the truffle to cover the potatoes and allow to cool to room
temperature before garnishing with chopped chives and serving.

The idea is for the truffle flavours to permeate the potato; to make sure,
flash the dish under the grill before garnishing.

SALADE DE L'ÎLE BARBE   Serves 4

This luxurious little salad relies on the very best produce; use Pink Fir
Apple, Jersey Royal or one of the French potato varieties.

> 1 lb (450 g) waxy-variety potatoes
> 2 cooked red or yellow peppers
> 2 oz (50 g) smoked ham, diced
> 1 lobster or crawfish tail, cut in rounds
> 1 truffle, sliced
> black olives
> 2 fl oz (50 ml) olive oil
> juice of ½ lemon
> salt, pepper

Boil the potatoes in their skins, peel, slice and cool to room temperature.
Mix all the ingredients and pour over the olive oil, lemon juice, salt and
pepper. Serve with delicious brown bread.

WINTER VEGETABLES IN OLIVE OIL/KIS TURLUSU   <u>Serves 6</u>

This Turkish dish transforms winter root vegetables and is a useful winter appetiser. It is also very pretty.

> 1 sweet potato
> 1 celeriac
> 8 oz (225 g) Jerusalem artichokes
> 3 large carrots
> 1 tbs lemon juice
> 4 tbs olive oil
> 2 tsp sugar
> salt, pepper
> small bunch dill, finely chopped to garnish

Peel all the vegetables, cut into even-sized chunks and place together in a large pan. Add the lemon, oil and seasoning and half cover with water.

Cover and cook gently for 20 minutes or until the vegetables are cooked but still crisp. Drain, reserving a little of the liquor to be poured over the vegetables as a sauce. Allow to cool, sprinkle with the dill and serve.

COMFORT STARTERS

POTATO GNOCCHI

Gnocchi shares with soufflés and pâtés an unfair reputation for being tricky and difficult to get right. In fact, making potato gnocchi is child's play, a bit like making pastry but less likely to go wrong. Like pastry, best results come from working with cold ingredients.

The ratio of potato to flour, eggs and butter or oil makes less difference if you use a waxy potato but do experiment. You may find you prefer more potato and less flour, or oil rather than butter in the mixture.

Gnocchi is very versatile. Traditionally it is served from a hot buttered dish with diners helping themselves to a grating of fresh Parmesan, but it can be varied by adding herbs, other vegetables or scraps of ham to the mixture. It is delicious fried up with bacon for breakfast. At Joe Allen's Italian restaurant Orso, it is served with a basil-laced tomato sauce.

Basic Mixture, serves 6–8:

2 lbs (900 g) floury-variety potatoes
10 oz (275 g) plain flour
1 egg
1 dsp olive oil
salt, pepper, pinch of nutmeg

Boil the potatoes in their skins in well-salted water. Cool and skin. Dry mash, season and pile the potatoes on to a floured board. Make a well and add a small amount of the sifted flour, the egg and sprinkle on the olive oil. Quickly work the mixture to incorporate the flour, adding more as you do so. You will end up with a soft, light yet firm dough that is easy to mould. Leave it to rest for 20 minutes, while you put on a large pan of water to boil and butter a gratin dish ready to go into a warm oven.

Divide the mixture in half and roll each half into a long thin sausage. Chop into 1-in (2.5-cm) pieces. Carefully roll each gnocchi round the prongs of a fork to make a slight curl. Poach the dumplings in small batches; they are done when they pop up to the surface and this takes about 5 minutes. Scoop them out with a slotted spoon and keep warm in the gratin dish while you complete the cooking.

GNOCCHI À LA PIEDMONTAISE   Serves 4

This is an adaptation of a recipe from Fredy Giradet's book *Cuisine Spontanée*.

10½ oz (290 g) floury-variety potatoes
3½ oz (90 g) plain flour
1 egg yolk
2 heaped tbs green herbs such as parsley, basil and chervil
olive oil
salt, pepper, grated nutmeg

Proceed as previous recipe (page 107) but work in your chosen herbs at the same time as you incorporate the other ingredients. Divide up the mixture in ¾- × ⅜-in (1.5- × 0.9-cm) pieces and poach in well salted boiling water.

Serve with a herb-flavoured tomato sauce, sauté in a frying pan and sprinkle with Parmesan or smother in cream and place under a pre-heated grill until the top is nicely browned.

POTATO AND GARLIC RAVIOLI   Serves 6

This is my version of Sally Clarke's version of Alice Walters' original recipe.
It is often on the menu at Sally's restaurant, Clarke's, in Kensington.

    2 lbs (900 g) floury-variety potatoes
    ¼ pt (150 ml) double cream
    4 big cloves garlic, chopped
    few sprigs of fresh thyme, finely chopped

    For the ravioli:

    1 lb (450 g) washed spinach
    6 large egg yolks
    1 lb (450 g) strong flour
    pinch salt
    fresh Parmesan to garnish

To make the ravioli, first sweat the spinach in a covered pan with a little
salt. When cooked, squeeze dry, chop and, together with the eggs, whisk
in the food processor. Mix the egg and spinach into the flour, add a pinch
of salt and knead until you have firm, smooth and elastic dough. Wrap in
cling film and leave to rest for at least 15 minutes.

Meanwhile, boil the potatoes in their skins and at the same time put the
cream and garlic on to simmer for 20 minutes. Mash the peeled potatoes
and whisk in the cream and garlic until the potatoes fluff. Add the finely
chopped thyme and leave to cool.

On a lightly floured surface roll out the pasta into wafer-thin sheets. Cut
out circles (a cookie cutter is perfect for this) and pipe or spoon enough of
the potato mixture that you will be able to make moon shape pasties.
Brush the edges with an egg wash or beaten milk and pinch together.
Leave on a rack to dry for 20 minutes and then plunge in boiling salted
water for 30–40 seconds.

Drain and serve dusted with Parmesan or with a fresh tomato *concassé*
made with black pepper, olive oil, finely chopped thyme and lightly
reduced with cream.

POTATO BOREKS   Serves 4

This is the Turkish equivalent of the Indian samosa and the Tunisian *brik*.
They are delicious as part of a meze but they are popular in my household
with drinks. An excellent use for leftover mashed potato.

1 lb (450 g) floury-variety potatoes
3 fl oz (75 ml) milk
2 oz (50 g) butter
2 tbs each chopped parsley and dill
salt, pepper

For the pastry:

2 sheets filo pastry (available frozen from most Middle Eastern food
    stores)
2 oz (50 g) melted butter

Boil the potatoes in their skins. When cool enough to handle, skin and
mash dry. Add the warmed milk, butter, and seasonings and beat into a
smooth purée. Cool while you cut out the pastry. Carefully lay out both
sheets together and cut in 4, so you end up with 8 rectangles approximately 10 × 5 in (25 × 13 cm). Brush all over with the melted butter
before the pastry goes brittle. Divide the mixture amongst the 8 pieces of
pastry and roll into cork shapes. Fold the pastry around the corks sealing
with melted butter. Pre-heat the oven to 350°F/180°C/gas mark 4 and
cook the boreks on a baking sheet for approximately 20 minutes. Serve
straight from the oven; they are very delicious and you'll probably wish
you'd made more!

SPICY APPETISERS

POTATOES WITH CHEESE, WALNUT AND HOT PEPPER
SAUCE/OCOPA AREQUIPEÑA   Serves 6

Last year TV cook Glyn Christian hit on the very good idea of persuading
leading chefs and cookery writers to give short demonstrations at a
specially equipped kitchen in the West End. I went along to *KitchenClass*
specially to watch Latin American cookery expert Elisabeth Lambert Ortiz
cook this Peruvian dish.

6 medium-sized Jersey Royal potatoes, boiled and cut in half
    lengthways
6 dried red chillies, about 1½ in (3.5 cm) long

4 fl oz (110 ml) peanut oil
1 medium onion, cut into 3 crosswise slices
2 cloves garlic, finely chopped
4 oz (110 g) walnuts, ground to a paste
4 oz (110 g) ricotta, mild goats' cheese or white Cheshire, crumbled
8 fl oz (225 ml) milk
salt, pepper

For the garnish:

lettuce leaves
6 hard-boiled eggs, halved lengthways
12 black olives
strips of sweet pepper, blanched and skin removed

Remove the stems and shake the seeds out of the chillies and put them to soak in 4 tbs of hot water for 30 minutes. Drain and set aside.

Heat the oil in a small heavy saucepan and sauté the onion over a very low heat until it is golden. Add the garlic – don't allow it to brown – and sauté for 1 or 2 minutes longer. Put the oil, onion, garlic, chillies, walnuts and cheese in a food processor or blender. Add the milk and salt and process to a smooth sauce about the consistency of heavy mayonnaise. Add milk and oil in equal quantities to thin the sauce if necessary.

Arrange a bed of lettuce leaves on a large warm plate. Arrange the potatoes, cut side down, on top of the lettuce. Pour the sauce over the potatoes and garnish with the egg – sunny side up, symbolising the sun – black olives and strips of pepper.

INDIAN POTATO APPETISERS

For me no Indian meal is complete without at least one potato dish; an *alu*, or *aloo* as it's more commonly spelled. As far as I've been able to discover, Indian chefs in London don't go out of their way to find specific varieties of potato for their many and varied potato dishes. They do though seem to have considerable success with their aloos, puris, samosas, batis and bondas. Spices, chillies and peppers seem to enhance the potato's flavour and the cooking and success rate of Indian potato dishes seems foolproof. These are some of my favourite dishes and all go well with a cucumber raita.

ALOO CHAT   Serves 6–8

     6 medium-sized potatoes, boiled and cut into ½-in (1-cm) cubes
     3 fl oz (75 ml) water
     1 tbs chat masala
     2 medium-sized onions, finely chopped
     1 lb (450 g) ripe tomatoes, peeled and chopped
     3 or 4 tbs coriander leaves, chopped
     1 tsp ground, roasted cumin seeds
     2 tbs lemon juice
     salt

Mix the water into the chat masala. You can buy a proprietary brand or
make your own by mixing together ¾ tsp ground roasted cumin seeds,
¼ tsp each of red pepper, ground asafetida and mango powder, ½ tsp
black salt and ¾ tsp coarse salt. Pour the mixture over the potatoes. Stir
well and leave for 15 minutes or so, giving the occasional stir. Add the
tomatoes, onions and coriander, cover the dish and leave to cool. Stir in
the cumin, salt and lemon juice.

BATI   Serves 4

This is another but very different recipe for a potato ball or patty; this one
is cooked in the oven and has a pastry case. They are good eaten with a
garlicky dal.

     8 oz (225 g) mashed potato
     1-in (2.5-cm) piece fresh ginger, finely chopped
     1–2 tbs fresh coriander leaves, chopped
     1 tsp cumin seeds
     ½ tsp chilli powder
     8 oz (225 g) wholemeal flour
     3–4 fl oz (75–110 ml) water
     salt

Mix the ginger and coriander with the cumin, salt and chilli and stir into the
mashed potatoes. Make a dough with the flour and water and divide the
mash and dough into an equal number of piles.
     Roll the dough into approximately 3-in (7.5-cm) circles and place a pile
of mash in the centre. Fold the dough around the mixture, pinch together
in whatever way is easiest and bake for 15–20 minutes in a moderate
(350°F/180°C/gas mark 4) oven.

SAMOSAS

Serves 6–8 (16 samosas)

For the filling:

1 lb (450 g) potatoes, boiled
oil for deep frying
1½ tbs fresh ginger, peeled and grated
2 tbs ground coriander seeds
2 large onions, finely chopped
4 large cloves garlic, finely chopped
2 fresh chillies, finely chopped
1 tbs salt
1 tbs fresh mint, chopped
4 tbs coriander leaves, chopped
1 tbs garam masala

For the pastry:

6 oz (175 g) margarine
10 oz (275 g) flour
6 tbs cold water

Make the pastry ½ hour before you begin on the filling. Rub the marge into the flour; when it begins to look like breadcrumbs gradually work in the water (I always use a knife), and knead thoroughly. Put the dough in a polythene bag and leave somewhere cool for at least an hour.

Dice the potatoes and then heat some oil in a heavy frying pan and sauté the ginger and ground coriander. Add the onions and after a couple of minutes the garlic, chillies and salt. Stir around and add the potatoes, mint and a little water if the mixture is very dry. Continue cooking over a low flame for 10 minutes and mix in the coriander leaves and garam masala. Set aside to cool slightly while you give the dough another kneading.

Divide the dough into 8 balls and roll each ball into a 9-in (23-cm) circle. Cut the circles in half and curl each half into a cone. Fill the cone with the potato mixture and attempt to fashion a triangle by fixing the edges with water. Heat the oil very hot (to 375°F/190°C) and drop in 5 or 6 samosas. This will lower the oil temperature which you should maintain. The pastries will puff and blister; they are ready after about 10 minutes when they will be golden brown. Drain on absorbent paper. The pastries can be reheated in a warm oven.

15.

Soups

Take a potato, a pinch of salt and half a pint of water and you have the basis of a delicious, subtle, nourishing and inexpensive soup that is quick and easy to make. Even with so few ingredients the end result can be varied depending on whether you want a smooth broth or prefer the texture of grated, chopped or sliced potatoes.

This basic soup can be enlivened with the addition of almost any herb or spice – thyme, sage and rosemary are favourites – and is vastly improved with a pat of butter, a sliced onion and a clove or two of garlic. With minimal imagination these few ingredients can be embellished to look more attractive and to add variety of texture. Cubed or larger triangular croûtons fried in bacon fat with or without garlic transform the soup and a sprinkling of fresh parsley or chives both look and taste good. Equally good are crisply fried scraps of bacon or toasted almond slices strewn on the soup just before serving. In *New English Cookery* Michael Smith suggested making mini balls of potato as a garnish to a potato soup; this would only work with a firm or waxy variety of potato. Using a melon scoop, make a minimum of six balls per serving. Rinse and drop the balls into briskly boiling salted water and cook for two minutes. Drain and serve with the soup.

The addition of cream, yoghurt, *crème fraîche* or an egg yolk creamed with a small amount of the hot soup adds body and richness. Floury varieties of potato are perfect for puréed soups; if the recipe demands diced or sliced potatoes then choose a waxy variety.

POTAGE PARMENTIER   Serves 4

This is a classic potato and onion soup devised by the French chef Parmentier who popularised the potato in France. The recipe is never the same twice but is generally a mixture of twice the quantity of potato to onion sweated in fat and then puréed in a broth of beef, veal or chicken stock and milk and garnished with chopped parsley. In his book *101 Ways of Cooking the Potato*, published in 1932, Marcel Boulestin omits the onion altogether.

1 lb (450 g) floury-variety potatoes
½ lb (225 g) onions
1½ oz (40 g) each butter and flour
1¼ pts (700 ml) stock
5 fl oz (150 ml) milk
salt, pepper
parsley, finely chopped and croûtons

Boil the potatoes in salted water, skin and mash. Meanwhile, in a heavy bottomed 2 pt (1.1 l) casserole, sweat the finely sliced onion in the butter for five minutes over a low flame. Add the sifted flour to make a roux and gradually add the hot stock. Bring to the boil and allow to simmer for five minutes. Add the potato, simmer for a further five minutes and add the milk. Check the seasoning and whisk in a blender for two minutes to amalgamate.

Serve with a sprinkling of finely chopped parsley and croûtons.

JANE GRIGSON'S POTATO SOUP   Serves 4

12 oz (350 g) potatoes, peeled and diced
2–3 oz (50–75 g) onion, chopped
2–3 large cloves garlic, finely chopped
2 big tbs lard or pork fat
1¾ pts (1 l) light beef or veal stock or water
parsley, chopped
salt, pepper
cubes of bread fried in lard with garlic

Cook the potatoes, onion and garlic in the lard over a gentle heat for about 10 minutes, turning them over occasionally. This process should not be hurried, or the vegetables will brown and the special flavour of garlic and lard will be spoiled.

Add the stock or water and simmer until the potato is tender. Sieve or purée in the blender. Reheat and check the seasoning. Stir in the parsley and serve with the bread in a separate bowl.

GREEK POTATO SOUP/PATATA SUPA

2 large Cyprus potatoes, chopped
1 onion
2 tbs olive oil
1 carrot, chopped
2 ripe tomatoes, chopped
4 fl oz (110 ml) yoghurt
1 tsp marjoram or oregano
½ tsp fennel seed
2 pts (1.1 l) vegetable or chicken stock
1 tsp salt, pinch of pepper, freshly ground
2 tsp mint leaves, chopped

Gently fry the onion in the oil until transparent, add the potato, carrot and
tomatoes. Season with salt and pepper and mix well to coat all the
vegetables with oil. Stir in the yoghurt, pour over the stock and bring to the
boil. Cover and simmer gently for 20 minutes.

Serve sprinkled with fresh herbs. This soup can be varied by stirring in
the juice of a lemon or 2 tbs tomato purée just before serving.

SWEET POTATO SOUP   Serves 4

2 lb (900 g) sweet potatoes or yams, peeled and diced
1½ pts (900 ml) water
1 onion, sliced thinly
1 tbs sunflower oil
8 fl oz (225 ml) natural yoghurt
½ tsp salt
finely chopped parsley and grated orange rind, to garnish

Cook the potatoes in the water until tender. Meanwhile, sauté the onion in
the oil until transparent. Add the onion to the potato and purée in batches
until smooth. Return to the pan and stir in the yoghurt. Serve garnished
with parsley and the orange rind.

POTATO AND LEEK SOUP/POTAGE AUX POIREAUX ET
POMMES DE TERRE   Serves 6

Leek and Potato is one of those culinary made-in-heaven combinations.
When prepared as a soup it is called *Bonne Femme* if the vegetables are

left in chunks and vichyssoise if they are puréed. Vichyssoise is traditionally served cold.

In his marvellous book *Simple French Food* Richard Olney gives this definitive recipe which is far more delicious than you would think possible.

1 lb (450 g) potatoes
1 lb (450 g) leeks
3½ pts (2 l) boiling water
1½ oz (40 g) unsalted butter
salt

Peel, quarter lengthways and slice the potatoes. Remove the tough green parts of the leeks, clean the remaining part and slice finely. Add the vegetables to the salted, boiling water and cook, covered, until the potatoes begin to fall apart. This takes about ½ an hour to 40 minutes, depending on the density of the potatoes. Add the butter at the moment of serving after removal from the heat.

CRÈME VICHYSSOISE MICHEL AND ALBERT ROUX   Serves 8

12 oz (350 g) potatoes
1 lb 9 oz (700 g) leeks
12 oz (350 g) onions
2 oz (50 g) butter
1½ pts (900 ml) water
1½ pts (900 ml) chicken stock
16 fl oz (450 ml) double cream
salt
2 tbs snipped chives

Trim, wash and finely chop the leeks, keeping only the white parts and the first inch (2.5 cm) of green. Peel, wash and finely slice the onions. Peel the potatoes and cut them into large even-sized chunks.

Melt the butter in a saucepan and gently sweat the leeks and onions. Add the water, chicken stock and potatoes and leave to simmer for 20 minutes. Add the cream and cook for a further 5 minutes. Purée the mixture in a blender or food processor, then rub through a sieve into a bowl set in crushed ice. Stir the soup gently from time to time and season with salt. Sprinkle with chives just before serving.

Note that if you don't have any chicken stock, you can make the soup entirely with water.

CALDO VERDE   Serves 8

In his swan song from editing the *Guardian*'s food page Christopher Driver gave this recipe for the famous Portuguese cabbage and potato soup. The dish travels well and adapts to the use of kale, which is similar to the fibrous Portuguese cabbage. This authentic version is adapted from Jean Anderson's book *The Food of Portugal*.

> 6 large potatoes
> 1 large onion, finely minced
> 1 large garlic clove, finely minced
> 4 tablespoons olive oil
> 4 pts (2.3 l) cold water
> 6 oz (175 g) *chouriço* or other dried garlicky sausage, thinly sliced
> 1 lb (450 g) collards, kale or turnip greens (assuming, that is, that the Portuguese Galician *couve gallego* is unattainable)
> 2½ tsp salt, ¼ tsp freshly ground black pepper

Sauté the onion and garlic in the oil in a large heavy saucepan over a moderate heat for a couple of minutes, until they begin to colour. Add the potatoes and sauté, stirring constantly for two to three minutes. Add the water and boil until the potatoes are mushy. Meanwhile, fry the sausage over a low heat until most of the fat has run out and drain.

When the potatoes are soft remove the pan from the stove and, with a potato masher, mash the potatoes right into the soup mixture. Add the sausage, salt and pepper, cover and return to the heat for 5 minutes.

Wash the greens, trimmed of coarse stems, slice them filament thin and add to the soup with a spoon of olive oil. Check the seasoning and ladle into large soup dishes. With the traditional accompaniment of yeast-raised corn bread (called *broa*) this constitutes a main course.

JERSEY ROYAL AND MINT SOUP   Serves 4

Any firm or waxy variety of potato is suitable for this soup but I particularly like the special flavour of the Royals.

> 1 lb (450 g) potatoes
> 6 spring onions
> 1½ oz (40 g) butter
> 1½ oz (40 g) flour
> 2½ pts (1 l) chicken stock or water
> 6 sprigs mint, finely chopped
> salt, pepper

Discard the root and any tough outer leaves and finely slice the spring onions. Sweat in the butter until the onions soften and then add the potatoes which have been scraped, rinsed and finely sliced. Coat the potatoes with the butter, mixing around to prevent sticking, and continue cooking for 5 minutes.

Next, stirring all the time, sift in the flour to take up the fat. Allow to bubble up and add the stock. Add half the finely chopped mint, bring back to the boil and turn down to simmer for approximately 15 minutes until the potatoes are cooked. Season and sprinkle with the remaining chopped mint.

GARLIC SOUP   Serves 6

This is a pretty pale yellow purée that belies its savoury hotness. Devised by Colin Spencer for his book *The New Vegetarian*, it goes particularly well with a pint of cider and crusty bread for dunking.

   1½ lb (700 g) floury-variety potatoes, peeled and chopped
   3 heads of garlic, peeled
   6 tablespoons olive oil
   generous pinch saffron
   2 pts (1.1 l) water
   ½ pt (275 ml) single cream
   2 tbs parsley, finely chopped
   salt, pepper

Roughly chop the garlic and sauté it in the oil for 3 or 4 minutes until soft but not brown. Add the potatoes, saffron, seasoning and water. Simmer for 30 minutes, then cool and purée. Reheat gently and add the cream and parsley.

POTATO SOUP WITH CORIANDER   Serves 6

   1½ lb (700 g) Cyprus potatoes
   1 medium-sized sweet onion
   1 tablespoon olive oil
   2 big cloves garlic
   6 sprays of fresh coriander leaves
   2 pts (1.2 l) water
   salt, pepper

Finely chop the onion and cook in the oil over a low flame. When the onion has started to soften add the roughly chopped garlic, cover and cook for 5 minutes. Add the peeled, sliced and rinsed potatoes, season with salt and pepper and mix to cook evenly. Lay 2 sprigs of coriander over the vegetables, add the water and simmer for about 30 minutes until the potatoes are cooked. Remove the coriander, purée and adjust seasoning. The soup should be the consistency of double cream; if it's too thick add more water. Stir in the rest of the coriander leaves, finely chopped, and serve.

This is a particularly pungent soup which is delicious served with thick slices of hot Greek cow-pat bread either dribbled with olive oil or spread with olive paste.

POTATO SOUP WITH A 'WHITE RUFFLED PETTICOAT'/FEHER ROKOLYAS PITYOKALEVES   Serves 6

In 1985 Paul Kovi, who co-owns the fashionable Four Seasons restaurant in New York City, came over to London to publicise his weighty tome *Transylvanian Cuisine*. He spoke with special affection for this unusual soup that has a sour-sweet flavour. It gets its name from the whisking in of thick cream at the end of cooking which gives a lacy rim to the soup.

    2 lb (900 g) potatoes, peeled and diced
    3 pts (1.75 l) water
    3 oz (75 g) butter
    2 oz (50 g) flour
    2 egg yolks, beaten
    ¼ pt (150 ml) double cream
    small bunch fresh tarragon
    vinegar, salt and sugar to taste

Drop the potatoes in the boiling salted water and cook until tender. Using 2 oz (50 g) of the butter and the flour make a roux. To this add a ladleful of the potato water and whisk until smooth. Return this to the soup and continue boiling until it has thickened and formed a purée. Season with vinegar, tarragon and a generous pinch of sugar and bring back to the boil. Remove from the heat and stir in the beaten egg yolks. Stir in a liberal amount of the cream and the remaining butter. Remove tarragon and bring to a boil to create a white foam round the edge of the soup before serving.

POTATO AND WATERCRESS SOUP/SOUPE
DE CRESSON   Serves 4

This is another of the great classic combination soups. My favourite is
Elizabeth David's recipe adapted from *French Country Cooking*, which is
really a potato soup with raw watercress and tomato.

     2 lb (900 g) potatoes, peeled and diced
     2 onions, sliced
     2 pts (1.1 l) water
     ½ pt (275 ml) milk
     2 bunches watercress, finely chopped
     2 raw tomatoes, chopped
     dash of white wine
     salt, pepper, nutmeg or mace to taste

Boil the potatoes and onions until soft. Purée, return to the heat and add
milk, plenty of pepper and a scraping of nutmeg or mace.
    When ready to serve stir in the watercress leaves and chopped tomato.
Check seasoning and add salt. The dash of white wine, added cautiously
so as not to curdle the milk, gives the soup a lift.

CREAM OF CUCUMBER SOUP/CRÈME DE CONCOMBRE   Serves 6

This delicately flavoured soup is particularly refreshing served cold when a
sprinkling of chopped mint makes it especially summery. The recipe is
adapted from *The Second Elle Cookbook*.

     1 lb (450 g) potatoes
     2 lb (900 g) cucumbers
     3½ pts (2 l) water
     2 oz (50 g) butter
     2 oz (50 g) flour
     3½ oz (100 g) crème fraîche
     salt, pepper

Trim and peel the cucumbers, split in half lengthways, remove pips and
dice. Blanch 1 heaped tsp of the diced cucumber in boiling salted water for
5 minutes. Drain and put to one side. Peel and dice the potatoes, add the
vegetables to the boiling salted water. Season with pepper and cook
covered for 20 minutes.

Meanwhile work the butter and flour together. When the potato is cooked purée the soup and bit by bit incorporate the butter paste. Bring the soup back to the boil, stirring constantly for 5 minutes, to ensure that the flour is cooked. Remove from the heat and beat in the *crème fraîche*.

Decorate with the blanched cucumber dice and serve. If serving chilled, stir carefully before garnishing.

CHILLED APPLE SOUP/LA POMMERAIE GLACÉE   Serves 4–6

The combination of apple and potato is particularly successful, surprising though that might seem the first time you try it. This recipe, adapted from *The Norman Table* by Claude Guermont with Paul Frumkin, is unadulterated bliss and combines many of the specialities of Normandy.

   ½ lb (225 g) potatoes, washed, peeled and diced
   6 tbs butter
   2 leeks, white part only, washed and coarsely sliced
   1½ lb (700 g) apples (Granny Smith or another crisp variety),
      peeled, cored and diced into ¼-in (0.5-cm) cubes
   1½ pts (900 ml) chicken stock
   ¼ pt (150 ml) heavy cream
   2 tsp Calvados
   ⅛ tsp cinnamon
   salt, pepper
   2 apples, peeled, cored and diced into ¼-in (0.5-cm) cubes to
      garnish

Melt 4 tbs butter, add the leeks and cook, covered, for 3–4 minutes. Add the apples and cook for 5 minutes more. Add the stock and the potatoes. Bring to the boil, reduce the heat and simmer for 45 minutes.

When the soup is cooked, purée in batches until smooth and then stir in the cream, Calvados and cinnamon, season and refrigerate for at least 3 hours. Just before serving, cook the 2 diced apples in the rest of the butter until the pulp begins to soften. Drain and use to garnish the soup.

SORREL SOUP/SOUPE À L'OSEILLE   Serves 6

The lemony flavour of wild sorrel is made more subtle when cooked with equal quantities of potatoes. The soup ends up a pretty pale green and should be served with a swirl of cream and croûtons fried in bacon fat. This is an almost free soup; throughout the summer you can pick your sorrel from country meadows and hedgerows. The French variety, however, has a more piquant flavour.

    1 lb (450 g) potatoes, washed, peeled and coarsely chopped
    2 oz (50 g) butter
    14 oz (400 g) sorrel leaves washed, stalks removed
    1 small onion, finely sliced
    1 shallot, finely chopped
    1½ pts (900 ml) chicken stock
    salt, pepper
    cream and croûtons to garnish

In a heavy-bottomed dish melt the butter and add the sorrel. Cover and sweat over a low heat until the leaves flop and turn a dark green. Add the onions and cook for a couple of minutes before adding the potatoes and stock. Simmer covered for about 40 minutes and blend in batches until smooth. Season and garnish with the cream and croûtons.

ROCKET AND POTATO SOUP/ZUPPA DEI POVERI
CON LA RUCOLA   Serves 4

In Italy *rucola*, or rocket, grows wild and as the bulk of this soup is made from potatoes and stale bread it is known as 'poor man's soup', explains Marcella Hazan in the second part of her definitive *Classic Italian Cookbook*. In this country rocket is not widely available and at the moment is a fashionable salad stuff. Cooked *rucola* imparts a pleasant bitter tang.

    4 medium waxy-variety potatoes (Italian, French or Cypriot are
        perfect), peeled and diced
    1¼ pts (700 ml) water
    2 oz (50 g) rocket leaves
    3½ oz (100 g) stale Italian or French bread, cut up
    4 tbs green, fruity olive oil
    salt, pepper

Bring the potatoes to the boil in the water. Carefully rinse the rocket in several changes of water to get rid of the sand. Halfway through the cooking, after about 15 minutes, add the rocket and 2 large pinches of salt. Cover and cook for a further 15–20 minutes, remove from the heat, add the bread and cover the pot. Leave to stand for 10 minutes and stir in the olive oil and a liberal sprinkling of pepper. Serve immediately.

POTATO AND FENNEL SOUP   Serves 6

This was devised by Jennifer Mason and Stephen Davy for their Lake District restaurant Lakeland Hedgerow. The aniseedy flavour of the fennel is unusual in a soup; be sure to cook its fibrous flesh thoroughly before attempting to purée.

> 2 large floury-variety potatoes, peeled and chopped
> 1 onion, finely chopped
> 2 heads fennel with tough core removed, washed and finely
>   chopped
> 1 pt (570 ml) each vegetable stock and milk
> dash of double cream
> salt, pepper, nutmeg
> chopped parsley to garnish

Sauté the onion in the oil until transparent. Add the potatoes and fennel and cook with the lid on for 5 minutes. Add the hot vegetable stock and simmer until the vegetables are soft. Purée in batches, return to the pan and add the milk. Heat through, season with salt, pepper and nutmeg. Serve with a dash of cream and a sprinkling of parsley.

POTATOES WITH PEAS

These two vegetables combine to make subtle soups; the four pea soups I've selected show the versatility of the combination.

FRANCES BISSELL'S POTATO, BASIL AND PEA SOUP   Serves 4

> 1 lb (450 g) potatoes
> 1⅓ pts (800 ml) vegetable or chicken stock
> 4 oz (110 g) fresh shelled peas
> 1 tbs skimmed milk powder
> 12 large basil leaves
> salt, pepper

Peel, finely dice and cook the potatoes in the stock. Purée half the mixture until smooth and return to the pot, reserving 2 tbs of stock. Bring back to the boil and add the peas, simmer for 2 minutes before seasoning.

Meanwhile, blend the skimmed milk powder with the reserved stock and add this to the soup. Just before serving tear the pungent basil leaves into shreds and stir these into the boiling soup.

POTATO, PEA AND BACON SOUP   <u>Serves 6</u>

    2 lb (900 g) new potatoes, peeled, sliced and rinsed
    5 slices smoked streaky bacon
    1 small onion, finely chopped
    1 tbs flour
    2 pts (1.1 l) vegetable or chicken stock
    4 oz (110 g) fresh shelled peas
    salt, pepper

Cut the bacon into ½-in (1-cm) pieces, fry over a low heat in a non-stick
pan and gradually increase the heat as the fat runs out. Cook until the
bacon pieces are crispy all over, remove with a slotted spoon and drain on
kitchen paper.

Cook the onion in the bacon fat until it turns transparent and then stir in
the sifted flour to take up all the fat. Add a small amount of stock and,
when smooth, add the rest of the stock and the potatoes. Bring to the boil
and simmer for 20 minutes. Add the peas and cook for 5 minutes, season
carefully.

Serve sprinkled with the chopped bacon.

GREEN SOUP/HARA SHORVA   <u>Serves 6</u>

This is India's version of cream of pea soup as demonstrated by Madhur
Jaffrey in her BBC series on Indian cookery in 1982. Though spicy, the
soup is surprisingly delicate. It's not worth making unless you have fresh
peas.

    4 oz (110 g) potato, peeled and roughly diced
    3 oz (75 g) onion, peeled and roughly chopped
    2 pts (1.1 l) chicken stock
    ¾ in (2 cm) cube of fresh ginger, peeled
    ½ tsp ground coriander seeds
    2 tsp ground cumin seeds
    10 oz (275 g) fresh shelled peas
    1 tbs lemon juice
    5 tbs fresh coriander leaves chopped
    ½ fresh hot green chilli
    ½ tsp ground roasted cumin seeds
    salt to taste
    ¼ pt (150 ml) double cream

Using a large heavy-bottomed lidded pan combine the potato, onion, chicken stock, ginger, ground coriander and cumin. Cover and simmer for 30 minutes. Discard the ginger and add the peas, lemon juice, coriander leaves, chilli, salt and roasted cumin. Bring to the boil and simmer uncovered until the peas are cooked – a couple of minutes. Blend the soup in batches, return to a clean pot and add the cream. Heat through and serve.

SPLIT GREEN PEA AND POTATO SOUP/ZUPPA DI PISELLI
SECCHI E PATATE   Serves 6

This is a marvellous winter stand-by soup from Marcella Hazan's *Classic Italian Cookbook*. As she says, this recipe is very easy to prepare and is comforting cold-weather soup. Served with *crostini* (croûtons) freshly made with a firm-bodied, ideally Italian or Greek bread and Parmesan it is extremely filling.

2 medium-sized potatoes, peeled and roughly cut up
8 oz (225 g) split green peas, washed and drained
2¼ pts (1.3 l) chicken stock (water will do)
2 tbs chopped onion
3 tbs olive oil
1½ oz (40 g) butter
3 tbs Parmesan, freshly grated
salt

Cook the peas and potatoes in half the stock until soft. Purée with the cooking liquid, return to a clean pot and add the rest of the stock.

Meanwhile, fry the onion with the oil and butter at a high temperature until a rich golden colour. Add to the pot, bring back to the boil and stir to dissolve the oil and butter. Just before turning off the heat stir in the cheese and check seasoning. Serve with additional cheese and the crostini.

ONION SOUP WITH CHEESE CROÛTONS/HELLIMLI
CORBA   Serves 2

This substantial Turkish soup cooked with eggs and cheese and served with croûtons manages to be both comforting and exotic at the same time. The recipe is by Nezih Simon who some years ago produced a Turkish vegetarian cookbook *Eats Without Meats*.

2 medium-sized potatoes, peeled and sliced
2 eggs
2 medium onions
4 oz (110 g) butter
1¼ pts (700 ml) water
1 or 2 slices bread
1 cup grated Hellim, Feta or Gruyère cheese
salt, pepper

Place the potatoes in cold salted water and bring to the boil. When cooked, drain, mash and mix in the beaten eggs. Meanwhile, sauté the onions lightly in the butter, then add the 1¼ pts (700 ml) water, allowing it to bubble up with the onions for a minute or two before mixing with the egg mash. Season carefully as the cheeses for the croûtons are very salty.

Serve with croûtons made by frying the bread that you've sprinkled with the cheese.

POTATO SOUPS WITH FISH AND SHELLFISH

POTATO SOUP GARNISHED WITH LOBSTER   Serves 4

Not, as you might expect, a fancy nouvelle cuisine recipe but an old British one as unearthed by Theodora Fitzgibbon in her *Art of British Cooking*. The end result is a rich, creamy, thick soup which is incredibly luxurious and well worth the expense of lobster. Shrimps make a good cheap substitute.

2 lb (900 g) potatoes, peeled
1 pt (570 ml) milk
1 medium-sized onion, sliced
2 oz (50 g) butter
8 oz (225 g) diced lobster or shrimps
1 tbs parsley, finely chopped
¼ pt (150 ml) cream
salt, pepper

Cook the potatoes in boiling salted water. When soft, strain and mash thoroughly. Scald the milk with the onion, remove the onion when soft and carefully add the milk to the potatoes. Beat the mixture with a whisk and stir in the butter cut into little pieces. Add the diced lobster or shrimp and the finely chopped parsley and finally the cream. Gently heat through, check seasoning and serve.

POTATO SOUP WITH MUSSELS AND LEEKS/PARMENTIER
DE MOULES AUX POIREAUX   <u>Serves 4</u>

Although the potato plays a small part in this delicious soup devised by Fredy
Giradet and included in his book *Cuisine Spontanée*, its part is a vital one.

    7 oz (200 g) potatoes
    1 small leek
    2 pts (1.1 l) small mussels
    1 small shallot
    1¾ oz (50 g) unsalted butter
    ½ pt (275 ml) dry white wine
    3 tbs water
    salt, pepper, cayenne

Wash the leek and finely chop the white and pale green part, discarding
the dark green. Wash the potatoes and cook in salted water. When
cooked, skin and mash.
    Meanwhile, scrape, debeard and wash the mussels. Peel and chop the
shallot and cook gently in the butter in a large saucepan. Add the white
wine and mussels, cover the pan and shake it occasionally to ensure even
cooking of the mussels – which takes about 5 minutes. Strain off the liquid
and shell the mussels. Add 3 tbs cold water to the strained cooking liquid,
reheat and add the leeks to cook for 4 minutes. Whisk the potato into the
saucepan with the leeks and, if necessary, thin the soup down with a little
water. Adjust the seasoning with the salt, pepper and cayenne.
    Divide the mussels between the dishes and pour the soup over.

A SIMPLE GREEK BOUILLABAISSE/KAKAVIA   <u>Serves 6–8</u>

    2 lb (900 g) Cyprus potatoes, peeled
    2 onions
    1 lb (450 g) ripe tomatoes (*not* moneymakers)
    ½ pt (275 ml) olive oil
    water
    handful celery leaves
    3 lb (1.4 kg) small varied fish
    juice of 2 lemons
    salt, pepper

Roughly chop the peeled potatoes, onions and tomatoes and put them all in a large pan. Add the oil, cover with water, bring to the boil and simmer until the potatoes and onions are cooked. Add the celery leaves and fish (either whole or cut into similar-sized chunks) and continue cooking for 15–20 minutes.

Check the seasoning and squeeze in the lemon juice just before serving. Serve Greek cowpat-style bread for mopping up the liquid.

CHILEAN FISH SOUP/CALDILLO DE PESCADO   Serves 6–8

Elisabeth Lambert Ortiz produced this substantial, red-hot fish soup for the BBC series *A Taste of Health*. As you'll discover, soup is something of a misnomer.

        2 lb (900 g) small new or waxy-variety potatoes
        2 lb (900 g) skinned filleted cod, cut into 4 steaks
        2 fl oz (50 ml) lemon juice
        2 medium-sized onions
        2 cloves garlic, crushed
        1 red pepper
        1 fresh red or green chilli
        2 tbs corn oil
        ½ tsp dried oregano or 1 tsp fresh chopped marjoram
        ½ pt (275 ml) dry white wine
        1½ pts (900 ml) fish stock
        salt, pepper
        fresh chopped herbs to garnish

Season the cod steaks with salt and pepper and sprinkle with the lemon juice. Meanwhile, finely chop the onions and garlic, de-seed and chop the pepper. De-seed and finely chop the chilli and be sure to wash your hands before you peel and slice the potatoes wafer thin.

In a large heavy casserole, heat the oil and gently fry the onions, chilli and pepper until soft. Add the garlic, cod steaks and after a couple of minutes, the potatoes. Sprinkle on the herbs and pour on the wine and fish stock. Simmer covered for 20 minutes or until the potatoes are cooked.

Serve in large bowls garnished with a few fresh herbs and accompanied by crusty bread.

CULLEN SKINK   Serves 6–8

A rich soup from the Moray Firth which is the home of the Finnan
haddock. If Finnan is unavailable, use any smoked haddock but avoid
those bright yellow fish that have been dyed.

      8 oz (225 g) potato, mashed
      1 onion, peeled and chopped
      2 oz (50 g) butter
      1 lb (450 g) Finnan haddock
      1 pt (570 ml) water
      1 pt (570 ml) fish, chicken stock or milk
      ½ pt (275 ml) single cream
      1 tbs parsley, finely chopped
      salt, pepper

Soften the onion in the butter in a large pan and then add the fish cut into
large pieces. Cover with the water and simmer for 20 minutes. Remove
the fish to cool, remove any bones and flake the flesh off the skin. Stir the
potato into the cooking liquid and when it's nicely incorporated add stock
or milk. Add the fish, onion and butter, check the seasoning and cook for a
further 10 minutes. Serve with a swirl of cream and a sprinkling of parsley.

MEAT STOCK SOUPS

Almost without exception the soups mentioned here will be as good, and
on occasion benefit, by being cooked in water rather than a vegetable
stock. The following three soups rely on their particular meat stock and
bits of that meat for their specialness.

CHINESE BROAD BEAN, POTATO AND
BELLY-OF-PORK SOUP   Serves 6–7

One of the most successful cookery books of the decade has been
Chinese cook and restaurateur Ken Lo's *Cheap Chow*. The potato features
a lot in the book and this soup is well worth the hassle of preparing the
trotters – and is actually more of a meal than a soup.

1½ lb (700 g) potatoes
1 pair pig's trotters
3¼ pts (2.1 l) water
1 lb (450 g) broad beans
2 chicken stock cubes
2 tbs soya sauce
12 oz (350 g) belly of pork, diced
salt, pepper to taste
3 tbs sherry

Cover the trotters with water and bring to the boil. Skim, reduce heat, simmer for 1 hour and skim away fat again. Add the potatoes and broad beans, bring back to the boil and simmer for another hour. Add stock cubes and soya, stir to mix thoroughly and add the diced belly of pork and season. Simmer for 10 minutes and just before serving sprinkle with sherry.

ARMENIAN MEAT AND LENTIL SOUP WITH
DRIED FRUIT   Serves 6

This is my favourite bizarre potato soup, one that never fails to revive a jaded palate. It's one of many hearty soups in *Best Food of Russia* by Sonia Uvezian.

2 medium-sized waxy-variety potatoes, peeled and cubed
1 lb (450 g) boneless lean lamb or beef, cubed
4½ pt (2.4 l) water
8 oz (225 g) dried lentils
2 tbs butter
dash sunflower oil
4 oz (110 g) each dried apricots and dried pitted prunes
3 oz (75 g) walnuts, chopped
salt, pepper
chopped fresh coriander or tarragon to garnish

In a large heavy pot combine the meat, water, salt and pepper, cover and simmer for an hour. Skim off any foam that forms and stir in the lentils. Cook for 15 minutes.

Meanwhile, in a heavy and spacious frying pan, heat the butter and oil over a moderate heat and sauté the potatoes evenly. Add to the soup with the fruit and walnuts and simmer for a further 30 minutes. Check seasoning and stir in the chopped coriander or tarragon before serving.

RUSSIAN VEGETABLE SOUP   <u>Serves 8–10</u>

I came across *The Jewish Holiday Kitchen* by Joan Nathan in the course of the research for this book. All the recipes are tied to Jewish holidays and the book is packed with historical and Nathan-family anecdotes. This soup is served at Hanukkah with Russian rye bread.

    2 medium-sized potatoes
    1 sweet potato
    3 carrots
    1 gal (4.5 l) water
    2 lb (900 g) top rib, cut in stewing pieces
    2 oz (50 g) dried mushrooms or 1 cup fresh sliced mushrooms
    4 oz (110 g) each lima beans, green split peas, large whole barley
        and fresh string beans diced
    4 ribs celery, diced
    salt, pepper to taste

Grate the peeled carrots, potatoes and sweet potato on the large holes of a grater or using a food processor.

Bring the water to the boil and add all the ingredients. Cover and simmer for 2 hours, stirring occasionally. Adjust seasoning and serve with black rye bread and unsalted butter.

16.

Salads

'Two large potatoes, passed through kitchen sieve
Unwonted softness to the salad give;
Of mordant mustard add a single spoon
Distrust the condiment which bites too soon;
But deem it not, thou man of herbs, a fault
To add a double quantity of salt;
Three times the spoon with oil of Lucca crown,
And once with vinegar, procured from Town;
True flavour needs it, and your poet begs
The pounded yellow of two well-boiled eggs;
Let onion atoms lurk within the bowl,
And, scarce suspected, animate the whole;
And lastly, in the flavoured compound, toss
A magic teaspoon of anchovy sauce.'

Sydney Smith, recipe for Potato Mayonnaise, 1843

The single most important ingredient in a potato salad is the potato. Don't bother with a potato salad if you haven't got some dense-fleshed, waxy potatoes that won't disintegrate in the cooking and collapse into bits when sliced or diced.

GARNISHING

The look and flavour of a simple potato salad can be improved hugely by garnishing with some finely chopped parsley before serving. Use chives, other fresh herbs and scraps of crisply fried bacon sparingly as they change the salad.

THE BEST VARIETIES FOR SALADS

Cornish new potatoes, Jersey Royals, kidney-shaped Egyptian and Cypriot varieties, Charlotte, Pink Fir Apple, Kipfler, the French Belle de Fontenay (La Ratte, Cornichon); less reliable are Maris Piper, Home Guard, Wilja and Estima.

POTATO SALAD DRESSINGS

Vinaigrette, oil and fresh lemon juice, sour cream, mayonnaise, yoghurt dressings and combinations of these are all delicious with a potato salad. Dressings can be varied with the addition of fresh chives, parsley, dill, mint, basil or thyme and given body with mustard, capers, anchovy and other pungent relishes.

OLD ENGLISH DRESSING

    1 large cooked potato, mashed
    ½ tsp English mustard
    1 tsp salt
    ¼ tsp onion, minced
    1 hard-boiled yolk of egg
    2 tbs sunflower oil
    1 tbs cider vinegar
    1 tsp anchovy sauce

Add the mustard, salt, onion and egg to the potato. Mix in the oil and vinegar stirring briskly. Lastly add the anchovy sauce.

BASIC VINAIGRETTE

Whisk together vinegar and oil in a proportion of 1 to 3. Season with a pinch of salt and several grinds of black pepper. Unless a recipe specifically demands it, use either the best olive oil you can afford (my preference is for the fruity Greek, Portuguese and Italian oils from Lucca) or sunflower oil. Finely chopped garlic and/or shallots or a few anchovies rinsed of salt pounded with a clove of garlic give the vinaigrette more flavour. Nut oils give a very distinctive flavour to a vinaigrette. Similarly, flavoured vinegars radically alter a dressing.

MAYONNAISE

Assemble your ingredients a little while before you start making this sauce and use a warmed bowl.

> 2 egg yolks
> 1½ tbs white wine vinegar or lemon juice
> 10 fl oz (275 ml) sunflower or olive oil
> salt, pepper

Using either a wire whisk or wooden spoon beat the egg yolks until they are thick and creamy. Continue beating while you add a dash of vinegar or lemon juice and begin a trickle of oil. Continue until you have a shiny, thick sauce. Taste for seasoning. Mayonnaise can be made in a food processor by blending all the ingredients save the oil which should be added in a thin stream while the blades are running.

If the sauce separates it can be saved by adding the curdle to a new egg yolk and beating thoroughly.

AÏOLI

A very garlicky version of mayonnaise. Proceed as for mayonnaise but first pound the garlic with the salt; traditionally 8–15 cloves are used but you may prefer a less stinging aïoli in which case use only 4 or 5. If you make aïoli in a food processor, start with the garlic and salt.

CLASSIC FRENCH POTATO SALAD/SALADE DE POMMES DE TERRE   Serves 8–10

This salad is delicious on its own, or with cold or barbecued meats. The classic accompaniment is kippered herring or boiling sausage.

> 2 lb (900 g) waxy-variety potatoes
> 6 tbs white wine
> 2 tsp fresh thyme, chopped
> 10 tbs olive or sunflower oil
> 2 tbs red wine vinegar
> 2 tbs Dijon-style mustard
> 2 shallots, finely chopped
> 1 clove garlic, crushed with a few grains salt
> salt, freshly ground pepper
> 3 tbs flat parsley, chives if preferred or a mixture of both

Boil the potatoes in their skins, peel while still hot and slice into a large dish. Meanwhile boil up the wine and thyme and pour over the potatoes. Bring 8 tbs oil and the vinegar to the boil and mix in the mustard, shallots and garlic, stir around and pour over the potatoes. Season and mix thoroughly and transfer to a serving dish. Dribble the remaining oil over the salad and sprinkle on the herbs.

BOULESTIN'S POTATO SALAD   Serves 4

1 lb (450 g) waxy-variety potatoes

For the dressing:

2 hard-boiled eggs
2 tbs olive oil
1 tbs chopped parsley, chives or spring onions
salt, pepper, dash vinegar

Boil the potatoes in their skins and allow to cool before peeling. Slice the potatoes into a bowl and add the whites of the eggs cut into neat pieces.

Meanwhile, make the dressing by mashing the egg yolks into a bowl and carefully adding the olive oil, stirring all the time, to make a sauce the consistency of thick cream. Add the salt, pepper, vinegar to taste and the chives, parsley or onions. Pour the dressing over the potatoes and stir.

HOT POTATO SALAD   Serves 4

1½ lb (700 g) waxy-variety potatoes, boiled in their skins
1 medium-sized onion or 4 spring onions, finely chopped
4 rashers streaky bacon
2 tbs white wine vinegar
2 tbs chopped parsley
salt, pepper

Slice the hot potatoes (peeled or unpeeled, whichever you prefer) into a warm bowl and mix in the onions. Season with minimal salt but plenty of pepper. Meanwhile dice the bacon and fry slowly until crisp. Remove the bacon pieces to drain and then add to the salad. Pour the vinegar into the bacon fat, stir around and heat through before pouring into the salad. Stir and add the parsley.

YOGHURT MAYONNAISE POTATO SALAD   Serves 4

1½ lb (700 g) waxy-variety potatoes, cooked in their skins
1 tbs lemon juice
2 tbs olive oil
4 spring onions, chopped
1 tbs chives, chopped

For the dressing:

2 egg yolks
8 fl oz (225 ml) olive oil
8 fl oz (225 ml) yoghurt
1 tsp Dijon mustard
salt, pepper

Peel and slice or dice the potatoes while still hot into a marinade made with the lemon juice, oil and seasoning. Add the spring onions. Stir the mustard into the yoghurt. Make the mayonnaise following the basic recipe (page 131) omitting lemon juice or vinegar, and beat into the yoghurt. Pour sufficient mayonnaise over the potatoes to coat them generously, sprinkle over the chives and serve.

INTERNATIONAL VARIATIONS

SILVER PALATE AMERICAN PICNIC POTATO SALAD   Serves 20

4 lb (1.8 kg) waxy-variety potatoes, peeled and cooked in salted water
¼ pt (150 ml) each white wine vinegar and olive oil
4 oz (110 g) each purple onions, thinly sliced, celery cut into 1- × ¼-in (2.5- × 0.5-cm) strips and flat-leaf parsley, chopped
3 cucumbers, peeled, seeded and sliced
1 pt (400 ml)/14 oz (400 g) jar Hellmann's mayonnaise
5 tbs Dijon-style or herb mustard
20 hard-boiled eggs, peeled and quartered
1 tsp salt, ¼ tsp pepper

While still hot, roughly chop the potatoes into a large bowl or bowls.

Sprinkle on the vinegar, olive oil, salt and pepper. Add the onions, celery, cucumber, mayonnaise and mustard; toss gently to combine. Add the quartered eggs and parsley, toss, correct seasoning and serve.

CREOLE POTATO SALAD   Serves 4

  1 lb (450 g) waxy-variety or new potatoes
  4 tbs olive oil
  1 tbs wine vinegar
  2 cups shelled prawns
  1 tsp salt, pepper
  2 hard-boiled eggs, peeled and sliced, to garnish

Boil the potatoes in their skins and, while still hot, peel and slice. Mix the oil, vinegar, salt and pepper to make a dressing and pour over the potatoes. Mix in the prawns and decorate with sliced eggs.

HOT DANISH POTATO SALAD   Serves 6

  2 lb (900 g) waxy-variety or new potatoes, boiled and peeled
  2 small onions, sliced
  ½ pt (275 ml) milk, stock or water
  2 oz (50 g) butter, melted
  ¼ pt (150 ml) vinegar
  salt, pepper, sugar

Simmer the onions in the milk, stock or water with the butter until tender. When cooked add the vinegar and seasoning and slice the potatoes into the mixture. Cook for a few minutes and serve hot.

KARELIAN POTATO SALAD FROM FINLAND/KARJALAN PERUNAT   Serves 6

  2 lb (900 g) small, waxy-variety potatoes, scrubbed and boiled in their skins

For the dressing:

4 oz (110 g) butter
3 hard-boiled eggs, chopped
1 tsp salt, ¼ tsp black pepper
1 tbs fresh dill

Melt the butter in a saucepan, add the potatoes, salt and pepper and stir around to coat the vegetables. Stir in the eggs and transfer to a bowl. Sprinkle with the dill and serve warm or chilled.

3 TRADITIONAL FRENCH SALADS

EPIPHANY SALAD/SALADE DES ROIS   Serves 6

4 medium-sized waxy-variety potatoes, boiled in their skins, peeled
   and sliced
1 lb (450 g) dried white haricot beans
bouquet garni
4 sharp eating apples, cored and diced but not peeled
3 heads chicory, trimmed and sliced in rounds
1 head chicory, few sprigs watercress to garnish

For the dressing:

6 tbs olive or sunflower oil
3 tbs white wine vinegar
salt, pepper

In a covered pan bring the beans slowly to the boil. Skim, strain and repeat, but this time add the bouquet garni and simmer covered until cooked, then add salt to your taste. This takes approximately 1½ hours depending on the age of the beans. Allow to cool before you begin the rest of the preparations.

Whisk together the dressing and then prepare the other ingredients of the salad. Put the cooled beans, potatoes, apples and sliced chicory in a bowl, pour over half the dressing, adjust seasoning and mix thoroughly.

Line a round serving dish with the whole chicory leaves and pour the salad into the middle. Garnish with watercress and more chicory and serve with the remainder of the dressing in a jug.

AUVERGNE POTATO AND WATERCRESS SALAD/LA SALADE AUVERGNATE
Serves 4–6

1½ lb (700 g) new potatoes, boiled in their skins and diced while
   still hot
1 bunch watercress, stalks removed
5 oz (150 g) Cantal cheese, cut into ¼-in (0.5-cm) dice

For the dressing:

4 tbs walnut oil
2 tbs wine vinegar
1 tsp Dijon mustard
2 shallots, finely chopped
sprig of watercress, finely chopped
salt, pepper

In a salad bowl stir together the potatoes, watercress and cheese. Whisk
the dressing ingredients, allow to rest for a few minutes and pour over the
salad. Mix well and serve.

COUNTRY SALAD/SALADE PAYSANNE
Serves 6

1½ lb (675 g) waxy-variety or new potatoes, boiled in their skins
   and peeled
2 red peppers
7 oz (200 g) saucisson (cooked pork sausage)
2 shallots, very finely sliced
4 firm but ripe tomatoes, quartered
2 hard-boiled eggs, chopped and then sieved, 3½ oz (100 g) black
   olives to garnish

For the dressing:

3½ fl oz (100 ml) olive oil
2 tbs vinegar
fresh mixed herbs of your choice
salt, pepper

Slice the potatoes in thick rounds into a large dish. Carefully remove the core and seeds of the peppers and slice into uniform rings. Cut the saucisson into slices. Meanwhile make the dressing. Add the pepper, onion, tomatoes and saucisson to the potatoes, season and mix thoroughly. Turn into a serving dish and garnish with olives and egg.

GERMAN WARM POTATO SALAD/WARMER KARTOFFELSALAT
Serves 8

This recipe is adapted from Jane Grigson's marvellous *Observer Guide to European Cookery* and goes well with sausages.

3 lb (1.4 kg) new potatoes
4 tbs hot veal or beef stock

For the dressing:

6 oz (175 g) sweet onion, chopped
4 tbs wine vinegar
4 oz (110 g) piece smoked bacon, diced or rashers cut into strips
butter
1 level dsp cornflower
1 heaped tsp brown sugar
4 tbs water
2 oz (50 g) each chives and parsley, chopped
3 tbs soured cream or whipping cream
lemon juice to taste
salt, pepper

Scrape and steam the potatoes. Slice them into a bowl, add the very hot stock and keep warm while you make the dressing.

Mix the onion and vinegar. Fry the bacon in a very little butter. Mix the cornflour, sugar and water, then stir into the bacon. Add the onion and vinegar. Stir until the mixture clears and thickens slightly, and stops tasting floury – this does not take long. Take off the heat, quickly stir in the herbs and the cream with lemon juice to taste. Finally check seasoning, adding salt and plenty of pepper. Pour over the potatoes while still very hot. Mix gently, garnish with more chives and parsley and serve.

GREEK POTATO SALAD/PATATA SALATA   Serves 6

2 lb (900 g) waxy-variety potatoes, boiled

For the dressing:

1 onion, finely sliced
1–2 cloves garlic, finely chopped
4 tbs Greek or other fruity olive oil
2 tbs wine vinegar
1 tbs coriander leaves, chopped
1 tsp salt, ½ tsp freshly ground pepper

If preferred peel the potatoes, then chop into dice. Meanwhile whisk all the dressing ingredients together reserving a few of the coriander leaves for garnish. Pour over the dressing, mix well and garnish.

GREEK POTATO AND BEETROOT SALAD/PATATA KE KOKINOYULI SALATA   Serves 4

1 lb (450 g) waxy-variety potatoes, boiled
¼ of average-sized cucumber, thickly sliced
2 medium-sized cooked beetroot, diced
1 cup yoghurt
2 spring onions or chives, chopped
½ cup Greek or other fruity olive oil
1 tsp salt, ½ tsp freshly ground pepper
1 tbs chopped coriander leaf to garnish

Sprinkle salt over the cucumber and set aside to draw out the water while you peel and dice the potatoes and beetroot. Place the yoghurt in a bowl and stir in the potatoes with the salt and pepper. Next add the beetroot, cucumber and onion and gradually mix in the oil. Serve garnished with coriander.

This salad can be varied by adding chopped mint instead of coriander.

HUNGARIAN POTATO SALAD/BURGONYSALATA   Serves 4

1 lb (450 g) waxy-variety potatoes, boiled
2 hard-boiled eggs, sliced to garnish

For the dressing:

1 ½ tbs French mustard
1 tsp caster sugar
2 tbs tarragon vinegar
1 tbs sour cream, water
salt, pepper

Slice the potatoes into a serving dish. Make the dressing by mixing the mustard with the sugar and vinegar and seasoning. Mix in the cream and thin with a little water. Pour over the potatoes and leave for at least an hour before serving, garnished with sliced egg.

RUSSIAN POTATO SALAD WITH BEETROOT/VINEGRET IZ
KARTOFELYA I SVYOKLY   Serves 8–10 (as part of a buffet)

Russian salad is that unappetising mixture of diced vegetables in a pink mayonnaise that is always available at the delicatessen counter. It's usually a depressing-looking affair but made properly is delicious. According to Darra Goldstein in *A Taste of Russia*, beetroot is not an integral ingredient but added for festive occasions.

2 lb (900 g) waxy-variety or new potatoes, boiled and diced
1 large beetroot, boiled and diced
3 hard-boiled eggs, chopped
1 large cucumber, diced
3 oz (75 g) dill pickle, diced
3 spring onions, chopped
1 heaped tsp capers
9 tbs oil
3 tbs white wine vinegar
2 tsp fresh dill
1 tsp salt, freshly ground black pepper to taste
¼ pt (150 ml) sour cream

Put the potatoes and beetroot in a large bowl and add the hard-boiled eggs, cucumber, pickle, onions and capers and mix well. Mix together the oil, vinegar, salt, pepper and dill and pour over the salad. Finally stir in the cream until all the vegetables are coated. Chill overnight, give a final stir and serve.

RUSSIAN SALAD/STOLICHNYI SALAT/SALAT OLIV'YE

<u>Serves 10</u>

This is Russia's other universally famous salad. It was in fact invented by a French chef, Olivier, who became the toast of Moscow when in 1860 he served cooked chicken, potatoes and mayonnaise at a fashionable banquet. This embellished adaptation from *A Taste of Russia* makes a fine centrepiece for a buffet.

> 2 lb (900 g) waxy-variety or new potatoes, boiled and cut into
>   chunks
> 1 carrot, scraped, sliced and boiled
> 2 spring onions, chopped
> 4 oz (110 g) freshly shelled peas, boiled for 5 minutes
> 2 tart apples, cored and chopped but not peeled
> 1 orange, peeled and cut into chunks
> 8 oz (225 g) cooked chicken in bite-sized pieces

<u>For the dressing:</u>

> 3 hard-boiled egg yolks
> 2 tbs olive oil
> 2 tbs white wine vinegar
> 8 tbs mayonnaise
> 8 tbs sour cream
> salt, freshly ground white pepper to taste

<u>For the garnish:</u>

> 4 tbs mayonnaise
> 4 tbs sour cream
> fresh parsley or dill

While still warm put the potatoes, carrots, spring onions and peas in a large dish, add the apple, orange and chicken and mix thoroughly.

Prepare the dressing by pounding the egg yolks and mixing in 2 tbs of olive oil to make a smooth paste. Stir in 2 tbs vinegar, 8 tbs each of the mayonnaise and sour cream, season and pour over the vegetables. Mix well, cover and chill overnight.

To serve, form the salad into a high mound on a decorative plate. Mix together the remaining mayonnaise, sour cream, olive oil and vinegar and pour this over the salad. Garnish with fresh parsley or dill.

SPANISH POTATOES VINAIGRETTE/PATATAS FRITAS A LA VINAGRETA   Serves 4

This dish forms part of the tapas in and around Rioja and is unusual in that all the ingredients of the salad are cooked.

    1 lb (450 g) waxy-variety potatoes, peeled and thinly sliced
    3 tbs olive oil
    ½ tsp salt

    For the dressing:

    2 fl oz (50 ml) vinegar
    2 cloves garlic, sliced
    ¼ tsp freshly ground pepper
    4 fl oz (110 ml) olive oil

Wash and dry the potatoes and season lightly with the salt. Gently heat the 3 tbs oil in a large heavy frying pan and add the potatoes. Cook gently without browning and transfer to a shallow dish. Meanwhile bring the vinegar, garlic and pepper to the boil, add the 4 fl oz (110 ml) of oil and pour over the potatoes. Allow to rest for 10–15 minutes, pour away any excess oil and serve slightly warm.

SPANISH POTATO SALAD/EL AJO DE LA MANO   Serves 6

The combination of chillies cooked with the potatoes and raw crushed garlic makes this a spicy hot salad.

    2 lb (900 g) waxy-variety potatoes
    3 fresh green chillies

    For the dressing:

    2 tbs olive oil
    2 tbs lemon juice
    4–6 cloves garlic, crushed
    1 tsp paprika
    2 tsp salt

Add the potatoes and chillies to a pan of boiling salted water. When the potatoes are cooked, drain and cool. Peel and dice into a salad bowl, chop and add the chillies. Mix the dressing and pour over the salad. Serve warm or cold.

SCANDINAVIAN POTATO SALAD   Serves 2–3

1 lb (450 g) small new potatoes
dill to garnish

For the dressing:

¼ pt (150 ml) sour cream
2 oz (50 g) purple onion, finely chopped
2 oz (50 g) fresh dill, chopped
salt, pepper

Scrub the potatoes and drop into a pan of cold salted water. Bring to the boil and cook for 10 minutes or until the potatoes are just cooked.

In a salad bowl mix the dressing ingredients and add the hot potatoes. Stir until all the potatoes are coated in the dressing, cover and chill for at least 2 hours.

Before serving, check seasoning, add a little more sour cream if the salad seems dry and garnish with a few sprays of dill.

TURKISH POTATO SALAD/YUMURTALI PATATES SALATASI   Serves 2

1 lb (450 g) new potatoes, boiled in their skins
2 medium-sized onions, sliced in rings
2 hard-boiled eggs, sliced
salt
1 tbs parsley, finely chopped
black olives to garnish

For the dressing:

juice of 2 lemons
2 fl oz (50 ml) olive oil

Slice the potatoes into a shallow serving dish. Spread the onions over the potatoes, the eggs over the onions and sprinkle first with salt and then with the parsley. Whisk together the lemon and olive oil and dribble over the salad. Garnish with olives if liked.

FISH AND POTATO SALADS

POTATO AND HERRING SALAD/SALADE DE POMMES DE TERRE ET HARENGS FUMÉS   Serves 4

1 lb (450 g) waxy-variety potatoes, boiled
1 medium-sized onion, finely sliced
1 packet of vacuum packed matjes herrings
2 hard-boiled eggs
handful of frisée leaves
1 tbs vinaigrette
1 tbs mayonnaise (optional)
salt, pepper
1 tbs flat-leaf parsley, chopped

Begin by putting the sliced onions in a shallow dish and adding any onions that are packed with the herring. Cut the herring into lengths and then into 2-in (2.5-cm) pieces. Lay the pieces over the onion and pour over the oil from the packet. Cover and leave while you slice the potatoes, quarter the eggs and tear the frisée into bite-sized pieces.

Pour the vinaigrette (see basic recipe page 130) over the potato pieces while still hot, season and mix thoroughly. Mix the herring and onions with the potatoes and stir in the mayonnaise (see basic recipe page 131) if using. Transfer to a serving dish and arrange the egg on top, sprinkle with parsley and serve with plenty of crusty bread and cold beer.

This recipe can be varied by the omission of the frisée and inclusion of a cored and diced Cox's Orange Pippin. It is also rather good served with diced cooked beetroot.

BETTY HELLER'S SWEDISH HERRING SALAD   Serves 4

This is a more elaborate version of the French herring salad. Ms Heller was given this recipe by a Swedish friend and it won her a bottle of Tuscan olive oil in an *Independent* cookery challenge.

8 oz (225 g) new potatoes, boiled
1 salt herring
8 oz (225 g) pickled or plain boiled beetroot
1 medium-sized apple
1 medium-sized onion
1–2 oz (25–50 g) pickled gherkins
4 tbs white wine vinegar
2 tbs water
2 tbs sugar
6 grinds of black pepper or ½ tsp ground pepper
4 fl oz (110 ml) sour cream
2 fl oz (50 ml) whipping cream
2 hard-boiled eggs, parsley to garnish

Clean the fish, removing the head. Rinse, drain, skin and fillet. Dice the fish, potatoes, beetroot, apples, onion and gherkins. Mix thoroughly – but carefully.

Blend vinegar, sugar and pepper and add to mixture, stirring gently. If desired, add the whipping cream at this point. Pack into a mould rinsed in cold water and chill in the fridge.

Unmould and garnish with sliced egg and parsley. Serve with sour cream beaten stiff.

SALADE NIÇOISE   Serves 6

In her series on Mediterranean Cookery for the BBC, Claudia Roden explained that a true *salade niçoise* as served in the south of France would never contain potatoes or any other boiled vegetables. Like Russian salad it is a salad that is much bastardised; this is my bastardised version – naturally with potatoes!

1 lb (450 g) small waxy-variety potatoes, boiled and sliced
8 oz (225 g) French beans
2 green peppers, thinly sliced
6 spring onions, thinly sliced
12 anchovy fillets, washed and cut into pieces
8 oz (225 g) can of tuna, flaked
4 oz (110 g) black olives
3 hard-boiled eggs, shelled and quartered

For the dressing:

1 clove garlic
3½ fl oz (100 ml) olive oil
2 tbs red wine vinegar
6 basil leaves, finely chopped
salt, pepper

Rub the garlic around the salad bowl, mix the dressing in the bowl and add all the ingredients. Mix around taking care not to break up the eggs.

BLOATER AND POTATO SALAD   Serves 6

In *English Food* Jane Grigson elevates the bloater to dinner party status with this simple yet delicious recipe. The same quantity will feed 4 for lunch, when it should be served with plenty of good bread and butter.

1 lb (450 g) waxy-variety potatoes; first choice would be Pink Fir
   Apple
3 fine bloaters
1 heaped tbs chopped chives to garnish

For the dressing:

5 tbs olive oil
1½ tbs lemon juice
salt, pepper, sugar

Strip the skin from the bloaters, remove fillets from the bone and set aside roes for another dish. Divide the fish into strips or cut the fish into pieces if the fillets look messy.

Meanwhile, boil the potatoes in their skins and when done peel and slice. Make up the vinaigrette with the oil, lemon juice, salt, pepper and sugar. Put the fish in the centre of a spacious serving dish and sprinkle 1 tbs of the vinaigrette over the bloaters. In a separate bowl toss the potatoes in the rest of the vinaigrette while still hot.

When cool, arrange the potatoes around the fish, chill and serve garnished with the chives.

SPANISH POTATO SALAD WITH TUNA AND
EGG/PATATAS ALIÑADAS   Serves 2 (or 4 as tapas)

Serve this as part of a tapas meal (indeed the recipe is adapted from Penelope Casas's book *Tapas*) or as a lunch dish.

    12 oz (350 g) waxy-variety or new potatoes
    3 tbs olive oil
    1½ tbs white wine vinegar
    1 tbs flaked tuna
    1 hard-boiled egg, sliced and each slice cut in half
    ½ small onion, finely chopped
    1 tbs parsley, chopped
    2 tbs tomato, diced
    salt, freshly ground pepper

Cook potatoes in boiling salted water for 10 minutes, remove from heat and leave covered until tender – about 15 minutes. Peel and cut into thin slices.

Whisk the oil, vinegar, salt and pepper. Spread a thin coating of the dressing over the bottom of a deep serving dish. Arrange half the potato slices on top, then sprinkle with salt, half the tuna, half the egg slices, half the onion and half the dressing. Repeat for a second layer. Top with parsley and tomato and leave to stand for at least an hour before serving.

WARM MUSSEL AND POTATO SALAD   Serves 6

    2 lb (900 g) waxy-variety potatoes, boiled and sliced while still hot
    4 pts (2.3 l) mussels
    1 glass white wine
    2 medium onions, chopped
    6 fl oz (175 ml) vinaigrette
    black pepper
    1 tbs chopped parsley to garnish

Scrub the mussels and rinse in several changes of water. Put them with the wine, onions and pepper in a large pan. Cover and bring the liquid to the boil as quickly as possible. Shake the pan to ensure that all the mussels get cooked. They are done when they open and that takes about 5 minutes. Strain and retain the liquor. Remove the mussels from their shells, discarding any that have not opened, and set aside to cool. Pour the hot liquor over the hot potatoes, leave to cool and then drain.

Mix the mussels in with the potatoes and stir in the vinaigrette (see recipe page 130). Transfer to a serving dish and garnish with the parsley and more black pepper.

CRAB AND POTATO SALAD   Serves 4

1 lb (450 g) waxy-variety potatoes, boiled in their skins
6 tbs each of olive oil and fresh lemon juice
1 lb (450 g) fresh crab meat
¼ pt (150 ml) homemade mayonnaise
2 oz (50 g) parsley, finely chopped
salt, pepper
2 hard-boiled eggs, quartered and 8 black olives to garnish

Slice the potatoes while still hot and sprinkle with the previously whisked olive oil, lemon juice, salt and pepper. Set aside 2 tbs of the crab meat, mash up fine and mix in with the mayonnaise (see recipe page 131). Carefully mix the parsley and the bulk of the crab meat in with the potatoes. Spoon the crab-mayo over the salad, garnish with the eggs and olives. Serve.

SPICY POTATO SALADS

INDIAN SPICED POTATO SALAD/ALOO RAITA   Serves 4–6

1 lb (450 g) new potatoes, boiled, peeled and sliced
8 fl oz (225 ml) plain yoghurt
½ tsp cumin seeds
½ tsp cumin seeds
1 dsp coriander leaves, chopped
½ tsp salt, pinch black pepper, chilli powder

Cream the cumin, salt, pepper, chilli powder and half the coriander leaves into the yoghurt. Add the potatoes and tomatoes, mix thoroughly and garnish with the rest of the coriander.

GUJARATI-STYLE YOGHURT WITH POTATOES/BATATA NU RAITA

This is a variation on Aloo Raita (above) but the potatoes are diced and fried, sizzled with the cumin seeds, allowed to cool and then mixed with the other ingredients. Omit the tomatoes.

PERUVIAN-STYLE POTATOES/PAPAS AREQUIPEÑAS   <u>Serves 6</u>

2 lb (900 g) waxy-variety potatoes, boiled in their skins
6 hard-boiled eggs quartered, olives, sliced tomato, cucumber and
   radishes to garnish

<u>For the dressing:</u>

2 fl oz (50 ml) oil
¼ pt (150 ml) milk
2 oz (50 g) unsalted, shelled peanuts
1 green chilli, seeded
1 small onion, chopped
2 oz (50 g) crumbled Feta or grated Gouda
tsp salt, ¼ tsp pepper

Skin and halve the potatoes. Place on a serving dish flat side down.
Meanwhile, liquidise all dressing ingredients and pour over the potatoes.
Garnish with the egg, olives, tomato, cucumber and radish and serve.

UNUSUALLY DRESSED SALADS

CARDAMOM DRESSING   <u>Serves 4</u>

Inspired by the use of cardamoms with milk-based products in Eastern
cooking, Judy Ridgway devised this recipe for her book *The Vegetable
Year Cook Book*. The flavour is very exotic and the salad is good with
barbecued lamb kebabs.

1½ lb (700 g) new potatoes, cooked and sliced
6 cardamom pods
8 oz (225 g) yoghurt
salt, pepper

Remove the cardamom seeds from the pods and crush in a pestle and
mortar. Mix with the yoghurt and seasonings and pour over the sliced
potatoes. Cover and leave in the fridge for at least 2 hours before serving.

SPICED POTATO SALAD WITH FRESH CORIANDER   Serves 4–5

The recipe is served at the Everyman Bistro in Liverpool.

  1 ½ lb (700 g) small new potatoes
  2 tbs sesame seed oil
  2 oz (50 g) sesame seeds
  1 tbs mustard seeds
  1 in (2.5 cm) fresh root ginger, peeled and finely grated
  ½ tsp chilli powder or hot pepper sauce
  juice of ½ lemon
  2 tbs fresh coriander leaves, chopped
  salt to taste

Boil the potatoes until just tender. Drain and put in a salad bowl. Meanwhile, heat the oil in a frying pan and stir in the sesame seeds, mustard seeds, ginger, chilli and salt. Fry and stir for 3 minutes. Mix the oil and spices into the potatoes, add the lemon juice and stir. When completely cool, stir in the coriander leaves.

SWEET POTATOES WITH TAHINI AND
SOY SAUCE DRESSING   Serves 4

This rich salad comes from *The Covent Garden Cookery Book*.

  4 sweet potatoes weighing 5–6 oz (150–175 g) each

  For the dressing:

  2 tbs tahini
  2 tbs soy sauce
  5 tbs water
  6 spring onions, finely chopped
  salt, pepper

Boil or bake the potatoes until soft. Split open and scoop out the flesh. Chop roughly into a salad dish and mix in the previously whisked dressing. Serve with a crisp lettuce salad.

17.

Lunch, High Tea and Supper Dishes

'We have come to you with the Potato-man
Who no longer can maintain himself in the field
Seeing how cold and wet it now is
He demands a feast of bacon and pancakes.'

A. de Gubernatio, *La Mythologie des Plantes*, 1882

I am especially fond of this section of the book.

The recipes aren't collated because of a particular cooking technique, don't especially rely on leftovers (though some of course *do*) or on exotic additional ingredients. These are knock-up recipes, homely dishes that show the potato's role as a comfort food. Most of the recipes are also quick to make or 'make themselves' while you are doing something else. Also these recipes are easy to expand and ingredients are adaptable.

There are of course many other recipes throughout the book that would fit within this section; most particularly the sections on Soups, Bake, The Gratin and Leftovers.

PANCAKES, BAKES AND FRY-UPS

POLISH POTATO PANCAKES/PLACKI ZIEMNIACZANE   Serves 4

In the very early days of the research for this book I had lunch with a Polish friend at the Polish Centre's restaurant Lowiczanka. After a delicious lunch my friend boasted that his mother's *placki* knocked spots off what we'd just eaten. Now that I've cooked Mrs Olga Rymaszewska's recipe I know what he means.

1 lb (450 g) floury-variety potatoes
1 small onion
4 oz (110 g) self-raising flour
2 eggs, beaten
oil for frying
salt, pepper

Wash, peel, grate and rinse the potatoes. Drain and dry them carefully. Finely chop the onion and mix it together with the potato, flour, eggs, salt and pepper. Continue mixing for at least 2 minutes and don't worry about the slight discolouration.

Heat up ¼ in (0.5 cm) depth of oil and drop in pancakes formed on a serving spoon. Cook over a gentle heat for about 7 minutes a side until they are golden brown but the inside is cooked thoroughly. Drain and serve directly with sour cream or cottage cheese.

LATKES

Latke is the Yiddish for pancake and, while the ingredients are almost identical to the Polish version, a good latke is thin and crisp.

1 lb (450 g) potatoes
1 small onion (optional)
2 tbs self-raising flour or matzah meal
2 eggs, beaten
oil for frying
salt, pepper

If using an onion grate it first and then the potatoes. Rinse the potatoes, drain and dry in a tea towel. Mix the potatoes, onion, flour, egg and seasoning to make a batter.

Heat ½ in (1 cm) oil and drop about 1 tbs of the mixture per latke into the pan. Quickly spread the mixture round with the back of the spoon and cook for a few minutes on each side. Drain and serve immediately on their own, with cold meat, sour cream or a tart apple sauce.

CRIQUE/MATAFAIM   Serves 4

This dish comes from the south of France where it is the traditional kill-hunger (matafaim) for the farmers after the long slog of the end of summer harvesting. It's a cake-sized latke without flour and, as you might expect, with garlic.

1½ lb (700 g) peeled and grated potatoes
2 eggs, beaten
2 cloves garlic, crushed and chopped
olive oil for frying.
salt, pepper

Rinse and dry the potatoes and mix with the eggs and garlic. Heat a large frying pan and add the oil; when it begins to smoke pour in the mixture and spread evenly round the pan. Turn down the heat and cook for 15 minutes giving the pan the odd shake in the hope of preventing it sticking. Turn the cake and cook for a further 5 minutes or finish under the grill. Season well before serving with a bitter green salad.

BOXTY   Serves 4

'Butter on the one side
Gravy on the other,
Sure them that gave me Boxty
Were better than my mother.'

Old Irish rhyme

Boxty originates from the word *bochty* or *boch*, meaning poor.

8 oz (225 g) raw potatoes
8 oz (225 g) mashed potatoes
4 oz (110 g) self-raising flour
3–4 fl oz (75–100 ml) milk
bacon fat for frying
salt, pepper

Grate the potatoes on to a clean cloth and squeeze out all the starch. Mix with the mash and mix in the sifted flour, salt and milk to make a thick batter. Heat the bacon fat and drop in spoonfuls and squash into pancakes in the pan. Fry on a gentle heat for about 4 minutes a side until golden brown.

Boxty can be made with a little grated onion or parsnip in the mixture. They are particularly good with bacon but go with anything.

PAN HAGGERTY   Serves 4

This is a Northumberland pan-fried potato cake.

1 lb (450 g) potatoes
dripping for frying
8 oz (225 g) onions, sliced
4 oz (110 g) cheese, grated
salt, pepper

Cut the potatoes into very thin slices, rinse them well and dry in a tea
towel. Heat up a generous tbs of dripping in a heavy-bottomed or
non-stick pan over a gentle heat and make layers of potatoes, onion and
cheese finishing with potatoes. Season each layer. Cook for 30 minutes
until the bottom is nicely brown and top layer is soft. Either turn or finish
under the grill.

STOVIES/STOVED POTATOES   Serves 2

Choose a heavy-based pan with a tight-fitting lid for making Scottish
stovies, a slow way of cooking firm-fleshed new potatoes in butter or
dripping and water.

12 oz (350 g) small new potatoes
2–3 tbs butter
2–3 tbs water
salt, pepper

Melt the butter with the water and put in a closely-packed layer of
scrubbed potatoes. Season lightly and press a buttered paper over the
potatoes and then the lid. Check the potatoes are browning nicely after 20
minutes, and cook for another 20 minutes. The flavour of these potatoes
is indescribably delicious. Give the pan the odd shake throughout the
cooking to prevent the potatoes sticking.

CORNISH POTATO FRY   Serves 1

2 large potatoes, peeled and finely sliced
1 rasher bacon
bacon fat for frying
1 small onion, finely chopped
1 tbs flour
salt, pepper

Remove the rind from the bacon and cut the bacon into little bits. Fry the bacon bits in a little fat, add the onion and when it begins to soften add the potatoes. Season and stir in the flour, sifted. Pour in just enough water nearly to cover the contents of the pan. Cover the pan with a plate and leave on a very low heat for about 1 hour.

This is a variation on Scottish stovies. All the water will be absorbed and the potatoes will have a crisp under layer. A delicious mess.

DUBLIN CODDLE   Serves 6–8

A Saturday night supper dish that is varied according to what's to hand. This is the authentic version from the Irish Tourist Board Information Sheet No. 29.

> 8 large potatoes, peeled and sliced
> 1 lb (450 g) pork sausages
> 8 thick slices streaky or back bacon
> 2 pts (1.1 l) water
> salt, pepper

Boil the sausages and bacon for 5 minutes in enough water to cover. Remove, keeping the liquid. Put all the ingredients in a casserole dish, adding seasoning to taste. Add the cooking liquid and water. Cover and cook in a slow oven (300°F/150°C/gas mark 2) for at least an hour or until the ingredients form a semi-thick stew.

POTATO AND ONION BAKE   Serves 4

> 1 lb (450 g) potatoes, sliced and rinsed
> 1 large onion, finely sliced
> approximately ½ pt (275 ml) milk
> 2 oz grated cheese
> salt, pepper

Grease an ovenproof dish and fill with alternate layers of potatoes and onions, seasoning with salt and pepper. Add just enough milk to cover and sprinkle the cheese – Parmesan, Cheddar or Mozzarella are especially good – on top. Cook for about 1 hour at 350°F/180°C/gas mark 4.

CZECHOSLOVAKIAN POTATO CAKES/
BRAMBOROVY GULAS

    3 lb (1.4 kg) potatoes, peeled and diced
    2 onions, finely chopped
    ¼ pt (150 ml) olive oil
    3 oz (75 g) flour
    1 tbs paprika
    4 tbs parsley
    2 bay leaves
    ½ pt (275 ml) yoghurt
    salt, pepper

In a large heavy-based pan sauté the onions in a little of the oil until transparent. Stir in the sifted flour and let it bubble up for a minute or two and stir in the dried but unwashed potatoes. Sprinkle on the paprika, salt, pepper, parsley and bay leaves and then the yoghurt. Simmer over a gentle heat for about 15 minutes until the potatoes are tender.

Heat up a little oil in a frying pan and gently sauté a cupful of the mixture. When it's nicely crispy flip over and crisp up the other side. Keep warm while you cook the other pancakes.

GREEK SPINACH AND POTATO PIE

    1 lb (450 g) waxy-variety potatoes
    1 small onion, chopped
    4 oz (110 g) butter
    1 clove garlic
    ½ tsp each mint and ground cumin
    1 tsp each ground coriander and turmeric
    ¼ tsp chilli powder
    1 tbs fresh coriander, chopped
    1 tsp lemon juice
    8 oz (225 g) spinach
    1 lb (450 g) filo pastry
    salt, pepper

Peel and dice the potatoes and cook in boiling water for 5 minutes. Drain. Sauté the onion in a little butter until transparent, add the garlic and spices. Continue cooking over a low heat for two minutes stirring continuously. Add the potatoes, mint, lemon juice, salt and pepper, stir a few times and remove from the heat.

In another pan sweat the spinach with a little butter and mix in with the potatoes. Butter an appropriate ovenproof dish and brush more melted butter over at least 6 sheets of filo.

Working quickly build up the layers of filo in the pan. They will all hang over the edges of the dish and these spare bits will be tucked in to completely enclose the filling. Pour in the filling, tuck it up with the overhang and seal with more butter. If you wish you can build up more layers on top but they must be painted with butter.

Bake for 30 minutes at 375°F/190°C/gas mark 5. The pastry will be golden.

POTATO KIBBEH   Serves 6–8

Kibbeh is a popular Middle Eastern dish of cracked wheat (burghul) and minced lamb mixed with onions and spices. It is either used to form a shell around a stuffing of more of the same mixed with pine nuts and then deep fried, or eaten raw with onion and fresh mint and a sprinkling of olive oil. This recipe is Claudia Roden's idea – to bake the kibbeh 'like an oriental shepherd's pie' but it can be formed into stuffed balls and deep fried.

A vegetarian version of this dish with the stuffing made from mint and pine nuts and the pie cooked in a round pan under the grill is served at my favourite Lebanese restaurant, The Phoenicia in Kensington. Both versions are very delicious but very, very filling.

For the shell:

1½ lb (700 g) mashed potato
12 oz (350 g) coarse burghul
3 eggs
4 oz (110 g) butter
½ tsp allspice
salt, pepper, pinch nutmeg

For the stuffing:

1 large onion, chopped
1½ lb (700 g) minced lamb
2 tbs sultanas
3 tbs pine nuts
1 tsp cinnamon
salt, pepper

Soak the *burghul* in cold water for 1 hour. Drain and squeeze out. Mix into the mashed potato and beat in the eggs, 2 oz (50 g) of the butter, melted, spices, salt and pepper.

To make the filling, fry the onion until it's limp but not brown. Add the meat and stir-fry until it changes colour. Add the other ingredients and 3–4 tbs of water. Cook gently for a few minutes until the water is absorbed.

Butter a large ovenproof dish with the remaining 2 oz (50 g) and spread out half the potato mixture, then the meat and finally the remaining potato on top. Bake for about 40 minutes at 375°F/190°C/gas mark 5 until the top is golden.

CHINESE POTATO CAKES   Serves 4

This recipe is adapted from Yan Kit So's *Wok Cookbook*. If you don't have a wok, a heavy-based frying pan will do. Like the French, the Chinese always use potato flour in their sauces although it is rare to see potato on the menu in a Chinese restaurant. Dried shrimps can be found at any Chinese food store.

1 lb (450 g) mashed potato
6 oz (175 g) pork with a little fat, finely minced
½ oz (15 g) dried shrimps, rinsed
8 tbs vegetable oil
2 large shallots or small onions, chopped
2 tbs potato flour or 2½ tbs flour

For the marinade:

2 tsp sherry
2 tsp soy sauce
1 tsp sesame oil
½ tsp potato flour or ¾ tsp flour
¼ tsp sugar
½ tsp salt, 6 turns of white pepper mill

Mix the marinade ingredients together and stir in the pork. Leave for at least 15 minutes. Pour 2 tbs very hot water over the shrimps and leave for 15 minutes, then rinse, chop and add to the pork.

Heat the wok to smoking point and add 2 tbs of the oil and swirl it around. Add the shallot, stir around 6 times before you add the pork. Using a spatula, turn and flip continually for about 45 seconds and remove. Stir into the mashed potato, mixing well. Wash and dry the wok. Sift the flour into the mixture and divide into 8 portions and mould each into little cakes approximately 2½ ins (6 cm) wide.

Reheat the wok, add 2 tbs oil and swirl around. Lower the heat and put in 4 of the cakes. Fry them for about 5 minutes, carefully turn the cakes over, add a trickle more oil and fry until golden brown. Keep these cakes warm while you cook the others.

POTATO STEWS

POTATOES WITH CHEESE, TOMATO AND ONION SAUCE
Serves 6

This is one of The Great Combinations, and variations on this dish are known to everyone. Call it by its Colombian name of *Papas Chorreadas* and it sounds quite exotic.

> 1½ lb (700 g) waxy-variety potatoes
> 1 onion, finely chopped
> 1 oz (25 g) butter
> 2 large tomatoes, peeled and chopped
> ¼ pt (150 ml) double cream
> 4 oz (110 g) Cheddar cheese, grated
> salt, pepper

Boil the potatoes in their skins, peel and cut into chunks. Keep warm while you prepare the sauce. Soften the onion in the butter, add the tomatoes, salt and pepper to taste and cook, stirring, for 5 minutes. Stir in the cream and cheese and keep on stirring until the cheese is almost melted. Pour the sauce over the potatoes.

This can be topped with equal quantities of grated cheese and breadcrumbs and finished under the grill.

POTATOES AND APPLES WITH BACON   Serves 4–6

This is a popular combination and one of many that recur in different forms throughout the book. This is a German recipe called *Himmel und Erde*, meaning heaven and earth.

> 2 lb (900 g) small new or waxy-variety potatoes
> 2 lb (900 g) apples, Cox's would be perfect
> 8 oz (225 g) thin sliced, smoked, streaky bacon
> salt, pepper

Scrub and/or peel the potatoes; cook in salted boiling water and 5 minutes before the end of cooking add the peeled, cored and quartered apples. Drain and put into a warmed serving dish. Dice the bacon and sauté it gently in a non-stick pan. When it's crispy, mix the bacon and juices into the potato mixture.

The Dutch do a similar dish called *hete bliksem* (hot lightning). I prefer this German version where the bacon is crisp and there is no sugar.

VEGETABLE MOUSSAKA   Serves 4–6

> 1 lb (450 g) waxy-variety potatoes, peeled, sliced and rinsed
> 2 aubergines
> 2 onions, chopped
> 3 tbs clarified butter, for frying
> 4 cloves garlic, crushed and chopped
> 1 tsp ground cinnamon
> 8 oz (225 g) mushrooms
> 4 tomatoes, peeled and quartered
> 8 oz (225 g) courgettes, cut in thick pennies
> 2 oz (50 g) butter, for the sauce
> 3 tbs flour, sifted
> ½ tsp freshly grated nutmeg
> 1½ pts (900 ml) milk
> salt, pepper

Trim and slice the aubergines, sprinkle with salt and leave to drain while you prepare everything else.

Gently sauté the onions in a little of the butter; when they begin to wilt add the garlic, potatoes, salt, pepper and cinnamon. Cook for 5 minutes and empty into a large dish. Rinse the salt off the aubergines, pat dry and fry on both sides in a little butter. Set aside separately. Cut the mushrooms into quarters and cook for a couple of minutes in a little butter. Stir in with the other vegetables.

Grease a suitable ovenproof dish and make layers of aubergine and the vegetable mixture. In a small saucepan melt the rest of the butter, stir in the flour and nutmeg and carefully incorporate the milk. Keep stirring while it thickens, season to taste and pour the white sauce on top of the vegetables. To make the sauce richer you can beat in 1 or 2 egg yolks. Bake at 375°F/190°C/gas mark 5 for 30–40 minutes until the top is scorched and the vegetable juices are bubbling.

STEWED POTATOES WITH ONIONS AND TOMATOES/PATATE IN UMIDO   Serves 6

> 1½ lb (700 g) waxy-variety potatoes, peeled, cut into 1 in (2.5 cm) dice, rinsed and dried
> ¼ pt (150 ml) olive oil
> 2 large sweet onions, very finely sliced
> 1 green pepper, cored and cut into ½ in (1 cm) wide strips
> 1 12–14 oz (350–400 g) tin Italian plum tomatoes
> salt, pepper

Heat the oil and sauté the onions until they start to soften, then add the peppers. Cook for a few more minutes and add the tomatoes, roughly chopped, and their juice, salt and pepper. Turn the heat down and let the tomatoes simmer for 15 minutes. Add the potatoes and turn the heat right down. Cover the dish and simmer for about 30 minutes or until the potatoes are done. Serve with crusty bread to mop up the delicious juices.

POTATO RATATOUILLE   Serves 4

> 1 lb (450 g) potatoes, diced
> 2 fl oz (50 ml) olive oil for frying
> 1 large onion, sliced
> 1 clove garlic, finely chopped
> 1 large green pepper, cored and sliced
> 4 tomatoes, peeled and quartered
> 2 courgettes, sliced
> 1 bay leaf
> 1 spray fresh, or 1 tsp dried, thyme
> salt, pepper

Heat the oil in a frying pan and gently cook the onion until limp; then add the garlic and pepper. Cook for 5 minutes before adding the tomatoes, potatoes, courgettes, herbs and seasoning. Stir, cover and simmer gently for about 30 minutes.

YUGOSLAVIAN POTATO NOODLES WITH CHEESE   Serves 4

    1 lb (450 g) dry mashed potato
    8 oz (225 g) flour
    1 egg, beaten
    1 tbs milk
    butter, for greasing
    4 oz (110 g) grated cheese
    4 oz (110 g) diced bacon
    salt, pepper

Sieve the flour into the potatoes, beat in the egg, milk and seasoning and work into a stiff paste. Flour a board and roll out the paste into a long ½-in (1-cm) wide sausage. Cut off 2-in (5-cm) lengths and drop them into boiling salted water. When they float to the surface they are done.

Drain and arrange in a buttered gratin dish. Smother with the cheese and diced bacon and bake for 15 minutes in a very hot oven (425°F/220°C/gas mark 7) or brown under a hot grill until the cheese has melted and the bacon bits are crisp.

If you omit the bacon and top with a mixture of crumbled blue and grated Swiss cheese and finally a dribble of melted lard you have a French dish called *Crozets*.

POTATO BADUN   Serves 2

    8 oz (225 g) potatoes
    10 fl oz (275 ml) thick coconut milk
    ½ tsp saffron
    1 dsp chilli powder
    1 dsp Bombay Duck
    1-in (2.5-cm) slice fresh ginger
    3 cloves garlic, chopped
    4 onions, finely sliced
    3 tbs oil for frying
    salt

Boil the potatoes in their skins, peel and slice thickly. Put in a pan with the coconut milk and simmer over a very low heat with the saffron, chilli, Bombay Duck, ginger and garlic. Meanwhile, gently fry the onion until it is soft. Mix in with the other ingredients, cover and cook until all the liquid has been absorbed and/or evaporated. Season to taste.

This is very good with lime pickle and some freshly cooked Indian bread.

KHUTTAH CURRY   Serves 4

1 lb (450 g) potatoes
½ oz (15 g) tamarind
1 dsp Demerara sugar
4 oz (110 g) each artichokes, sweet potatoes and carrots
8 oz (225 g) each pumpkin and tomatoes
1 onion, chopped
2 cloves garlic
½ tsp chilli powder
1 tsp each ground turmeric, coriander seed and onion seed
2 fl oz (50 ml) mustard oil
salt

Mash the tamarind and mix with a little water to make a paste. Make the water up to about ½ pt (275 ml) and stir in the sugar. Chop all the vegetables into fairly large pieces and put into a pan with the tamarind water, the garlic and spices and bring it all to the boil. While that's happening heat the mustard oil in a separate pan and cook the onion seed. When the seeds begin to pop pour the oil and seeds over the boiling vegetables. Turn the heat right down, jam on a tight lid and simmer for 20 minutes. This is very good cold.

MUSHROOM AND POTATO DISHES

Wild mushrooms and potatoes that taste of potatoes are made for each other. The following selection are perfection; so too is the gratin on page 83.

POTATOES WITH CEPES   Serves 2

This is a recipe from Jane Grigson's *Good Things* for eking out a few cepes after a bad woodland haul.

1 lb (450 g) waxy-variety potatoes, boiled and sliced
2 tbs olive oil or goose fat
a few cepes
1 clove garlic, chopped
salt, pepper, 1 tbs parsley

Heat the olive oil in a frying pan over a low flame and fill with sliced potatoes. Add the sliced cepe caps and stir them about until they're lightly browned. Cover and lower the heat. Chop the cepe stalks with a clove of garlic and some parsley and add them to the pan with some salt and pepper. Leave to cook for 15 minutes and you will find that the potatoes have absorbed the flavour of the cepes.

CEPES COOKED WITH POTATOES AND GARLIC/CÈPES À LA SARLADAISE   Serves 3–4

This is a recipe from Périgord, home of the wild mushroom as well as the truffle. It is a fabulously rich and aromatic dish; a culinary memory that won't fade in a hurry.

1½ lb (700 g) potatoes, waxy-variety is preferable
4 tbs goose or duck fat
1 slice smoked bacon, finely diced
1½ lb (700 g) cepes, chopped
3 large cloves garlic, minced
2 tbs flat-leaf parsley, chopped
salt, pepper

Peel and slice the potatoes finely. Rinse in plenty of cold water and drain while you heat up the fat. Fry the bacon until it begins to crisp and add the potatoes. Stir well to coat the potatoes with the fat and add the cepes. Cover and cook gently for 5 minutes. Add the garlic, parsley and seasoning. Cover and cook for a further 10–15 minutes until the potatoes are cooked, all the flavours have merged and you'll be going crazy with the smells.

POTATOES BAKED WITH MUSHROOMS/PATATE ALLA BOSCAIOLA   Serves 4

Despite claiming that Italians aren't very good with potatoes, Marcella Hazan managed to find several marvellous recipes for her *Classic* and

Second Classic Italian Cookbook. This is a recipe from Liguria, one of the few parts of Italy where potatoes, garlic and mushrooms are justly venerated. Ms Hazan quite reasonably assumes that wild boletus mushrooms are more or less out of the question. This is a dish that is cooked and eaten immediately.

  1 lb (450 g) small, new potatoes
  ¾ oz (20 g) dried boletus mushrooms
  12 fl oz (350 ml) warm water
  8 oz (225 g) fresh, firm mushrooms
  8 tbs olive oil
  2 cloves garlic, peeled and very finely chopped
  2 tbs parsley, chopped
  salt, pepper

Soak the dried mushrooms for at least 30 minutes in advance in a small bowl with 12 fl oz (350 ml) warm water. Afterwards rinse them but save their water. Boil the reconstituted mushrooms and their filtered water (pour through a filter paper or piece of muslin) until all the liquid has boiled away.

Pre-heat the oven to 400°F/200°C/gas mark 6. Peel the potatoes, rinse them in cold water and cut them in slices no thicker than ¼ in (0.5 cm). Rinse the fresh mushrooms swiftly under cold running water then wipe them dry. Cut them lengthways in slices the same thickness as the potatoes.

Choose an oven dish in which all the ingredients will fit without being piled deeper than 1½ ins (3.5 cm). Put in the olive oil, garlic, potatoes, mushrooms, parsley and a few liberal grindings of pepper. Mix everything well and level off the contents of the dish. Place at the top of the oven. Bake for 15 minutes, then add 2 or 3 large pinches of salt and mix all the ingredients well. Bake for 15 minutes more or until the potatoes are tender. Allow to rest for a minute or two and remove some of the excess oil before serving.

HARD BOILED EGGS WITH POTATOES/OEUFS DURS
AUX POMMES DE TERRE   Serves 6

This is Richard Olney's interpretation of a hearty Lyonnaise dish he first encountered in Ali Bab's monumental tome *Gastronomie Practique.* The vinegar-finished sauce gives what appears to be a rather ordinary dish an unusual twist.

2 lb (900 g) potatoes, boiled in their skins
2 tbs shallots or onions, finely chopped
4 oz (110 g) butter
6 hard-boiled eggs
2 tbs parsley, chopped
3 tbs wine vinegar
salt, pepper

Drain the potatoes, peel and leave while you sauté the shallots in the butter over a very low flame. Slice the potatoes and mix them in a serving dish with the roughly chopped eggs. When the shallots are soft, sprinkle with salt and pepper, turn up the flame, throw in the parsley and then vinegar, stir and pour over the potatoes and eggs.

SPICED HARD-BOILED EGGS WITH POTATOES/UNDAY AUR ALOO Serves 2–4

I once saw Madhur Jaffrey cook this dish on one of her TV programmes and I have been cooking it regularly ever since. With a little bit of cheating you can make a very good version from the store cupboard.

1 lb (450 g) waxy-variety potatoes, peeled
1 in (2.5 cm) fresh ginger, peeled and chopped
2 cloves garlic
6 tbs vegetable oil
5 oz (150 g) onions, peeled and finely chopped
1 tbs ground coriander seeds
1 tsp plain flour
4 tbs plain yoghurt
11 oz (300 g) tomatoes, peeled and chopped
½ pt (275 ml) water
½ tsp garam masala
1 tbs coriander, finely chopped (at a pinch flat-leaf parsley will do
    but the pungency of coriander makes the dish)
4 hard-boiled eggs
1½ tsp salt, pinch cayenne

Pound the garlic, ginger and 2 tbs water to make a paste. Cut the potatoes into fat chips. Heat the oil and sauté the potatoes gently until they are golden brown. Remove. Fry the onions in the same oil until they are browned but not crisp. Stir in the garlic-ginger paste and stir fry for a minute before adding the cayenne, coriander seeds and flour. Add the yoghurt and stir to make a sauce. Next add the tomatoes and stir fry for 2 minutes before you add the ½ pt (275 ml) water and salt. Bring to the boil, cover and simmer for 10 minutes.

Add the potatoes and continue simmering until they are quite cooked – probably about 10 minutes – stir in the garam masala and coriander.

Halve the eggs, crosswise, and carefully put them into the frying pan with the cut sides up. Try not to let the yolk fall out. Spoon some of the sauce over the eggs, simmer covered for 5 minutes and serve with plain rice and chutney. It is not at all hot but fragrant and very delicious.

ANGLESEY EGGS/WYAU YNYS MON   Serves 4

This is a marvellously soothing dish.

> 1½ lb (700 g) mashed potato
> 3 oz (75 g) butter
> 2 lb (900 g) leeks, sliced and carefully rinsed to remove all the grit
> 1 tbs flour
> ½ pt (275 ml) milk
> 3 oz (75 g) Cheddar cheese, grated
> 8 hard-boiled eggs
> salt, pepper

Melt half the butter and sweat the leeks in a covered pan. When soft beat them into the mash, season and pour into a buttered gratin dish leaving a space in the middle for the eggs.

Melt the rest of the butter in a small saucepan, stir in the flour and gradually beat in the milk. Allow it to cook for a few minutes before adding 2 oz (50 g) of the cheese. Put the eggs in the middle of the dish and pour over the sauce. Sprinkle the remaining cheese over the eggs and bake until golden brown at 400°F/200°C/gas mark 6.

POTATO PURÉE WITH EGGS/OEUFS AU NID   Serves 4

Mashed potatoes and soft-fried eggs are a delicious combination; baked with a sprinkling of grated cheese it is even better.

> 1½ lb (700 g) well-beaten mashed potato
> 2 oz (50 g) butter
> 4 eggs
> 4 tbs cheese, grated
> salt, pepper

Pre-heat the oven to 400°F/200°C/gas mark 6. Liberally butter an oven-proof dish and pile in the well-seasoned potatoes. Make 4 indents, pop in a little knob of butter and then crack in the eggs. Season and, with your fork, make deep grooves round each egg to make a nest. Sprinkle with cheese and bake for at least 15 minutes until the white is firm but the yolk runny.

PATENTLADA   Serves 4

This is a Swedish fry-up.

        4 large potatoes, boiled and diced
        oil for frying
        1 onion, finely chopped
        4 slices smoked ham
        8 eggs
        salt, pepper

Take a large frying pan and cook the potatoes gently in the oil. Add the onion and continue cooking until it is soft but don't let it brown. Add the ham, season and mix everything together. Keep warm while you fry the eggs. Arrange a line of the potato mixture with a fried egg on each side. Serve immediately.

SPANISH POTATO BAKE/HUEVOS A LA EXTREMEÑA   Serves 4

        2 lb (900 g) potatoes, peeled, boiled and diced
        2 onions, finely chopped
        4 tbs olive oil
        8 oz (225 g) tomatoes, skinned and chopped
        14 oz (400 g) peas, cooked
        5 oz (150 g) chorizo (spicy dried sausage), peeled and diced
        5 oz (150 g) smoked, prosciutto or serrano ham
        8 large eggs
        salt, pepper

Fry the onions in the olive oil until limp but not brown. Drain off any excess oil and add the tomatoes. Simmer for 15 minutes until they are thoroughly cooked and then whizz them up in the blender to make a purée. Stir in the potatoes, peas, chorizo, ham, salt and pepper to taste and put in an ovenproof dish.

Preheat the oven to 450°F/230°C/gas mark 8. Make indentations in the mixture and break the eggs on top. Put the dish in the oven and check if the eggs are cooked after 6 minutes; the yolks should be runny. Serve with crusty bread to mop up the delicious sauce.

POTATO SOUFFLÉ   Serves 2

> 1 lb (450 g) well-beaten mashed potato
> 4 eggs, separated
> 2 oz (50 g) butter
> Parmesan, grated
> salt, pepper, pinch grated nutmeg

Whisk the egg yolks, seasoning and nutmeg into the mash and allow to cool. Whisk the egg whites to form stiff peaks and gently fold into the potatoes. Pour into a buttered soufflé dish and dust with freshly grated Parmesan. Bake in a hot oven (425°F/220°C/gas mark 7) for 25 minutes until the soufflé is golden and well-risen. Serve immediately.

POTATO OMELETTES

The most famous potato omelette is the Spanish tortilla, cooked like a cake and served cold or warm in wedges (page 98). In France Parmentier's name prefaces potato omelette; in Persia the *Kuku Sibzamini* is cooked with spring onions and finely chopped parsley; and in Greece *Omeletta Me Patates* is cooked in olive oil with chopped coriander, and served with lemon and cucumber. Here are three slightly more unusual potato omelettes.

PARSI POTATO OMELETTE   Serves 2

> 4 potatoes, diced
> ghee for frying
> 1 onion, finely chopped
> ½ tsp each paprika and turmeric
> 1 tbs coriander leaves, chopped
> 6 eggs, beaten
> 1 tsp salt

Heat 2 tbs of the ghee and fry the onion. When the onion is transparent add the potatoes and cook until both are golden. Stir in the salt, paprika, turmeric and coriander. Allow to cool in a bowl and then add the eggs. Heat 1 tbs of ghee in a frying pan and add half the mixture. Cook for a minute or two until the eggs have set. Fold omelette in half and keep warm whilst cooking the second omelette.

SWEDISH PEASANT OMELETTE/BOUDOMELETT   <u>Serves 4</u>

7 oz (200 g) potatoes, boiled and cubed
7 oz (200 g) lean fresh belly of pork or salt-cured streaky bacon
2 oz (50 g) butter
1 onion, chopped
8 eggs, whisked
salt, pepper, chives, parsley

Sauté the bacon in the butter and when it has begun to crisp add the onion. Allow the onion to get limp and then add the potatoes. Whisk the eggs with the salt and pour over the mixture. Cook for a couple of minutes, sprinkle with chives and parsley and serve from the pan. It should be creamy and slightly under-done.

SHRIMP AND POTATO OMELETTE/CUAJADO
DE CAMARONES   <u>Serves 4</u>

As Elisabeth Lambert Ortiz explains in her book *Latin American Cooking*, in Colombia *cuajado* means a dish of meat, fish or fruit made in a frying pan with eggs to hold it together.

2 medium-sized new potatoes, boiled
2 onions, finely chopped
1½ oz (40 g) butter
1 tsp paprika
3 large tomatoes, peeled and chopped
6 eggs, separated
1 lb (450 g) raw shrimp or prawns, peeled and cut into ½-in (1-cm) pieces
salt, pepper

Choose a large frying pan and gently sauté the onions in the butter. When they are soft stir in the paprika, tomatoes, salt and pepper and cook until it thickens. Add the diced potatoes and warm through.

Remove from the heat while you beat the egg yolks until they are thick and in a separate bowl whisk the egg whites until they form peaks. Fold the peaks into the yolks.

Return the pan to the heat and add the shrimps to the sauce, cook for 2 minutes and then fold in the eggs. Mix around and cook until the eggs are lightly set. Serve with a green salad.

POTATO PIZZA

Not a lot of people know that the Pizza Express boss, Peter Boizot, hails from Peterborough. An awful lot of King Edward potatoes are grown in and around Peterborough and that is why you will find this pizza on Boizot's flagship branches Kettners in Soho and Pizza on the Park at Hyde Park.

KING EDWARD'S PIZZA   Serves 2

     1½ lb (700 g) King Edward potatoes, mashed
     1 oz (25 g) butter
     2 oz (50 g) Parmesan
     1 egg, beaten
     5 oz (150 g) sliced tomato
     2 oz (50 g) mozzarella, sliced
     8 thin slices salami
     1 oz (25 g) mushrooms, finely sliced
     salt, pepper, oil, oregano

Mix the mash with the salt, butter, Parmesan and egg. Press the mixture in a lightly floured 9-in (23-cm) pizza pan and give it a slightly raised edge by tapping the base all round ½ in (1 cm) from the edge. Top with tomato, then cover with the sliced cheese, salami and mushrooms. Sprinkle on oregano, pepper, salt and a trickle of oil.

Pre-heat the oven to 450°F/230°C/gas mark 8 and bake for 20 minutes.

PIZZA PARMENTIER   <u>Makes two 6–7-in (15–18-cm) pizzas</u>

Peter Boizot and Alastair Little both gave me almost identical recipes for a
potato pizza with rosemary. This is Alastair's; the only difference is the
addition of garlic.

While ready-prepared pizza bases are widely available in supermarkets,
the end result is far better if you make your own pizza dough. Authentic
pizza dough is made with yeast, requires proving and is consequently a
long business. This recipe is a quickie version adapted from Josceline
Dimbleby's *Favourite Food*.

For the dough:

8 oz (225 g) strong white bread flour
1 level tsp each bicarbonate of soda, cream of tartar and salt
¼ pt (150 ml) milk soured with 1 tbs vinegar
4 tbs olive oil

For the topping:

1 lb (450 g) waxy-variety potatoes
2 fat or 4 regular sized cloves garlic, peeled and crushed
1 tbs fresh rosemary
2 oz (50 g) grated or wafer-thin sliced Parmesan
salt, pepper

To make the dough, first pre-heat the oven to its highest level (probably
475°F/240°C/gas mark 9). Sift the flour, bicarbonate of soda, cream of
tartar and salt into a bowl. Using a wooden spoon, gradually stir in the
soured milk and keep stirring to make a soft dough. Remove to a floured
board and knead lightly and form into a ball. Halve the ball and roll out 2
circles. If you don't have special pizza trays place the dough on a dry and
flour-dusted heavy baking tray. Make slightly ridged edges and paint the
dough with olive oil.

Peel the potatoes and slice them wafer thin using either a mandoline or
razor-sharp knife. Imagining you are making a French apple tart with the
slices arranged in patterns, cover the dough with potato. When the dough
is entirely covered, divide the garlic equally between the two pizzas.
Gently brush the remaining olive oil over the potatoes, sprinkle with
rosemary and cover with the Parmesan. Bake for 20 minutes. Peter
suggests adding small pieces of bacon.

POTATO PIES WITHOUT PASTRY

POTATO KUGEL   Serves 2

This is rather like a giant *latke* but is cooked in the oven.

> 4 large floury-variety potatoes
> 1 onion
> 2 eggs
> 2 oz (50 g) flour
> 2 tbs chicken fat, butter or oil
> salt, pepper

Peel and grate the potatoes. Sprinkle with salt and leave to drain (the salt draws out the moisture and softens the potatoes) for 20 minutes. Rinse and squeeze to get all the water out. Grate the onion. Whisk the eggs and mix with the potato, onion, seasoning and the sifted flour.

Put the fat into a metal baking dish and pop into a very hot oven (450°F/230°C/gas mark 8) for 5 minutes. Remove the pan and pour in the mixture, spreading it quickly around the dish. Return to the oven and bake for 15 minutes and then lower the heat to 350°F/180°C/gas mark 4. Cook for a further 30 minutes until the *kugel* is crusty brown and cooked right through.

MEDITERRANEAN POTATO PIE   Serves 6

> 3 lb (1.4 kg) waxy-variety potatoes, boiled and sliced
> 1 lb (450 g) tomatoes, peeled, cored and sliced
> 10 oz (275 g) onions, chopped
> 5 oz (150 g) Gruyère cheese, grated
> ¼ pt (150 ml) olive oil
> salt, pepper, fresh thyme

Oil a large gratin dish and make layers with the potatoes, tomatoes, onions and cheese seasoned with a little salt, lots of pepper and a few leaves of thyme. Hold back some of the cheese to cover the top and sprinkle the oil over the dish. Bake for 30 minutes in a hot oven (425°F/220°C/gas mark 7) until the pie is golden brown.

CAULIFLOWER AND POTATOES   Serves 4–6

This is a Hungarian variation on cauliflower cheese and is exceedingly filling.

> 1 lb (450 g) waxy-variety potatoes, boiled and sliced
> 1½ lb (700 g) cauliflower
> 1½ oz (40 g) butter
> 5 eggs; 3 hard-boiled and sliced, 2 whisked
> 4 oz (110 g) grated cheese
> 2 fl oz (50 ml) yoghurt
> 1½ oz (40 g) fine breadcrumbs
> salt, pepper

Divide the cauliflower into florets and chop the stalk into similar-sized pieces. Boil for 3 minutes in salted water. Drain carefully. Butter a suitable ovenproof dish and make layers of potato, egg and cauliflower, sprinkling each layer with cheese and seasoning each with salt and pepper. When you get to the top, cover with cheese and pour over the whisked eggs mixed with the yoghurt. Sprinkle on the breadcrumbs and bake in a pre-heated hot oven (400°F/200°C/gas mark 6) for 30 minutes until the top is golden brown.

POTATO AND MUSHROOM PIE   Serves 4–6

> 1 lb (450 g) mashed potato
> 1 lb (450 g) mushrooms
> ¾ pt (400 ml) milk
> 1 oz (25 g) butter
> 1 tbs flour
> 1 tbs parsley, chopped
> salt, pepper

Wash the mushrooms and halve them if they are very large. Simmer very gently in the milk for about 10 minutes, season lightly with salt and generously with pepper. Drain and keep the juices. Melt the butter, stir in the sifted flour and add the mushroom liquid. Stir until the sauce has thickened and add the parsley. Pour the mushrooms into the sauce and then into a suitable ovenproof dish. Top with mashed potatoes making swirl patterns on the top, dot with butter and bake for 30 minutes at 400°F/200°C/gas mark 6 until the top is golden brown.

SALT COD AND POTATOES/BACALHAU COM BATATAS
Serves 6

This is a Brazilian dish that is both comforting and exotic.

2½ lb (1 kg) waxy-variety potatoes, boiled and roughly chopped
1½ lb (700 g) salt cod, soaked for 24 hours in several changes of
   cold water
olive oil for frying
2 onions, sliced
2 green peppers, cored and sliced
1 clove garlic, chopped
3 hard-boiled eggs
20 black olives
salt, pepper

Drain the fish, cut into 2-in (5-cm) pieces and remove any bones. Put the fish in cold water, bring it to the boil and cook for 15 minutes. Drain. Heat some oil and fry the fish quickly on both sides.

To make the green pepper sauce (*refogado*) heat a little oil and gently cook the onion until soft, then add the peppers, garlic and 5 minutes later the tomatoes. Cook until it amalgamates in a delicious sloppy mess.

Oil a suitable ovenproof dish and pile in the fish, potatoes, green pepper sauce, sliced egg and olives. Season with a little salt and lots of pepper and finish with potatoes. Bake for 30 minutes at 400°F/200°C/gas mark 6 and serve with a fresh tomato sauce seasoned with what fresh green herbs you have to hand.

POTATO PIES WITH PASTRY

POTATO PASTRY
Makes ½ lb (225 g) pastry; to line or top a 7-in (18-cm) pie

Potato pastry is light yet adds bulk to savoury pies. The quantities are variable according to what you have available; potato pastry is a good way of using up leftover mash. It can be used instead of ordinary pastry for any pie but is most successful with savour pies.

4 oz (110 g) mashed potato
4 oz (110 g) flour
3 oz (75 g) fat
salt, pepper, water

Add the seasoning to the flour and rub in the cooking fat until it resembles fine breadcrumbs. Mix in the potatoes, kneading firmly, and adding a little water – sufficient to make a stiff dough. Leave to rest for 15 minutes before use.

SHORT PASTRY

Makes 1 lb (750 g) pastry; to line or top a 7-in (18-cm) pie

5 oz (150 g) butter or lard
10½ oz (290 g) plain flour, sifted
2½ fl oz (60 ml) cold water

Cut the butter into pieces and quickly work into the flour. Using a knife (or fork if you're superstitious) stir in the water, a little at a time, until it forms into one big lump. Knead quickly and leave to rest until you're ready to use it. Always make pastry with cold hands and touch it as little as possible.

CORNISH PASTIES   Serves 2

'Pastry rolled out like a plate,
Piled with turmut, tates and mate
Doubled up and baked like fate,
That's a Cornish Pasty.'

The fat ridge of pastry that is the hallmark of the Cornish pasty dates back to when Cornish miners had to eat their lunch on the job. The 'handle' was discarded. Another tradition was to use pastry trimmings to identify the pasty with the owner's initials.

For the pastry:

4 oz (110 g) lard
8 oz (225 g) plain flour
pinch salt, water to mix

For the filling:

8 oz (225 g) each potatoes, turnip, chuck steak
1 lb (450 g) onions
butter
salt, pepper

Rub the lard into the sifted flour, add the salt and enough water to form a decent dough. Leave in the fridge while you make the filling. Pre-heat the oven to 400°F/200°C/gas mark 6.

Dice the meat and vegetables and finely chop the onion, season generously and keep everything in separate piles. Divide the pastry in two and roll into 2 circles. On half the circle of pastry put half the turnip, ½ in (1 cm) from the edge. Sprinkle with salt and cover with half the meat. Sprinkle with pepper and cover with half the sliced potatoes and half the sliced onion. Put a knob of butter on top of the onion and sprinkle with salt. Fold over the empty half of pastry, damp the edges and crimp them together. Brush with milk or egg and punch a few air-holes with a fork. Repeat with the second pasty.

Place the pasties on a baking sheet and cook for 20 minutes; lower the heat to 325°F/170°C/gas mark 3 and cook for a further 30 minutes. Serve wrapped in a paper napkin. A pasty is *never* eaten with a knife and fork.

EMPANADAS

This is the Argentinian version of a pasty. *Empanadas* are smaller; this filling will make about 16 small pasties.

> 1 lb (450 g) short pastry, recipe page 175

> For the filling:

> 2 medium-sized potatoes, finely diced
> 2 onions, finely chopped
> 1 lb (450 g) best quality lean mince
> 3 tbs beef stock
> salt, pepper

Mix all the filling ingredients together and proceed as for the pastry recipe (page 175). The oven temperature should be lowered after 10 minutes of cooking.

ARABELLA BOXER'S POTATO AND HERB PIE   Serves 4–6

I have been cooking variations on this pie since I first came across the recipe in Arabella Boxer's delightful *Garden Cookbook*, a cookbook that is rare in that all the recipes not only work but taste good too.

1 lb (450 g) new or waxy-variety potatoes, peeled
1½ lb (700 g) short pastry, recipe page 175
2 oz (50 g) butter
1 egg yolk
¼ pt (150 ml) cream
4 tbs chopped fresh chervil, chives, parsley, dill
salt, pepper, nutmeg

Line a 9-in (23-cm) flan dish with the pastry. Slice the potatoes wafer thin and arrange in layers in the pastry. Dot each layer with butter, salt, pepper and nutmeg. Cover with a pastry lid and brush with the beaten egg yolk. Bake for 1 hour at 350°F/180°C/gas mark 4. Heat the cream, season with salt and pepper and stir in the herbs. Lift off the lid and pour the cream over the potatoes. Replace the lid and cook for a further 5 minutes.

POTATO QUICHE

Serves 4–6

1 lb (450 g) potatoes, boiled
2 oz (50 g) butter
2 tbs flour
4 fl oz (110 ml) double cream
2 rashers good bacon, chopped
1 clove garlic, crushed
2 oz (50 g) Gruyère cheese, grated

Peel and dry mash the potatoes and mix with the butter and sifted flour. Knead until you have a firm dough. Roll it out ¼ in (0.5 cm) thick and lay it in a buttered and floured flan tin. Prick the base a few times with a fork and fill with the cream and bacon and stir in the garlic. Sprinkle the top with the cheese and bake at 400°F/200°C/gas mark 6 for about 20 minutes. This is good hot or cold.

TARTE SAVOYARDE

This is an idea from Alastair Little. Make a puff pastry case (or buy it ready-made) and make a filling with the Roux brothers' Savoyard (page 82). If possible add a truffle, a few slices of blanched bacon or some chopped Cantal cheese. When you have lined the pie dish with pastry, freeze it before you add the Savoyard. Seal the top and bottom layers of pastry very carefully with egg so that the cream can't leak out.

Start the pie in a very hot oven (450°F/230°C/gas mark 8) for about 10 minutes, then turn down and follow the Savoyard recipe.

SEVENTEENTH-CENTURY POTATO PIE   Serves 4

This recipe was first published in *The Perfect Cook*, 1656.

> 1 lb (450 g) potatoes, boiled and diced
> 4 oz (110 g) dates, stoned and chopped
> 4 oz (110 g) grapes, stoned and halved
> ¼ pt (150 ml) chicken stock
> ¼ tsp each grated nutmeg, mace and cinnamon
> 1 lb (450 g) short pastry
> 2 oz (50 g) butter
> salt, pepper

Mix the diced potatoes with the dates and grapes. Season with the nutmeg, mace, cinnamon, salt and pepper. Roll out the pastry (see recipe page 175) and line a suitable pie dish, liberally buttered. Pile in the mixture and cover with the pastry.

Bake at 400°F/200°C/gas mark 6 for 15 minutes, turn down the heat to 325°F/170°C/gas mark 3 and remove the pie. Lift the pie lid and pour in the chicken stock. Cook for a further 15 minutes.

APPLE AND POTATO PIE   Serves 4–6

> 1 lb (450 g) potatoes, 2 additional potatoes, sliced
> 1 lb (450 g) apples
> 1 onion, finely sliced
> 4 oz (110 g) butter
> 1 egg yolk, beaten
> 8 oz (225 g) short pastry
> salt, pepper

Peel, chop and fry the potatoes and apples in butter. Butter a suitable gratin-style dish and cover with a layer of sliced potatoes. Pile in the potatoes and apples mixed with the onion, season with salt and pepper, cover with water and dot with butter. Top with a layer of thin potato slices and bake for 30 minutes at 400°F/200°C/gas mark 6. Remove from the oven, cover with the pastry – follow recipe page 175 using half quantities. This is a little tricky so be careful not to burn yourself. Paint with the beaten egg and bake for 15 minutes until the pastry is golden.

This pie can be made more substantial by adding 8 oz (225 g) cubed and browned lamb. If you substitute 12 oz (350 g) diced gammon, 2 tsp sugar, a little thyme and stock rather than water you have the Shropshire dish Fidget Pie.

PIQUANT PIE   Serves 4

12 oz (350 g) potato pastry
1½ lb (700 g) lean pork, diced
1 oz (25 g) cooking fat
8 oz (225 g) onions, sliced
1 oz (25 g) plain flour
½ pt (275 ml) stock or water
2 tbs vinegar
4 tbs brown sugar
1 dsp Worcester sauce
2 medium-sized cooking apples
milk
salt, pepper

Fry the pork in the fat until brown. Remove from the pan and gently fry the onions. When they are soft stir in the flour and make a sauce with the stock. Let it bubble for a couple of minutes and add the vinegar, sugar, Worcester sauce and season with salt and pepper. While the mixture is bubbling, peel, core and chop the apples and stir them into the sauce. Return the meat and cook for 5 minutes before you load the mixture into a pie dish. Roll out the pastry (see recipe page 179) and cover the pie. Make some steam holes with a fork, brush the top with milk and bake at 400°F/200°C/gas mark 6 for 35 minutes.

POTATO AND FISH DISHES

SALT COD FRITTERS/BOLINHOS DE BACALHAU   Serves 4–6

I once wrote an article about the Portuguese restaurants of London directly after a mid-season holiday in a tiny fishing village near Lisbon. The difference in the quality of food was so marked as to make the two experiences incomparable. One unifying ingredient was the salt cod which is a major feature of Portuguese cooking wherever and however it is prepared. There is a claim that *bacalhau* can be cooked differently every day of the year. This is a favourite way for me.

1½ lb (700 g) dry mashed potatoes
1 lb (450 g) salt cod
2 tbs parsley, chopped
1 small onion, finely chopped
5 eggs
oil for deep frying
pepper (you will *not* need salt)

For the chilli/tomato sauce:

1 oz (25 g) butter
1 small onion, peeled and finely chopped
2 red chilli peppers, de-seeded and chopped (wash hands
    immediately after doing this)
2 cloves garlic, peeled and finely chopped
1 lb (450 g) ripe tomatoes
salt, pepper

To prepare the *bacalhau* cut it into 3-in (7.5-cm) pieces and leave to soak in a bucket of water for 24 hours. Change the water a few times. The smell is rather off-putting, so if possible leave it covered outside.

Drain the pieces, put in a pan and cover with water, bring slowly to the boil and simmer for about 30 minutes.

Mince the fish and beat it, the parsley, pepper and onion into the potatoes. Beat in 4 of the eggs, one at a time. If you have a fairly stiff smooth dough you won't need the fifth egg. If it is sloppy beat in a little sifted flour.

Heat up the chip pan and form the mixture into balls with the help of two spoons. When the oil is hot (350°F/180°C) drop in the balls and fry until golden brown. Drain and serve with a chilli-hot tomato sauce.

To make the sauce, melt the butter and gently cook the onion until transparent. Add the chilli and garlic and cook for 5 minutes before adding the tomatoes, peeled and cored. Turn up the heat and boil hard for 5 minutes, reduce heat and leave to simmer for 10 minutes. Taste for seasoning.

FISH WITH SOUR CREAM AND POTATOES/RACHAL   Serves 4

Rachal is a Hungarian fish dish which Jews prepare on the Friday night of *Shavuot*.

    6 medium-sized potatoes, boiled
    4 oz (110 g) butter
    1 tsp paprika
    2 lb (900 g) haddock, cut into 4 steaks
    1 tbs fresh dill
    4 fl oz (110 ml) sour cream
    1 tbs breadcrumbs
    salt, pepper

Butter a gratin dish and cover the bottom with sliced potato. Sprinkle with salt, pepper and paprika. Make a layer with the fish, sprinkle with dill, a little more paprika and cover with potatoes. Pour over the sour cream and top with the breadcrumbs. Dot with butter and bake for 30 minutes at 400°F/200°C/gas mark 6.

CORNISH HERRING PIE   Serves 6

    1½ lb (700 g) mashed potato
    6 pickled herrings
    2 gherkins, chopped
    ½ pt (275 ml) milk
    3 large tomatoes, skinned and sliced
    4 oz (110 g) breadcrumbs
    butter
    salt, pepper

Clean and bone the fish and soak overnight. In the morning, skin the herrings and steam until tender. Flake the flesh and mix with the chopped gherkins and milk and turn the mixture into a gratin dish. Cover with seasoned sliced tomatoes and then with the mash. Sprinkle with breadcrumbs and dot with butter.
    Bake for 40 minutes at 375°F/190°C/gas mark 5.

JANSSONS'S TEMPTATION   Serves 4

Anna Hegarty of Anna's Place tells me that the correct name for this dish should be Janzon's Frestelse. Behind the name of one of Sweden's most popular dishes is a tale of self-improvement. Adolf Janzon (1844–1889) was the son of a fisherman and expected to follow in his father's footsteps. But the young Adolf's outstanding voice won him a place at Stockholm's Royal Opera House where he came to earn a reputation for his singing, his suppers and his flirtations. Adolf fell in with a sophisticated set and after his performance he would cook them supper in his rooms. The dish he most liked to cook was a peasant-style casserole of fish and potatoes. As his status improved Adolf changed his name to Jansson. His famous dish became known as Jansson's Temptation.

Of the many marginally different recipes for this dish here's the one devised by Anna and served at her delightful Swedish restaurant in North London.

Swedish anchovies are less salty than the Italian variety and, while they need to be rinsed, they don't require soaking. Whole tinned anchovies are ideal for this recipe. They can be bought by mail order from Swedish Table, 7 Paddington St, London W.2.

> 6 medium-sized waxy-variety potatoes
> 14 anchovy fillets
> 2 tbs butter
> 2 onions, finely sliced
> 3 fl oz (75 ml) each single cream and double cream
> 2–3 tbs homemade breadcrumbs

Rinse and chop the anchovy fillets. Liberally butter a gratin dish. Peel and grate the potatoes and make layers of potato, onion and anchovy finishing with potatoes. Press the mixture down firmly, smooth the surface and pour the cream mixture over the top so that the potatoes can be glimpsed but aren't smothered. If you need more liquid use some of the liquor from the anchovy tin. Sprinkle the breadcrumbs on top, dot with butter and bake at 400°F/200°C/gas mark 6 for 1 hour. Serve with a glass of Schnapps and a cold beer.

FISH AND POTATO BAKE   Serves 6

> 1½ lb (700 g) potatoes, peeled and sliced
> 1 tbs lard
> 2 lb (900 g) mixed fish, cut in chunks

2 tbs parsley, chopped
4 cloves garlic, chopped
2 tbs olive oil
salt, pepper, cayenne and saffron threads

Grease a large casserole with the lard and make layers of potato and fish, seasoning each layer with parsley, salt and pepper, garlic, cayenne and saffron. Cover with cold water and dribble the olive oil over the top. Bring to the boil, turn down to simmer and cook for 15–20 minutes.

WELSH SUPPER HERRINGS/SWPER SGADAN/SGADAN ABERGWAUN   Serves 4

1½ lb (700 g) potatoes, peeled and thinly sliced
4 herrings, filleted
1 tbs made English mustard
2 oz (50 g) butter
1 large cooking apple, cored, peeled and sliced
1 large onion, finely sliced
¼ tsp dried sage
salt, pepper

Spread out the herrings, spread with mustard, sprinkle them with salt and pepper and roll up from the tail end. Butter a large gratin dish and make a layer with half the potato, then apple and then onion. Lay the herrings in the middle, sprinkle with the sage and make layers with the rest of the onion, apple and potato. Pour in boiling water to come halfway up the dish, dot with butter, season well and cover with foil.

Punch a few holes in the top to let the steam out and bake for 30 minutes at 350°F/180°C/gas mark 4. Remove the foil, turn the heat up to 400°F/200°C/gas mark 6 and cook for a further 20 minutes until the top potatoes are nicely browned and the liquid has been reduced.

ANNA HEGARTY'S LAX PUDDING   Serves 8

This classic Swedish dish is an ideal way of making a small amount of fresh salmon go a long way. It is also a cheap and spectacular way of feeding a lot of people. It is not worth making for less than 8 but any leftovers are delicious cold the next day.

2 lb (900 g) big waxy-variety potatoes
2 lb (900 g) fresh salmon, preferably a middle section which is oilier
  than the head and tail
bunch of dill stalks
4 tbs white sugar
2 medium-sized onions, finely sliced
4 eggs
½ pt (275 ml) milk
8 tbs salt, 20 white peppercorns, finely crushed

Ask the fishmonger to fillet the salmon removing any bones but leaving the skin intact. You will probably have to go over the fish again with tweezers to remove any stragglers.

Twenty-four hours in advance marinate the fish with the salt, sugar and pepper which you have thoroughly mixed with half a cupful of roughly chopped dill stalks. To do this sprinkle some of the marinade mixture into a dish that can comfortably hold the fish. Place one fillet skin side down and cover with most of the marinade. Place the second fillet flesh side down to make a sandwich (the fish is now reconstituted) and sprinkle the rest of the mixture over the top. Cover the fish with foil, top with a heavy weight and leave for 12 hours.

When the fish is ready, rinse off the mixture and, using a very sharp knife, cut the fish in diagonal slices. Boil the potatoes the skins, cool, peel and slice in ½-in (1-cm) rounds. Butter a gratin dish and make alternate layers with the potato, fish and onion, starting and ending with potato. Whisk the eggs and milk with a pinch of white pepper and pour over the pudding.

Bake for 30 minutes in a hot oven (400°F/200°C/gas mark 6) to enable the egg mixture to cook through and the top layer of potatoes to crisp. Serve with a green salad, Schnapps and beer.

POTATOES AND SAUSAGES

What that really means to the entire British nation is Bangers and Mash. And there are few dishes so universally loved as a steaming plate of good firm mash, slightly burnt sausages and a pile of fried onions. Here, however, are some interesting variations on that theme.

BRATWURST WITH WARM POTATO SALAD   <u>Serves 4</u>

This dish originates in Alsace and is classified as an authentic brasserie dish. Serve with German mustard and chilled lager.

 2 lb (900 g) waxy-variety potatoes, boiled, skinned and sliced
 8 Bratwurst sausages
 6 tbs olive oil
 2 tbs wine vinegar
 1 tbs parsley, finely chopped
 4 shallots, finely sliced
 salt, pepper

Slice the potatoes while they are still warm and pour over the dressing made by whisking together the oil, vinegar, parsley, shallots and seasoning. Grill the sausages to be ready to serve with the warm salad.

PAPRIKA POTATOES WITH SMOKED SAUSAGES   <u>Serves 4</u>

 1½ lb (700 g) waxy-variety or new potatoes
 1 oz lard
 4 oz (110 g) onion, chopped
 2 tbs flour
 1 tsp paprika
 1 tbs wine vinegar
 ½ pt (275 ml) stock or water
 1 lb (450 g) smoked sausages
 salt

Melt the fat and fry the onion. When soft stir in the flour and paprika, mix well and add the vinegar and stock. Stir until it boils. Peel and cut the potatoes into pieces about the size of an egg and add to the sauce. Cover the pan and boil gently, stirring occasionally. Grill the sausages and, 10 minutes before you think the potatoes will be ready, taste and season with salt then add the sausages to the pan.

HUNGARIAN LAYERED POTATO CASSEROLE/RAKOTT KRUMPLI   Serves 6–8

3 lb (1.4 kg) small new potatoes, boiled and sliced
4 oz (110 g) each sliced boiled ham and cooked sausage
6 hard-boiled eggs
1 tbs paprika
1 cup sour cream
4 oz (110 g) butter
salt, pepper

Butter a casserole dish and make layers of potato, meat and egg finishing with potato. Season each layer with salt, pepper and paprika and cut the bulk of the butter (3 oz/75 g) into pieces to dot over the pie between the layers. Mix any remaining paprika into the sour cream. Pour the cream over the pie and bake for 30 minutes at 300°F/200°C/gas mark 6.

SAUSAGES COOKED INDIAN-STYLE   Serves 4

1 lb (450 g) waxy-variety potatoes, peeled and cut like big chips
1 in (2.5 cm) fresh ginger, peeled and chopped
1 large or 2 small cloves garlic, peeled and finely chopped
2 tbs vegetable oil
1 lb (450 g) good quality pork sausages
4 oz (110 g) onion, chopped
1 tsp ground cumin
¼ tsp cayenne
8 oz (225 g) fresh tomatoes or 8 oz (225 g) tinned tomatoes, peeled
    and chopped
½ tsp salt

Blend the ginger and garlic with 4 tbs water until you have a paste. Heat the oil in a frying pan and brown the sausages all over and set aside. Cook the onions in the same oil and stir fry until they begin to brown. Add the ginger/garlic paste, stir fry for a couple of minutes and then add the cumin and cayenne. Stir for one minute. Add the tomatoes, salt and potatoes. Bring up to simmer, cover and cook for 15 minutes adding a little more water if the mixture is getting dry. Check that the potatoes are almost cooked and add the sausages cut into pieces. Simmer for a further 15 minutes and serve.

LOBSCOUSE/LABSKOVA   Serves 4

Lobscouse is the dish that exiled Mancunian Anthony Burgess needs as a
regular fix in his South of France home. Brisket of beef is first fried in
dripping then slowly stewed with plenty of potatoes and then left to
brown, rather like a meat version of stovies. In Denmark they do an
identical dish and call it *Labskova* and on the Baltic coast of Germany the
dish is made with fish and called *Fischlabskaus*. In Liverpool Lobscouse is
made with mutton or lamb and served with pickled red cabbage.
Lobscouse without meat is called Blind Scouse and the dish is the origin of
the word Scouser. It can be made with leftovers.

>   2 lb (900 g) potatoes, cut into chunks
>   2 oz (50 g) lard or beef dripping
>   1 lb (450 g) brisket with fat, diced
>   1 pt (570 ml) water
>   1 bay leaf
>   salt, pepper

Melt the lard in a large heavy frying pan and brown the diced meat. Add
the potatoes, turn them around to coat with lard and cook for 5 minutes.
Pour on the water which will almost cover the contents of the pan. Season
and add the bay leaf. Cover tightly and simmer over a very low heat for 1
hour. Remove the lid, turn up the heat and let it bubble away until the
base is brown and crispy and there is no liquid left. Serve with a knob of
butter on each helping.

A Dutch version of this is made with salf beef, and 2 lb (900 g) carrots
which are cooked, roughly chopped, with the potatoes in salted water;
the salted meat is then laid on top of the vegetables. A fried onion is
cooked separately and when it's done the carrots and potatoes are added
to that dish, leaving the meat to cook on in the water.

18.

Using Leftovers

To qualify for inclusion in this section all the dishes have to be made with a reasonable quantity of leftover potato. Baked, mashed and boiled potatoes are all eminently re-usable and will keep for several days in the fridge. Boiled potatoes are best stored in their skins otherwise they should be covered with clingfilm. Leftover mash should always be covered to prevent the top going hard. Baked potatoes can be reconstituted by 10 minutes in a hot oven, alternatively their flesh can be used for any of the recipes stipulating mash.

INDIVIDUAL LEFTOVER DISHES

Puffs, patties, fritters, cakes, pancakes, croquettes, balls and rissoles are our names for the acceptable face of leftovers. The common ingredient in all these dishes is the potato; most often it's mashed and apart from that almost anything goes.

Quantities can generally be adjusted to your particular leftover situation; the most important thing is to keep the proportions the same.

POTATO CAKES 1   Serves 4

> 1 lb (450 g) mashed potato
> 4 oz (110 g) sifted flour
> 4 oz (110 g) melted butter
> oil or clarified butter for frying
> salt, pepper

Using a fork work the flour into the potato. Season generously and beat in the melted butter. You will have a firm dough that can now be fashioned into little cakes about 1½ ins (3.5 cm) in diameter. Heat a little oil in a non-stick pan. When very hot drop in your cakes and immediately lower the heat. Cook for 5–10 minutes on either side until they are golden brown.

This recipe can be varied by mixing in chopped parsley, chives, thyme, rosemary, crushed garlic or 1 oz (25 g) grated cheese.

POTATO CAKES 2   Serves 4

    1 lb (450 g) mashed potato
    4 oz (110 g) sifted flour
    1 tsp dry mustard
    1 egg, beaten
    1 onion, chopped
    bacon fat for frying
    salt, pepper

Work the flour and mustard into the potatoes and beat in the egg. The mixture should be quite firm; if it isn't add more flour. Stir in the onion (fried gently in a little of the bacon fat) and if liked some parsley. Season and fashion into cakes. Sift a little flour over the cakes and fry at a medium temperature for 5–10 minutes each side.

Rather than have to do several batches, these can be cooked on a greased baking tray at 375°F/190°C/gas mark 5 for 15 minutes.

POTATO, CELERIAC AND BRUSSELS SPROUT CAKES   Serves 4

This recipe came about because all the ingredients happened to be left over at the same time. The combination could be almost anything so long as you follow the proportions given here.

    8 oz (225 g) mashed potato
    8 oz (225 g) mashed celeriac
    1 oz (25 g) flour
    1 egg, beaten
    8 oz (225 g) sprouts, finely chopped
    clarified butter or butter and oil for frying
    salt, pepper

Mix the potato and celeriac together and sift in most of the flour, season and stir in the egg and finally the sprouts. Form into little cakes and dust with the remaining flour. Heat enough butter to cover the bottom of the pan and when it is very hot add the cakes. Turn down the heat and cook for 10 minutes, turn and repeat. These are good with fried sausages.

LEEK PATTIES/KOFTA   <u>Serves 4</u>

Kofta are eaten at Passover by Greek Jews.

> 1 lb (450 g) mashed potato
> 2 lb (900 g) leeks
> butter
> 2 oz (50 g) Parmesan, freshly grated
> 3 eggs, beaten
> oil for deep frying
> salt, pepper

Finely slice the leeks into rounds and wash in several rinses of water. Melt a knob of butter in a large pan that has a well-fitting lid and sweat the leeks, sprinkled with salt, for 5 minutes. Drain and mix into the potatoes with the cheese, seasoning and eggs.

Bring the oil up to 375°F/190°C and when ready drop spoonfuls of the mixture into the hot fat. Cook until golden brown, about 5 minutes.

BRIKS AUX POMMES DE TERRE   <u>Serves 4</u>

Anyone who's been to Tunisia or eaten in a Tunisian restaurant will be familiar with the popular street snack, *brik à l'oeuf*. This is a potato version without the excitement of biting into a soft egg yolk.

> 12 oz (330 g) mashed potato
> 1 onion, chopped
> 1 large clove garlic, minced
> 2 tbs flat-leaf parsley, chopped
> 1 egg york, beaten
> 4–6 sheets filo pastry
> 2 oz (50 g) melted butter
> oil for deep frying
> salt, pepper

Fry the onion in 2 tbs olive oil until it is soft, add the garlic and cook for another minute. Stir in the parsley and remove from the heat. Beat into the potato and then incorporate the egg yolk and season generously.

Working with one sheet of filo at a time (keep the rest covered with a damp cloth because it dries and cracks very quickly) cut out 6-in (15-cm) squares and paint all over with melted butter. Put a generous teaspoon of the mixture in the middle of the pastry and form into tight triangles. Don't worry about them looking untidy, the butter acts as a glue and the whole thing will look better when cooked. Drop into hot oil (375°F/190°C) and cook until golden, about 5 minutes. Serve with halves of lemon.

HADDOCK FISH CAKES   Serves 4

    8 oz (225 g) mashed potato
    8 oz (225 g) smoked haddock
    milk
    1 oz (25 g) butter
    1 tbs flat-leaf parsley, chopped
    1 egg, beaten
    homemade breadcrumbs made with stale bread
    clarified butter or groundnut oil for frying
    salt, pepper

Place the fish flesh side down in a suitable pan, cover with milk and the butter and cook gently for 10 minutes. Skin, bone and flake, season with a little salt and a lot of pepper and mix with the parsley. Using your hands mix the potato and fish together and form into cakes. Roll in the egg and press into the breadcrumbs. Fry the cakes in the hot butter or oil for 10 minutes each side. Serve with homemade tomato sauce.

MOLLY KEANE'S FISH CAKES   Serves 4

From Molly Keane's lovely book *Nursery Cooking*, this is popular with children who claim they don't like fish.

    1 lb (450 g) mashed potato
    12 oz (450 g) white fish
    1 tbs tomato ketchup
    1 tbs parsley, chopped
    squeeze of lemon juice
    2 eggs, beaten
    approximately 2 oz (50 g) cornflakes, crushed
    oil for frying
    salt, pepper

Cook the fish in milk or water for 10 minutes, skin, bone and flake. Beat the fish, ketchup, parsley, lemon juice, seasoning and enough egg to bind the mixture into the potatoes. Divide into 4 portions and, with floured hands, shape into cakes. Dip each cake in the remaining egg and squash into the cornflakes. Heat the oil and brown the cakes all over. Serve with more ketchup.

KIPPER CAKES   Serves 4

  8 oz (225 g) mashed potato
  8 oz (225 g) kippers
  1 egg
  2 tsp Dijon mustard
  2 oz (50 g) Parmesan, freshly grated
  flour
  salt, pepper

Grill the fish, fillet and remove as many of the fine bones as possible. Flake and mash into the potatoes. Beat in the egg, mustard and cheese and form into little cakes about the size of a flattened golf ball. Roll in flour and cook quickly until brown and crispy on both sides.

ANCHOVY AND EGG CAKES/GALETTES POLONAISES   Serves 4

  1 lb (450 g) mashed potato
  2 fillets of anchovy, rinsed under cold running water
  1 hard-boiled egg
  flour
  oil for frying
  pepper

Chop up the anchovy and egg and mix into the potatoes with a good seasoning of pepper. Shape the mixture into cakes, dust with flour and fry in hot fat. Cook for one minute, turn down the heat and cook on both sides for 5–10 minutes until the cakes are golden.

TINNED FISH CAKES   <u>Serves 4</u>

    1 lb (450 g) mashed potato
    1 egg, beaten
    1 tbs parsley or dill, chopped (optional)
    two 7 or 8 oz (200 or 225 g) tins of salmon or tuna
    squeeze of lemon juice
    flour
    oil for frying
    salt, pepper

Beat the egg into the potato, season and if including parsley or dill mix it in
now. Drain the fish and remove any bones. Flake the fish, mix with the
potato and add a squeeze of lemon. Turn the mixture on to a floured
board, divide into cakes and dust with flour. Heat the oil and shallow-fry
the cakes over a moderate flame for 10 minutes on each side. These are
good with a tomato sauce.

FRIED COD PUFFS

    8 oz (225 g) mashed potato
    1 oz (25 g) butter, melted
    2 eggs, beaten
    8 oz (225 g) boiled, flaked fish
    1 tbs parsley, chopped
    oil for deep frying
    salt, pepper

Beat the melted butter, seasoning and eggs into the potatoes. Continue
beating until you have a fluffy mixture. Stir in the fish and parsley.
    Meanwhile slowly heat the oil to 375°F/190°C and when ready drop
spoonfuls of the mixture into the hot fat. They will take three or four
minutes to turn golden brown. Drain and serve.

IRAQI STUFFED POTATO CAKES

This dish 'evolved' after years of using Claudia Roden's inspiring *A Book of
Middle Eastern Food*.

2 lb (900 g) mashed potatoes
3 large eggs
2 tbs flour, sifted
homemade breadcrumbs or flour
oil for deep frying
salt, pepper

For the stuffing:

4 oz (110 g) quick-fried lean-minced lamb
1 oz (50 g) brown rice, slightly undercooked
1 oz (25 g) pine kernels
1 tomato, skinned and chopped
2 tbs parsley, chopped
½ tsp ground cinnamon

To make the cakes beat 1 egg, the flour, salt and pepper into the potatoes. Knead well and set aside while you make the filling. Using your hands mix all the ingredients together, including seasoning, until they are thoroughly blended. Shape the potato into balls the size of a walnut, make a hollow with your finger and fill with a little stuffing. Re-form the balls. Whisk the 2 remaining eggs, dip each ball into the egg then into the breadcrumbs and deep fry in very hot fat (375°F/190°C) until they are golden brown.

GREEK MEAT BALLS/KEFTEDES   Serves 4

4 boiled potatoes, skinned and grated
1 onion, chopped
olive oil for frying
6 slices bread
8 oz (225 g) minced beef
8 oz (225 g) minced lamb or pork
2 eggs, whisked
1 tbs each fresh or dried mint, oregano and flat-leaf parsley
¼ tsp salt, 6 grinds or ¼ tsp ground black pepper

Gently fry the onion in a little olive oil for a couple of minutes. Soak the bread in water, squeeze out as much as possible and break it into pieces. Mix all the ingredients together, season and form into egg-sized balls. Heat the oil and gently sauté the balls, turning to cook them evenly. This will take about 30 minutes in all.
   Serve with a Greek salad.

ARMENIAN KOFTA   Serves 4

  1 lb (450 g) mashed potato
  1 lb (450g) minced lamb
  1 egg, beaten
  2 oz (50 g) pine nuts
  butter
  2 oz (50 g) small seedless raisins
  flour
  oil for deep frying
  salt, pepper

Season the meat and mix with the egg. Cream into the potatoes.Quick fry the pine nuts in a little butter until they brown slightly and mix these, with the raisins, into the mixture. Knead everything together thoroughly and form into walnut-shaped balls. Roll them in flour and deep fry in hot oil (375°F/190°C) for 10–15 minutes when they will be crisp on the outside and cooked through.

PEA AND POTATO PATTIES/MATAR ALOO TIKKI   Serves 4

  1 lb (450 g) mashed potato
  2 oz (50 g) flour, sifted
  4 oz (110 g) green peas, boiled and mashed
  2 tbs grated or desiccated coconut
  2 chilli peppers, chopped
  ½ tsp turmeric powder
  ½ tsp paprika
  ghee for frying
  1 tbs lemon juice
  2 tbs coriander leaves
  semolina or flour for dusting
  1 tsp salt

Work the flour into the potatoes and divide up into balls the size of a small egg. To make the filling, fry the peas with the coconut, chillies and spices for a couple of minutes in a little ghee. Remove from the heat, stir in the lemon juice, coriander and salt. Poke a hole in each of the balls and stuff with a little of the filling. Close up the hole and roll in the semolina or flour. Gently flatten with your hand and fry in hot ghee for 5 minutes a side until they are golden. They can be served hot or cold and are delicious with a hot lime pickle. They make an excellent appetiser.

SPICY PATTIES   Serves 4

  1 lb (450 g) mashed potato
  1-in (2.5-cm) piece ginger
  2 green chilli peppers
  2 tbs flour, sifted
  1 tbs fresh coriander
  1 tbs crushed almonds or pine nuts
  2 tbs grated or desiccated coconut
  squeeze of lemon juice
  oil for deep frying
  salt

Peel and grate the ginger, chop the chilli and mix all the ingredients together. Form the mixture into little patties and deep fry until golden. The oil should be very hot (375°F/190°C) and it will take about 4 or 5 minutes. Drain and serve with Indian chutneys and cucumber raita.

HASHED POTATOES/HASH BROWNS

This is the American name for fried-up leftover potatoes. Mashed or grated cooked potatoes are sautéed in hot oil, oil and butter, fat or clarified butter to make a very crisp bottom layer. The addition of a chopped onion, fried first and mixed in with the potatoes before cooking, livens it up a bit. But like all the other recipes so far in this section, anything goes.

POTATO FRITTERS   Serves 4

  1 lb (450 g) mashed potato
  2 eggs and 2 extra yolks
  a few chopped pistachio or pine nuts
  2 oz (50 g) melted butter
  olive oil for frying

Separate one egg, lightly whisk the white and set aside. If using pine nuts, brown them in a little butter. Beat the eggs and mix them, the remaining butter and the nuts into the potatoes. Form into small rissoles, dip in egg white and sauté in hot olive oil until golden brown. Drain and serve immediately directly from the pan.

POTATO CROQUETTES   Serves 4

When is a fritter a croquette or when is a croquette a fritter? I think the answer lies in the fact that croquettes always have a breadcrumb coating. Perhaps because they look a bit like rissoles, croquettes are considered a bit low rent. They aren't. This basic recipe is delicious, is good munchies fodder, always welcome with children and can be jazzed up with chopped parsley, chives or any other fresh herb and served as an accompaniment. Equally it can be stuffed Middle-Eastern and Indian style, mixed with any other leftovers or filled with different things so you have croquette surprise! My favourite way is to grate 2 oz (50 g) Parmesan into the mixture. They can be pan or deep fried.

> 1½ lb (700 g) mashed potato
> 1 egg and 2 extra yolks
> flour
> fine dry breadcrumbs
> oil for frying
> salt, pepper, grated nutmeg

Beat the 2 egg yolks, one at a time, into the potatoes. With such a large quantity of potato (you will regret it if you make less), it is easier to halve the mixture and incorporate it again when it's softened by the egg. Season with plenty of black pepper, salt and a little grated nutmeg. Flour a board and the dough and form into little nuggets; you should be able to make about 16 but it depends on your favoured size. Coat in the whole beaten egg and then the breadcrumbs. Heat the oil – about ¼ in (0.5 cm) deep or using a chip pan – and cook until golden brown.

POTATO CROQUETTES WITH CRISP-FRIED NOODLES/PATATE SPINOSE

This is a novel idea from Marcella Hazan. Instead of breadcrumbs, as in the basic potato croquette recipe (above), crush 3½ oz (100 g) vermicelli or similar fine noodles into ⅛-in (0.25-cm) pieces and mix with a little flour. Dip the croquettes in the mixture and fry, uncrowded.

This is slightly easier if you make balls rather than the usual cork shape.

OATMEAL POTATO CROQUETTES

Similarly, John Tovey used porridge oats. Follow the basic potato croquette recipe (page 197) except dip the croquettes in beaten eggs and roll in oats before frying.

BUBBLE AND SQUEAK   Serves 4

'When 'midst the frying pan, in accents savage,
The beef so surly, quarrels with the cabbage.'

Dr Kitchner, Cook's Oracle, 1817.

The name of this familiar dish is a somewhat poetic interpretation of the sound of potato, onion and cabbage sizzling in the pan. The following recipe comes from Cassell's Dictionary of Cookery, 1877: 'Dissolve 2 or 3 ounces of beef dripping in a frying pan. Cut some thin slices of cold boiled or roast beef and fry them slightly, a nice brown. Mix some cold green of any kind with a few mashed potatoes, shred onion, if liked, salt and pepper and fry, stirring all the time.'

These days the dish is most often a way of using up leftover mash and sprouts or greens but is also enjoying a new lease of life on the menu of many of London's most fashionable restaurants. Here's my recipe:

    1 lb (450 g) mashed potato
    1 onion, finely chopped
    2 oz (50 g) dripping or oil
    8 oz (225 g) cooked cabbage or sprouts, finely chopped
    salt, pepper

Soften the onion in half the dripping and when cooked mix in with the potato and greens. Season generously and add a little more dripping. Press the bubble into the hot dripping and fry over a moderate heat until it's nicely browned underneath (about 15 minutes). Turn and do the other side, having added the last of the dripping.

BUBBLE AND SQUEAK WITH BACON

Follow the basic recipe (above) but dice a couple of rashers of streaky bacon, sautéeing slowly until the fat runs out. When the bacon is crisp, mix it in with the bubble and cook it in the bacon fat.

ALASTAIR LITTLE'S RESTAURANT BUBBLE AND SQUEAK

Serves 8–10

One day Alastair found himself with 2 lb (900 g) of mashed potato made with garlic and olive oil. It is unlikely that you or I are ever going to be in that position but here's the recipe anyway. It is of course terrific.

> 2–3 lb (900 g –1.4 kg) mashed potato made with olive oil and garlic
> 1 large onion, finely sliced
> olive oil
> 1 whole Savoy cabbage, cored and shredded
> 4 oz (110 g) butter
> salt, pepper

Slightly cook the onion in a little olive oil and blanch the cabbage in boiling salted water. Mix the onion, cabbage and potato together, season to your taste. Grease a heavy baking tray with olive oil and pile in the potatoes. Dot the top with butter and cook in your oven – pre-heated to its highest possible temperature – for 20 minutes. It will be deliciously crispy and coming away at the edges.

SIMON HOPKINSON'S BUBBLE WITH LEEKS

Serves 1

Being the perfectionist that he is, Simon's recipe is inextricably linked in with a whole meal. As you'll see, it's stretching it a bit to include this recipe in leftovers.

> 1 large boiled potato
> 1 new season's (summer) lamb's kidney in its suet
> 1 small leek, trimmed, sliced and washed
> salt, pepper

Trim the excess fat from the kidney and melt in a small frying pan. Boil the leeks in a little salted water (were you starting from scratch you'd use the potato water, says Simon) for a couple of minutes. Drain. Crush the potato and mix with the leek and season.

Heat up the fat and fry the bubble for about 10 minutes on each side until it is nice and crispy. At the same time, in a separate pan, sauté the kidney in its suet until golden all over and transfer to a very hot oven (425°F/220°C/gas mark 7) for 5–10 minutes. Allow to rest for a couple of minutes, remove remaining suet, slice and lay on top of the bubble.

RICHARD SHEPHERDS'S POTATO LEFTOVER   Serves 4

1 lb (450 g) potatoes, cooked and sliced
4–8 oz (110 g – 225 g) Cheddar or Mozzarella cheese
2 oz (50 g) butter

Butter an ovenproof dish and fill with well-seasoned layers of potato, strewing ¼-in (0.5-cm) pieces of cheese throughout. Dot the top with the rest of the butter and cook in a hot oven for about 35 minutes (424°F/220°C/gas mark 7) until the top is crispy and all the cheese melted.

When Escoffier retired to Monte Carlo in 1919 his cook was a Madame Jeanne. She created an almost identical dish to this but made alternate layers of potato and cooked rice and sprinkled each layer with a mixture of grated Gruyère and Parmesan. She then pressed the mixture down firmly and topped it with melted butter and sprinkled thickly with equal quantities of cheese and fine breadcrumbs.

BRUSSELS AND BACON TART   Serves 2

1 lb (450 g) mashed potato
2 oz (50 g) butter
8 oz (225 g) Brussels sprouts
1 oz (25 g) flour
2 oz (50 g) Cheddar, Parmesan, Gruyère or Emmenthal
8 rashers very thin smoked bacon
4 oz (110 g) fresh prawns
salt, pepper

Butter an ovenproof dish and line with mashed potato. Dot with butter and bake at 425°F/220°C/gas mark 7 for 15 minutes or until it begins to brown.

Meanwhile, parboil some even-sized sprouts for 5 minutes and set aside to drain thoroughly. Use some of the cooking liquid to make a cheese sauce and season well with pepper. Mix the sprouts into the sauce and pour into the mashed potato 'pastry'. Make a criss-cross pattern with strips of (ideally) thinly sliced, smoked, streaky bacon. Return to the oven for 10 minutes until the bacon is crisp and the juices have seeped into the pie.

FISH PIE

   1½–2 lb (700–900 g) mashed potato
   1 lb (450 g) each smoked and fresh haddock
   ¾ pt (400 ml) milk
   1 oz (25 g) butter
   1½ oz (40 g) flour, sifted
   1 tbs fresh parsley, chopped
   2 hard-boiled eggs
   4 oz (110 g) fresh prawns
   salt, pepper

Simmer the fish in the milk for about 10 minutes until it is just cooked. Leave the fish to cool slightly but reserve the liquid. Melt the butter and stir in the flour, let it cook for a moment before you add most of the milk to make a thick sauce. Let it cook for 5 minutes, remove from the heat and add the parsley and big flakes of fish. Chop up the eggs and peel the prawns.

   Butter a large ovenproof dish and pour in the sauced fish, mix the prawns and egg evenly throughout the pie, season well and top with the mash. Dot with butter and bake for 30 minutes at 400°F/200°C/gas mark 6 until the top is nicely browned.

PIGS IN BLANKETS

Variations on this recipe were given to me by masses of people. The wartime version using reconstituted potato and cooking the P.I.B.s in the fat from the sausage isn't a patch on this.

   1½ lb (700 g) mashed potato
   8 of your favourite sausages
   2 oz (50 g) melted butter
   1 tbs English mustard
   1 egg, beaten with 1 tbs milk
   breadcrumbs
   oil for deep frying
   salt, pepper

Fry the sausages how you like them while you beat the melted butter, 1 tbs mustard and seasoning into the potato. Allow the sausages to cool (this is also good for using up leftover sausages) and make each sausage a 'coat' of potato. Dip into the egg mixture and roll in the breadcrumbs. Fry in hot oil until golden brown. Drain on absorbent kitchen paper.

CORNED BEEF HASH   Serves 4

This is a chicken and egg dish; do you start with leftover corned beef or leftover potatoes? As a guideline there should be at least half as much beef to potato. Waxy-variety potatoes are best.

    1 lb (450 g) cooked potatoes, diced
    2 oz (50 g) clarified butter or dripping
    2 onions, finely sliced
    4 tomatoes, skinned and quartered (optional)
    8 oz–1 lb (225–450 g) corned beef, diced
    2 tbs parsley, chopped
    1½ tbs Worcestershire sauce
    salt, pepper

Heat the butter and cook the onions until softened. Stir in the tomatoes, beef and potatoes, seasoning, parsley and Worcester. Let it bubble away over a moderate heat for at least 15 minutes. To get it crispy takes quite a bit of time because all the fat comes out of the beef. It is very good served with triangular croûtons and crisp green salad dressed with a mustardy vinaigrette.

SHEPHERD'S PIE   Serves 6

In 1988 Prue Leith devoted her *Guardian* cookery column to English mince and to shepherd's pie in particular. The correct proportion of potato and mince, she said, was 50:50 and the mash should be firm and made without milk. In France their *hachis Parmentier* is often cooked with the meat sandwiched between two layers of potato. My own shepherd's pies are never exactly the same but I always include some chicken liver, if available a splash of red wine, Worcester sauce, a grated carrot and tomatoes to give the invariably tasteless mince a bit of body. Were I to follow a recipe, I'd choose Jane Grigson's Shepherd's Pie:

2 lb (900 g) mashed potato
1 or 2 raw potatoes, peeled and sliced very thinly
5 oz (150 g) onion, chopped
3 tbs butter, dripping or oil
1 lb (450 g) minced fresh or leftover roast lamb
3 cloves garlic, crushed and chopped
½ pt (275 ml) meat jelly, clear gravy and stock (in whatever
      proportions you have them)
1 level tbs flour or cornflour
tomato concentrate or paste
1 tbs each dry Leicester and Parmesan, grated
1 tbs Worcester sauce
salt, pepper, thyme, cayenne

Cook the onion in the fat until soft. Add the meat and garlic, stirring well,
then raise the heat so that the meat browns. Turn it over several times so
that it browns all over. Pour off surplus fat. Add some of the stock and
bubble gently for 5 minutes. Sprinkle on the flour, stir again and add the
remaining liquid. Let it bubble to a rich sauce, adding the various
flavourings to taste. Leave to simmer for 40 minutes.

Transfer to an ovenproof dish, allow to cool and top with the potato.
Make a ring round the edge with the slices of potato, scatter the cheese on
top and brown at the top of a hot oven (425°F/220°C/gas mark 7).

19.

Dinner Dishes

What do *Bouillabaisse*, *Mee Rebus*, *Bacalhau a Bras*, Lancashire Hot Pot, *Damalaki Aretousa*, *Carapulcra*, Cawl, *Ubi Kentang Kari*, *Pot au Four*, Lamb *Boulangère* and Irish Stew have in common? The answer of course is the potato. None of these dishes would work without it. Unlike shepherd's pie, bubble and squeak and corned beef hash, they aren't dishes that get knocked up, that rely on the store cupboard or fridge leftovers. These are dishes that demand special shopping, that require a bit more kitchen work than the 'everyday' supper dishes in the section on Leftovers and in Lunch, High Tea and Supper. They are the sort of dishes you might make if there are guests for dinner or a large family gathering.

VEGETARIAN POTATO DISHES

The potato is the vegetarian's life saver – it offers such scope for variety both on its own and mixed with other vegetables. Looking through this collection of recipes with hindsight, I've come to the conclusion that the potato as part of the meat and two veg syndrome is the potato at its least interesting. I've also come to the conclusion that the potato was designed with the vegetarian in mind. It fulfils so many needs.

For a start the potato is rich in vitamins and minerals, it is cheap and readily available. It keeps for ages without detriment and it is so versatile that there is no excuse not to enjoy a varied diet while dining on potatoes every night of the year. Think of the marvellous soups, the gratins, the salads and the different pancakes, patties, croquettes and fritters, the deep-fried potato dishes, the exotic Middle Eastern potato-stuffed pastries and spicy Indian curries, the heartening gnocchi, the pies and the pastries, salads and sauté dishes. Then of course there's chips and baked potatoes, potato breads, cakes and puddings.

Ironically the majority of the dishes that fit the categorisation for this chapter do involve meat or fish. The following dishes are all very special

for the vegetarian, they marry the potato with flavourings other than meat
to elevate it to dinner-party status.

GRENADIER MARCH/GRANOTASKOCHA   Serves 6–8

This heartening Hungarian dish is perfect for a winter's dinner. If you
make it with waxy-variety potatoes the dice will retain their shape, made
with a floury variety the dish is more of a slop. Both are equally delicious.
Serve with a crisp green vegetable, a tomato sauce and bear in mind that it
is a very filling dish.

> 1½ lb (700 g) potatoes
> 1 lb (450 g) flour
> 2 eggs, beaten
> 1 large onion, finely chopped
> 2 tbs sunflower oil or butter
> 1 heaped tbs paprika
> salt, pepper
> chives or flat-leaf parsley to garnish

Sift the flour and make a hard dough by mixing in the eggs, at least 2 fl oz
(50 ml) water and a generous pinch of salt. Knead it well and stretch it
several times before you leave it to rest for 1½ hours.

Meanwhile, peel the potatoes and chop up into small dice. Blanch in
boiling salted water for 5 minutes, drain and set aside while you brown
the onion in the oil or butter. Stir-fry for a few minutes until the onions are
soft, add the diced potatoes and paprika. Let the mixture sauté very
slowly, turning it every now and again to crisp the edges lightly. When the
potatoes are evenly cooked, roll and stretch the dough to a thin sheet and
cut it into 1½-in (3.5-cm) squares. Put a large saucepan full of salted
water on to boil and when it is boiling fiercely throw in the dough squares.
Cook for 5 minutes and drain.

Mix the noodles and potatoes, sprinkle with chives or parsley and
serve.

BRAISED GLOBE ARTICHOKES AND POTATOES/CARCIOFI E
PATATE   Serves 6

Artichokes and potatoes are both subtly-flavoured vegetables. In this dish
their flavours are accentuated by the garlic, lemon and salt which,
combined with a generous amount of olive oil, makes a rich and robust

dish. Serve this on its own with crusty Italian bread preceded by a light soup, followed by Italian cheese and a fresh fruit dessert.

1½ lb (700 g) waxy-variety potatoes
6 tiny or 3 medium-sized globe artichokes
juice of ½ lemon
1 onion, chopped
6 tbs olive oil
1 clove garlic, peeled and finely chopped
salt, pepper
1–2 tbs flat-leaf parsley, chopped

You will need a large sauté or casserole dish. Prepare the artichokes by snapping off the outer green parts of the leaves leaving only the tender, edible whiteish part. Squeeze lemon juice over each cut to avoid discolouring. When you get down to the central cone of pale translucent leaves cut off the top (about 1 in/2.5 cm) to reveal the prickly tipped leaves that cover the whiskery choke. Cut away these leaves and scrape out the choke, taking care not to damage the edible heart. Squeeze lemon over the heart and trim the tough leaves at the base of the stem and the stem itself. Quarter the artichoke hearts or halve the small ones and rub the cuts with lemon juice.

Peel the potatoes and cut into thick wedges like giant chips. Leave in cold water while you sauté the onion in olive oil until it turns translucent. Add the garlic and cook for a couple of minutes. Add the drained and dried potatoes, the artichokes, salt and pepper and sauté over a gentle heat for about 10 minutes, turning to make sure that every surface is cooked. Sprinkle on most of the parsley, 6 tbs of water, stir the dish and cover. Continue cooking over a gentle heat for about 40 minutes until the vegetables are tender. If the pan dries out during the cooking add a little more water. Season generously, sprinkle on the rest of the parsley and serve warm rather than piping hot.

COUNTRY-STYLE POTATO STEW/RAGOÛT DE POMMES DE TERRE THÉZY-GLIMONT   Serves 6–8

I was amused to read that the grandmother of the French chef Jean Conil used to make a potato liqueur which she called Spirit of Jesus, presumably a French version of poteen. She also devised this delicious ragoût which is based on the plentiful supply of vegetables in Thézy-Glimont. This area of France, just a half-kilometre from the site of the Battle of the Somme, is a marshy plain that supplies a plentiful harvest of vegetables that are sold in the markets of Paris. The ragoût was a daily ritual, served to her grandson Jean and the rest of the family after a hard day's spudding. The recipe is adapted slightly in favour of the potato. Serve with plenty of crusty bread and a fruity, light Beaujolais, and follow with cheese and a fruit tart with whipped cream.

    1½ lb (700 g) new potatoes, scrubbed and quartered
    2 fl oz (50 ml) olive oil
    2 oz (50 g) butter
    1 large onion, sliced
    1 clove garlic, crushed
    4 oz (110 g) each celery, carrots, turnips, swedes, cabbage, shelled
        peas or mangetout and runner beans
    1 spray fresh thyme
    1 bay leaf
    2 oz (50 g) tomato purée
    3 pts (1.7 l) water
    salt, pepper
    1 tsp each fresh chervil, parsley, marjoram and mint, chopped

Heat the oil and butter in a large heavy casserole. Stir fry first the onion and, when it has softened, the garlic. Cook for a few minutes and add the potatoes. Cover and turn the heat very low. Peel the carrots, turnips and swedes and chop into chunks slightly smaller than the potato. Slice the cabbage and beans and chop up the celery. Add all these vegetables to the pot, stirring to coat them all with the fat. Cover and allow to sweat for a couple of minutes, stir and repeat. Add the thyme, bay leaf, tomato purée and the water. Bring to the boil and simmer for 15 minutes. Season generously and add the cabbage, beans and peas. Cook for a further 10 minutes, check the seasoning and sprinkle the herbs. Serve in large soup plates.

CAPPELLACCI FILLED WITH SWEET POTATOES AND PARSLEY/
CAPPELLACCI DEL NUOVO MONDO   Serves 4

One of the muckiest and most-used cookbooks in my kitchen is Marcella Hazan's *Classic Italian Cookbook*. Like many pages, pages 144 and 145 are so familiar to me that I no longer need to consult them. The recipe in question is an adaptation of the dish *cappellacci di zucca*, pasta filled with pumpkin, which is an exclusive speciality of Ferrara – where Marcella Hazan was at university. This adaptation uses baked sweet potato flesh instead of the flat, yellow pumpkins peculiar to Ferrara and the chestnutty flavour is not dissimilar. Although normally served as an hors d'oeuvre, the *cappellacci* make a splendid main course especially if served with a crisp salad, plenty of red wine and ripe Italian cheese to follow.

For the stuffing:

1¾ lb (800 g) sweet potato flesh
4½ oz (125 g) freshly grated Parmesan cheese
3 tbs parsley, finely chopped
1 oz (25 g) prosciutto or green bacon, chopped (optional!)
1 egg yolk
salt, pepper, ½ tsp nutmeg
freshly grated Parmesan and finely chopped parsley to garnish

For the dough:

7 oz (200 g) plain flour
2 eggs
2 tsp milk

Puncture the potatoes all over and bake for 1 hour in a hot oven. Meanwhile, make the pasta. Sift the flour on to a flat surface and form into a mound. Make a well in the centre and pour in the eggs whisked with the milk. Using one hand to support the mound, incorporate the flour into the egg mixture with the other. Work the mixture until you have a crumbly paste. Knead and work the dough until it becomes slightly elasticated and pliable – this takes about 10 minutes of work. Roll it up into a ball and set aside while you dust the surface with flour. Roll out the dough into a big circle, working to create an even, thin sheet and using the rolling pin to help you stretch and shape the dough. Continue rolling and then curling and stretching the dough around the pin at least 12 times so that you end up with a wafer-thin sheet of pasta. All this can of course be done with consummate ease using a pasta machine.

When the potatoes are cooked, peel and purée them and mix in 2½ oz (65 g) of the Parmesan, the parsley, bacon (if you're not vegetarian), egg yolk, nutmeg and seasoning. Stir thoroughly. Place about 1 tsp of the mixture at 1½-in (3.5-cm) intervals in a straight line about 2 in (5 cm) from the edge of the pasta sheet. Fold over the edge to sandwich the stuffing and, using a fluted pastry cutter, cut along the three edges to make little squares. Press the edges together and if necessary use a little water to act as a glue. Continue until you run out of pasta or stuffing.

Bring a large pan of salted water to the boil. Fling in the pasta and cook for a couple of minutes, drain and pile into a warm buttered dish. Sprinkle on the remaining 2 oz (50 g) cheese, dot with butter and serve with more Parmesan and sprinkled with parsley.

JAMAICAN RUN DOWN   Serves 2

This Jamaican recipe comes from Huckleberry's in Bath. Serve with brown rice.

1 medium-sized potato, diced
1 sweet potato, diced
5 oz (150 g) creamed coconut
1 pt (570 ml) water
2 carrots, peeled and cut into 1-in (2.5-cm) sticks
1 green pepper, cored and sliced
1 medium-sized onion, finely chopped
1 bay leaf
2 sprigs thyme
2 cloves garlic, chopped
1 chilli pepper, seeded and chopped
1 parsnip, peeled and cubed
8 oz (225 g) kidney beans, soaked and cooked
salt, pepper, soy sauce

Put the creamed coconut in a pan with the water and bring it to the boil. When the coconut melts and oil separates out add the carrot, pepper and onion. Let the mixture simmer for 10 minutes and then add the potatoes, bay leaf, thyme, garlic and chilli. Continue cooking for a further 10 minutes and add the sweet potato and parsnip. When all the vegetables are almost done add the beans, the seasoning and the soy sauce to taste.

By the end of the cooking process the majority of the liquid will have evaporated or been absorbed. If the vegetables dry out before they are all cooked, add a little more water; conversely if there is too much liquid left by the time the vegetables are cooked, boil it vigorously to evaporate the excess. The vegetables should be soft but not mushy and coated with a creamy coconut layer.

MOROCCAN POTATO CASSEROLE   Serves 4–6

This is a marvellous example of how the potato can become extremely exotic with the addition of a few spices. Serve with a coriander-spiced dish of creamy sheep's yoghurt, two or three meze dips, a crunchy salad, plenty of black olives and hot pitta bread.

> 2½ lb (1 kg) waxy-variety potatoes
> 6 fl oz (170 ml) olive oil
> 3 green peppers, cored and sliced in strips, not rings
> 12 cloves garlic, minced
> 2 tsp each ground cumin and coriander
> zest and juice of 2 small lemons
> salt, pepper

Peel and quarter the potatoes, rinse and pat dry. Heat the oil in a heavy casserole dish, add the peppers and sauté gently for 5 minutes, turning once. Add the garlic, coriander and cumin and cook for 5 more minutes stirring continuously. Stir in the potatoes, lemon juice and zest and seasoning. Turn the heat down as low as possible, cover and leave to simmer until the potatoes are cooked; check after 30 minutes.

GOANESE POTATO CURRY   Serves 4

This and the next two curries are quite different but interchangeable. Serve as the centrepiece to a vegetarian Indian meal and accompany with a garlicky dal, rice, cucumber raita, pickles and chutneys, and nan.

> 1½ lb (700 g) potatoes, peeled and cut into large uniform chunks
> 4 tbs oil
> 3 tsp cinnamon
> 3 cloves garlic, chopped
> 1 small red chilli pepper, chopped
> 2 tsp coriander seed
> 2 medium-sized onions
> 6 oz (175 g) desiccated coconut
> 2 tbs ghee
> 1 lb (450 g) tomatoes, peeled and quartered
> 4 oz (110 g) shelled peas
> salt, pepper
> fresh coriander leaves, chopped, to garnish

Put 2 tbs of oil into a frying pan and sauté the cinnamon, garlic, chilli pepper and coriander seed for 2 minutes. In a separate pan heat the remaining oil and when the oil is very hot brown the sliced onions. Turn the heat right down and add the coconut. Gently cook for 5 minutes and mix with the cinnamon mixture. Pound into a paste.

Melt the ghee in a large frying pan or casserole dish and sauté the potatoes until they are tender and browned in places. In a separate pan boil the tomatoes with ½ pt (275 ml) water, cook to a pulp and sieve. Add the paste, tomato pulp, peas and seasoning to taste to the potatoes and simmer for 5 minutes. Serve garnished with chopped coriander.

NEPALI POTATO CURRY   Serves 6

2 lb (900 g) potatoes, diced
4 tbs ghee
2 onions, chopped
6 spring onions, chopped
6 cloves garlic, minced
1 bay leaf
4 green chilli peppers, chopped
1½-in (3.5-cm) piece fresh ginger, finely chopped
½ tsp turmeric powder
6 oz (175 g) peas (optional)
1 cauliflower, divided into florets and the stalk chopped into 1-in (2.5-cm) pieces
6 tomatoes, peeled and quartered
1 tbs fresh coriander leaves, chopped
2 tsp coriander seeds
1 tbs cumin seeds
2 tsp salt, ½ tsp black pepper

Melt the ghee and cook the onions until soft, add the spring onions and garlic and continue cooking over a gentle flame. Add the bay leaf, pepper, chillies, ginger, turmeric and salt. Stir fry for a couple of minutes, then add the potatoes and, stirring occasionally, sauté for 10 minutes. Add the remaining ingredients and ½ pt (275 ml) hot water. Cook gently until all the vegetables are tender; this will take between 15 and 20 minutes.

BENGALI POTATO CURRY   <u>Serves 4</u>

   1 lb (450 g) potatoes, diced
   1 tbs ghee
   ½ tsp each mustard seeds, paprika, fenugreek seeds and fennel
   1 tsp cumin
   1 bay leaf
   1 medium-sized aubergine, diced
   1 large courgette, diced
   4 oz (110 g) peas (optional)
   1 tsp soft brown sugar
   ½ tsp salt

Heat the ghee and stir fry the mustard seeds, fenugreek, fennel, cumin, paprika and bay leaf. When the seeds begin to pop stir in the potatoes. Turn the heat down very low and stir fry for 5 minutes and then add the rest of the vegetables. Continue stirring and frying for a further 5 minutes and then sprinkle on the salt and sugar and just enough water to cover the vegetables. Cover and simmer until the potatoes are tender and most of the liquid is absorbed.

RICH POTATO CURRY/UBI KENTANG KARI   <u>Serves 4</u>

This is a Malaysian dish that is an amalgamation of the previous Jamaican coconut curry (see page 209) and the chilli hot Indian dishes. It is very quick to prepare because the potatoes are boiled before the dish is prepared. Serve with rice and crunchy beansprout-packed spring rolls.

   1½ lb (700 g) waxy-variety potatoes, boiled and diced
   1 tsp chilli powder
   ½ tsp turmeric powder
   4 tbs oil
   1 tsp fresh ginger, finely chopped
   1 clove garlic, minced
   3 oz (75 g) sesame seeds, dry-roasted and finely ground
   1 tsp fenugreek seeds, dry-roasted and finely ground
   2 oz (50 g) creamed coconut, soaked in 4 fl oz (110 ml) hot water
   2 large peppers, 1 red, 1 green, seeded and sliced
   1 tbs coriander leaves, chopped
   ½ tsp salt

Mix the chilli, turmeric and salt to a paste with a little water. Heat the oil in a large frying pan or wok and gently sauté the ginger and garlic before adding the chilli mixture, sesame and fenugreek. Stir well and pour in the coconut milk. Bring it up to the boil, add the peppers and coriander leaves and simmer for a couple of minutes. Add the potatoes and let them simmer gently for several minutes to absorb and be coated by the sauce.

POTATO-STUFFED PARATHAS   Serves 4

This is one of those dishes that tastes exotic and looks impressive, but in fact it's like falling off a log to prepare. It should be served with lime pickle and mango chutney and perhaps a dish of cucumber raita.

To make 12 pancakes:

12 oz (350 g) wholewheat flour
6 oz (175 g) plain flour
10 tbs vegetable oil or melted ghee
7 fl oz (200 ml) water
½ tsp salt

For the stuffing:

1½ lb (700 g) floury-variety potatoes
2 medium-sized onions, finely sliced
5 large cloves garlic, crushed
4 tsp fresh ginger, grated
juice of ½ lemon
large pinch each paprika, cumin and turmeric
1 tbs coriander leaves, chopped

Begin with the pancakes. Sift the two flours into a bowl with the salt and dribble 3 tbs of the oil into the mixture. Working quickly, rub the mixture between your fingertips until it resembles coarse breadcrumbs. Gradually add the water and work together to make a soft dough. Rub all over with oil and leave to prove for at least half an hour in a covered bowl. Meanwhile make the stuffing.

Scrub the potatoes and cook them in boiling salted water. Drain, peel and dry mash. Sauté the onions in 3 tbs of the oil until transparent. Add the garlic and cook for a further 2 minutes. Remove from the heat and mix all the ingredients together. Cover.

Having made the stuffing, divide the dough into 12 balls and, working with one ball at a time, flatten, brush with oil and roll into a 6-in (15-cm) round. Spread 3 tbs of the filling on to one half of the paratha. Fold the remaining pastry over the filling and seal by pressing the edges together, using a little water as glue if necessary. Brush the top of the pastry with oil and gently sauté in a lightly oiled heavy frying pan. Cook for 2 minutes a side and keep warm while you repeat the process.

FISH

BAKED MACKEREL WITH POTATOES   Serves 6

> 1½ lb (700 g) floury-variety potatoes
> ½ pt (275 ml) olive oil
> 3 cloves garlic, chopped
> 6 small mackerel, filleted
> 2 oz (50 g) parsley, chopped
> salt, pepper

Peel and finely slice the potatoes, rinse in cold water and pat dry. Sluice a large baking dish with half the olive oil and pile in the potatoes, half the garlic, half the parsley and a generous amount of salt and pepper. Mix it all around with your hands and even it out.

Bake for 30 minutes or until the potatoes are almost cooked at 450°F/230°C/gas mark 8. Lay the mackerel fillets skin side down over the potatoes and divide the remains of the olive oil and the parsley between the fish. Season generously and return to the oven. After 15 minutes remove the dish and scoop up some of the juice to baste the fish. Bake for a further 5 minutes and serve.

BAKED HAKE WITH MAYONNAISE AND
POTATOES   Serves 4

This is a recipe devised by Sophie Grigson after a gourmandising visit to Spain.

> 1½ lb (700 g) waxy-variety potatoes, boiled, peeled and sliced
> 2 lb (900 g) hake

1 large onion, sliced
1 tbs olive oil
1 clove garlic, chopped
¼ pt (150 ml) mayonnaise
salt, pepper

Ask the fishmonger to clean and scale the fish but leave the head and tail in situ. Grease an ovenproof dish and spread with the potatoes.

Gently sauté the onion in the oil until limp, add the garlic and cook for a minute, then spread the mixture on top of the potatoes. Season and lay the hake on top, curving it round and catching its tail in its teeth. Bake at 400°F/200°C/gas mark 6 for 15 minutes. Remove from the oven and smear mayonnaise over the fish and the visible potatoes. Return for a further 15–20 minutes and serve directly.

JOHN DORY WITH POTATOES/SAINT-PIERRE À LA BOULANGÈRE
Serves 4

This is a similar idea but reversed with the potatoes on top of the fish.

3 lb (1.4 kg) waxy-variety potatoes, peeled and thinly sliced
4 large onions
2 oz (50 g) butter
1 clove garlic, chopped
1 John Dory weighing about 3 lb (1.4 kg)
2 pts (1.1 l) boiling chicken stock
1 sprig fresh thyme
salt, pepper
1 tbs fresh parsley, chopped

Slice the onions finely and cook them very gently in ¾ of the butter until they are thoroughly cooked – this will take about 20 minutes. Spread the onions in a large gratin-type dish, sprinkle with the garlic and lay the cleaned and gutted fish on top. Rinse and pat dry the potatoes and pile on top of the fish. Pour on the hot stock, sprinkle over the thyme, dot with butter, cover with foil and bake for 45 minutes.

If the liquid hasn't been totally absorbed by the potatoes during the cooking time, strain it off and reduce until it thickens, pour over the potatoes and serve sprinkled with parsley.

SQUID AND POTATOES FROM GENOA/TOTANI E PATATE IN TEGAME ALLA GENOVESE   Serves 6

This dish has become a great personal favourite and comes from Marcella Hazan's *Second Classic Italian Cookbook*. The squid turns out deliciously tender, the potatoes saturated with the rich juices. Serve with crusty Italian bread, for you won't want to leave any of the sauce.

>   2 lb (900 g) potatoes, cut into chunks
>   2 cloves garlic, chopped ·
>   1½ tbs parsley, chopped
>   5 tbs olive oil
>   1½ lb (700 g) cleaned and sliced squid
>   6 tbs dry white wine
>   8 oz (225 g) tin of Italian plum tomatoes
>   ¼ tsp oregano
>   salt, pepper

Sauté the garlic and parsley in the oil. When nicely browned add the squid, move it around to cook it slightly on all sides. Pour on the wine, let it bubble a little and then add a couple of pinches of salt, the chopped tomatoes with their juice and the oregano. Stir well, cover and simmer gently for 30 minutes. Add the potatoes, another pinch of salt, a few grinds of pepper, cover again and continue simmering until the potatoes are tender. This will take about 40 minutes.

Check the seasoning and serve sprinkled with more parsley.

BOUILLABAISSE   Serves 10–12

Down in the South of France there are several restaurants that specialise in this stupendous dish. It is a dish that doesn't travel well because of the unavailability of *rascasse* which is considered a vital ingredient. An authentic version is served at Pierre Martin's Fulham restaurant called Bouillabaisse. Not all recipes include potatoes in a bouillabaisse but most people expect beautiful pale yellow saffron-tinted potato slices as an integral part of the dish.

3 lb (1.4 kg) waxy-variety potatoes, peeled and sliced
4 fl oz (110 ml) olive oil
2 large onions, finely sliced
5 cloves garlic, crushed
1 lb (450 g) ripe tomatoes, peeled and chopped
2 bay leaves
sprig of thyme
fennel bulb, sliced
2-in (5-cm) piece of orange peel
5 pts (2.8 l) boiling fish stock or water
¼ tsp saffron
6 lb (2.7 kg) mixed fish chosen from John Dory, red mullet,
    monkfish, bream, bass, eel, gurnard, and including *rascasse*,
    cleaned, gutted and cut into chunks
2 tbs parsley, finely chopped
15 or so slices of toasted French bread, rubbed with garlic
salt, pepper

For the rouille:

2 cloves garlic
1 red chilli pepper
bread
1 egg yolk
olive oil

Heat the oil and fry the onions until golden but not browned. Add the garlic and a minute later the tomatoes. Simmer for 5 minutes and add the thyme, bay leaf, fennel and orange peel. Stir in the hot stock or water, raise the heat and let it boil for a few minutes. Add the saffron and the potato slices. Simmer for 10 minutes and adjust the seasoning. Lay the fish over the potatoes and cook for a few minutes starting with the denser-fleshed fish and gradually adding the soft-fleshed. Remove the fish as they are done and keep warm in a covered dish.

Serve the broth as a soup sprinkled with parsley accompanied by the bread and a bowl of *rouille*. According to Alan Davidson, who is something of an expert on bouillabaisse, the correct way to make a *rouille* is to pound 2 cloves of garlic with a previously soaked red chilli pepper, a little sodden bread, a few pieces of cooked potato from the bouillabaisse and an egg yolk. Olive oil should be dribbled and beaten in to finish. The next course is the fish and potatoes which is also eaten with the hot *rouille*.

POTATOES WITH FISH AND VEGETABLES/CAUSA A LA
CHICLAYABA   Serves 4

This is a Peruvian recipe, once again showing their inventiveness with the
potato. It's an extraordinary collection of ingredients and makes a good
centrepiece for a buffet. It was cooked by Elisabeth Lambert Ortiz for the
BBC programme *A Taste of Health*.

       2 lb (900 g) potatoes, boiled and peeled
       1 lb (450 g) sweet potatoes
       1 medium-sized onion
       3 fl oz (75 ml) lemon juice
       ¼ tsp cayenne
       8 fl oz (225 ml) olive or corn oil
       2 under-ripe or green bananas
       2 sweetcorn cobs
       1 lb (450 g) non-oily, firm-fleshed white fish fillets such as haddock,
          cod or halibut
       1 small red pepper
       8 oz (225 g) Cheshire, Wensleydale or fresh goat cheese
       salt, pepper
       olives and lettuce leaves to garnish

Finely chop the onion and marinate it with the lemon juice, cayenne, a
little salt and pepper. Mash the potatoes with the onion and its juices and
the oil. Make a mound of the potatoes in the centre of a large plate and
keep warm.
   Boil the sweet potatoes until tender, peel and cut each one into 4 slices.
Boil the bananas in their skins for 15 minutes. Cool, peel and cut each one
into 8 slices. Boil the sweetcorn for 5 minutes, drain, cool and cut into 8
slices horizontally. Set aside the vegetables, keeping them warm. Lightly
grill the fish on both sides. Thinly slice the de-seeded pepper, blanch in
boiling water for one minute and drain. Cut the cheese into chunks.
   To assemble the dish, garnish the edge of a large serving plate with
lettuce leaves and arrange the fish fillets and vegetables around the
mound of potatoes. Scatter the pepper over the potatoes and garnish with
black olives and chunks of the cheese.

THAI GREEN HERB CURRY OF SHRIMP AND
POTATOES/DOM KA GUNG MAN FARANG   <u>Serves 4</u>

The popularity of Thai food is on the increase in this country and most of the ingredients specified in this recipe from Jennifer Brennan's book *One Dish Meals of Asia* are widely available. Chinese food emporiums are the best source of the more obscure fish sauce, known in Thai as *nam pla*.

The dish has the characteristic sweet/sour flavour of Thai food. I have substituted prawns for shrimps, those most readily available raw are the big Pacific prawns.

For the curry:

2 large waxy-variety potatoes, peeled and cut into ½-in (1-cm) dice
2 tbs oil
2 small onions, peeled and finely chopped
12 fl oz (340 ml) thick coconut milk
2 tbs fish sauce (*nam pla*)
juice and grated rind of 1 lime
2 medium tomatoes, peeled and chopped
2 tsp dried basil
20 raw prawns, shelled, the black nerve removed and chopped
2 tbs coriander leaves, chopped

For the spice paste:

½ stalk of lemon grass (bottom end only) minced
8 stems coriander, chopped
3 cloves garlic, peeled and smashed
1 shallot, peeled and chopped
grated rind of ½ lime
3 small fresh green chilli peppers, minced
½ tsp each shrimp or anchovy paste, ground ginger, ground coriander, ground caraway and nutmeg
pinch ground cloves
1–2 tbs vegetable oil
½ tsp salt, ⅔ tsp black pepper

Put all the ingredients for the spice paste in the blender and grind to a smooth paste, adding a little extra vegetable oil if needed.

Heat 2 tbs oil to smoking point in a wok or large frying pan. Turn down to low and stir fry the spice paste for 3 minutes. Add the potatoes and onions and toss until they are thoroughly coated with the paste. Pour in the coconut milk and add the fish sauce. Stir in the grated lime rind, tomatoes and basil. Stir and raise the heat to medium high to bring the mixture to the boil. Immediately reduce the heat to low and simmer, stirring occasionally, for about 10 minutes until the potatoes are cooked. Stir in the prawns, half the coriander and lime juice and cook gently for a further 10 minutes.

Serve sprinkled with the remaining coriander and accompany with a dish of plainly boiled rice.

CHICKEN AND OTHER FOWL

CHICKEN CYPRESSA   Serves 4–6

This is a mild, soothing dish that has a subtle flavour. It needs no accompaniment.

    1½ lb (700 g) small new potatoes
    3 lb (1.4 kg) maize-fed chicken
    2 bay leaves
    4 oz (110 g) clarified butter
    ½ pt (275 ml) white wine
    ½ pt (275 ml) chicken stock
    bundle of asparagus, trimmed and boiled so that they still retain
        some bite
    salt, pepper

Season the chicken inside, cover with water, add the bay leaves and bring to the boil. Simmer for 15 minutes and add the potatoes 5 minutes after the water has started simmering. Drain, setting aside the potatoes and leaving the chicken to cool sufficiently so that you can cut it into serving pieces.

Heat the butter in a large casserole dish and brown the chicken pieces all over, then add the potatoes so that they brown too. Pour over the wine and chicken stock, bring up to the boil, season well and turn down low. Allow to simmer very gently for 20 minutes and then add the boiled asparagus for the last 5 minutes of cooking. Serve from the casserole.

CHICKEN WITH VEGETABLES IN A CREAM SAUCE/POULE AU BLANC   Serves 6

This is a peasant dish served all over France. Accompany with crusty bread, plenty of vin de table and finish with a green salad and some ripe French cheese.

        12 small new potatoes
        4–5 lb (1.8–2.3 kg) chicken
        6 turnips, trimmed and peeled
        6 small leeks, trimmed and tied together
        2 parsnips, trimmed and peeled
        1 onion, peeled, halved and each half studded with a clove
        bouquet garni
        5 tbs flour
        6 fl oz (170 ml) crème fraîche or double cream
        salt, pepper

Clean the bird, season inside and put in a large pot. Cover with water, bring to the boil and simmer gently for 1½ hours. If necessary skim the top. Add the vegetables, bouquet garni and seasoning and bring back to the boil. Simmer for a further 30 minutes.

Ten minutes before the end of cooking, skim approximately 2 tbs of melted chicken fat from the surface of the broth. Transfer to a small saucepan and mix in the flour, cook it gently for a couple of minutes before adding 1 pt (570 ml) of the cooking broth. Bring to the boil and then turn down to simmer for 5 minutes. Stir in the cream and simmer for a further five minutes.

Remove the bird from the pot and carve into serving pieces. Arrange the chicken on a serving platter and the vegetables around the meat. Pour over the sauce and serve. The broth can be used for a soup.

POTATOES AND EGGS IN PIGEON AND WALNUT SAUCE   Serves 6

Throughout this book there are recipes from Latin America and from Peru in particular. This dish from the Incas is characteristic in that the potato is treated to an extremely complex sauce. In this case it involves two pigeons, and the potatoes are also served with half a dozen hard-boiled eggs. To Incas the yellow yolk represented the sun.

3 lb (1.4 kg) Jersey Royal potatoes, scrubbed and steamed
3 medium-sized onion, peeled and sliced
2 pigeons
2 tomatoes, peeled and sliced
2 oz (50 g) crushed walnuts
4 oz (110 g) Wensleydale cheese
1 dried chilli pepper, soaked in hot water, seeded and chopped
¼ pt (150 ml) milk
6 hard-boiled eggs
salt, pepper
1 tbs flat-leaf parsley, chopped

Line the base of a large heavy casserole dish with 2 of the onions. Split the pigeons through the breast bone and lay them flesh-side down on top of the onions. Season with salt and pepper and cover with the tomatoes. Cover tightly first with foil and then with the lid and cook on the lowest flame possible for a couple of hours until the pigeons are tender. When you're satisfied that the pigeons are done take them off the heat and leave them to cool. Strain off the cooking juices for use later. Discarding the skin and tendons, remove all the meat from the birds and set aside. Gently fry the third onion until it is limp but not browned. Put the pigeon, onion, walnuts, cheese and softened chilli pepper in the blender to make a purée. Dribble in sufficient milk to make the sauce the consistency of mayonnaise.

To assemble the dish cut the potatoes in half horizontally and lay them flat side down on a large serving plate. Halve the eggs horizontally and make a pattern with them round the side of the plate. Pour over the sauce and sprinkle with the flat-leaf parsley and a few slices of raw red pepper, if liked. Everything should be lukewarm. This is a very good dish for a buffet.

SRI LANKAN ROASTED SPICED CHICKEN WITH NEW POTATOES/KUKUL THAKKALI   Serves 6

The spicy, fiery hot curries of Sri Lanka have so far failed to catch the imagination of the British restaurant diner. There are only four Sri Lankan restaurants in and around London, the oldest being the Prince of Ceylon in Hendon. This recipe is moderated to Western palates with the use of paprika rather than chilli. If you prefer it really authentic then just swop chilli powder for paprika. Serve with plain boiled rice.

2 lb (900 g) small, waxy-variety potatoes, peeled and halved
½ tsp fenugreek seeds
¾ tsp fennel seeds
1½ tsp cumin seeds
1 tbs coriander seeds
3 tbs ghee
3 onions, finely chopped
4 cloves garlic, finely chopped
1-in (2.5-cm) piece of fresh ginger, peeled and chopped
1 tsp each turmeric, cinnamon and cayenne
1 heaped tbs paprika
2 tbs white vinegar
3 lb (1.4 kg) chicken pieces
½ tsp cardamom seeds
3 cloves
1 stalk of lemon grass
¾ pt (400 ml) water
⅓ pt (100 ml) thick coconut milk
juice 1 lemon
1 tsp salt

Begin by roasting the spices. Heat a small heavy frying pan and add the
fenugreek seeds. Shake the pan until they change colour and become
aromatic. Set aside and repeat with the fennel, cumin and coriander. It is
important to follow this order and routine because this dry roasting
contributes to the specifically Sri Lankan flavour and dark gravy. Grind the
spices to a fine powder.

Using either a wok or a spacious casserole, heat up the ghee and gently
fry the onions. When they begin to soften add the garlic and ginger and stir
fry for a couple of minutes. Meanwhile stir the turmeric, cayenne and
paprika into the vinegar to make a paste and add this to the onion
mixture. Cook for 2 minutes and brown the chicken pieces (small serving
pieces – the breast divided into 4, the legs into 2, etc.) in the spices,
turning them on all sides. Next add the salt, cinnamon, cardamom, cloves
and lemon grass. Stir thoroughly and pour on the water. Add the potatoes
and bring the liquid up to the boil. Turn down to simmer and cook for 20
minutes or until the potatoes are done. Remove the lid, stir in the coconut
milk and simmer uncovered for 10 minutes.

Remove from the heat, stir in the lemon juice and turn into a serving
dish.

EGG NOODLES IN SWEET POTATO
GRAVY/MEE REBUS   Serves 4–6

I discovered this unusual and very delicious dish in a book by Rafi
Fernandez called *Malaysian Cookery*. Ms Fernandez evolved this recipe
after eating the dish at a Malay stall. It is most unusual and will appeal to
anyone who likes chilli-hot oriental flavours. It is a complete meal, perfect
for sharing and requires very little in the way of an aperitif or dessert. The
best drink would be Kingfisher lager, Chinese beer or sake.

> 2 large sweet potatoes, cooked and mashed
> 12 almonds
> 1 onion, finely chopped
> 1-in (2.5-cm) piece fresh ginger, peeled
> 1½ tbs coriander powder
> ½ tsp turmeric powder
> 1 tbs fermented soya beans
> ghee or oil for frying
> 4 chicken breasts, thinly sliced
> 2 pts (1.1 l) chicken stock
> 1 lb (450 g) fresh thick egg noodles, scalded in boiling water and run
>   under cold water

For the garnish:

> 4 hard-boiled eggs, cut into quarters
> 4 fresh red chillies, seeded and cut into thin strips
> 2 beancurd cakes, deep-fried until brown and cut into small cubes
> 6 spring onions, finely sliced
> 8 oz (225 g) beansprouts
> 2 lemons, cut into wedges

Begin with the garnish and arrange all the ingredients on a large serving
plate. Grind together the dried chillies, almonds, onion, ginger, coriander,
turmeric and soya beans and, when they are a fine paste, fry the paste in
hot ghee until fragrant. Add the chicken and stir fry until all the pieces are
coated with the paste and nicely sizzling. Add the stock, stir well and leave
to simmer for 10 minutes. Stir in the mashed potato to make a smooth
gravy.

Cook the noodles (if using dry noodles instead of fresh, follow the
packet instructions) just before the chicken mixture is ready and serve a
portion of noodles into each bowl, a portion of the chicken and gravy and
let people help themselves to the garnish. This can be adapted very easily
to feed more.

CHICKEN, PORK AND POTATOES IN PEANUT SAUCE/
CARAPULCRA   <u>Serves 6</u>

In her book *Latin American Cooking*, Elisabeth Lambert Ortiz tells of the
time when she decided to cook this Peruvian dish in New York. When it
became clear that it would be impossible to find one authentic ingredient
Ms Lambert Ortiz decided to do exactly as the Inca women do. Way back
in 2500 BC the Incas were the first people to cultivate the potato and they
very quickly realised the importance of the crop. To cope with storage
problems they devised the first ever attempt at freeze-drying. 'Raw,
unpeeled potatoes were put outside their houses at night in the icy cold of
the Andean highlands, where they froze solid. In the morning they thawed
in the sun and the water was trampled out of them by Inca women, and
the process repeated until they were thoroughly dry.' 3 large potatoes
were put in Ms Lambert Ortiz's freezer overnight and in the morning the
potatoes were put out in the sunshine to thaw. At the end of the day she
squeezed out the water. This process was repeated three times and the
end result was three potatoes 'like stone, strange skinny objects. The flesh
had turned quite dark, almost black.' Two of those potatoes were cooked
in the Carapulcra and one was kept for two years before it was used.

I rather wish I could tell you that this painstaking effort towards
authenticity makes all the difference to this dish. But I have Ms Lambert
Ortiz's word on it: 'It is perfectly all right to substitute fresh potatoes.'
Anyway, it will give you something to talk about round the dinner table.

> 2 freeze-dried potatoes or 2 fresh floury-variety potatoes
> 6 or 12 small waxy-variety potatoes (this depends on your estimate
>   of your guests' appetites)
> 2½ lb (1 kg) chicken, cut into small serving pieces
> 1 lb (450 g) loin of pork, cut into ¾-in (1.5-cm) cubes
> ¾ pt (400 ml) chicken stock
> 4 tbs lard or vegetable oil
> 1 large onion, finely chopped
> 4 cloves garlic, minced
> ½ tsp Spanish paprika (very hot) or cayenne
> ⅛ tsp ground cumin
> 2 oz (50 g) roasted peanuts, finely ground
> salt, pepper
> 3 hard-boiled eggs, sliced and 20 stoned black or green olives, to
>   garnish

If you have decided to use freeze-dried potatoes, soak them in warm water for about 2 hours, chop them coarsely and set aside. If using normal potatoes, peel and dice them. Set aside. Put the chicken and pork into a saucepan with enough stock to cover. Cover and simmer until tender. Drain and reserve the stock.

Bone the chicken and cut the meat into chunks approximately the same size as the pork. Melt the lard in a large heavyweight casserole and sauté the onion, garlic, paprika and cumin. When the onion is soft add the potato and about ½ pt (275 ml) of the reserved stock. Cover and gently simmer until the potato has disintegrated, thickening the mixture. This takes between 40 minutes and 1 hour. Season to taste and then stir in the peanuts and meat. The sauce should be thick but add a little more stock if you think it necessary. Simmer just long enough for the flavours to mingle and the meat to heat through.

To serve arrange the meat and its gravy on a large serving dish garnished with the hot small potatoes, the egg slices and olives.

POTATO AND CHICKEN STEW WITH CRESS/AJIACO
SANTAFEREÑO SIN GUASCAS   Serves 6

When I attended the lecture and cookery demonstration given by Elisabeth Lambert Ortiz on Latin American cooking she talked about a dish that used three different varieties of potato all with different ends in mind. One type softens and disintegrates to thicken the dish (as in the previous recipe), one type will stay firm and provide bulk and the third has a good flavour, colour and texture to provide interest. Thanks to the increased availability of different varieties of potato, it is now possible to cook this dish at home.

The traditional accompaniment to an *Ajiaco* from Bogotà is a sliced ripe avocado and a number of little dishes of relish that are used to embellish the dish. These should include capers, cream, chopped parsley and a hot sauce called *aji*. *Aji* is made from finely chopped onion, leek or spring onion, tomato, chilli and coriander mixed with a little lime juice or vinegar.

  1 lb (450 g) floury-variety potatoes
  1 lb (450 g) waxy-variety potatoes
  8 oz (225 g) Pink Fir Apple or Jersey Royal potatoes
  3 lb (1.4 kg) chicken
  2 onions, peeled and halved
  4 sprays fresh coriander
  3 corn cobs
  bunch watercress
  salt, pepper, chilli pepper to taste

Rip out any lumps of fat inside the chicken cavity and season inside the bird. Put the bird, onion and coriander in a large saucepan and cover with water. Bring to the boil, turn down to summer and cover. Cook for 15 minutes before adding the peeled and sliced floury potatoes and continue cooking (covered) for a further 30 minutes. Discard the onion and coriander and remove the chicken. Scrub or peel the other two lots of potatoes and add them to the pot. Bring back to the boil and simmer for 15 minutes. By this time the first lot of potatoes should be virtually collapsed and you can now mix them into the liquid.

Slice the corn into 3 pieces and add to the pot, bring it back to the boil and add the watercress. By now the chicken will have cooled sufficiently for you to rip all the meat off the carcass. Return to the pot and adjust the seasoning, making it as hot as you favour with the chilli powder. Simmer for 5 minutes and serve into large soup plates.

PORK, HAM AND VEAL

PORK CUTLETS IN WINE/CHIRINES
COTOLETTES KRASATES   Serves 4

This Cypriot dish is very similar to the Greek dish *Afelia* but without *Afelia*'s mushrooms. It is aromatic, rich and satisfying.

    1½ lb (700 g) Cyprus potatoes
    4 large pork chops
    1 tsp coriander seeds, crushed
    generous ½ bottle red wine
    salt, pepper

Trim the fat off the chops and melt it in a large frying pan. Add the peeled and quartered potatoes and sauté until browned and almost cooked. Transfer to a casserole dish. Sauté the chops, using a little extra lard if needed and add to the casserole with the coriander seeds, red wine and a generous amount of seasoning. Bring up to the boil and simmer covered for 30–45 minutes until the meat is tender and the potatoes turning red.

PORK CHOPS WITH WINE AND VEGETABLES/PORC AU
CORBIÈRES   Serves 8

This is a marvellous winter dinner dish of plainly sautéed pork chops with fresh chestnuts, salsify, carrots and potatoes that are glazed in goose fat. Everything is assembled on one serving dish and the complete meal is eaten with a mayonnaise made with sautéed and mashed chicken liver.

It is worth tracking down some goose fat for this dish but failing that use rendered pork fat; lard by any other name.

2½ lb (1 kg) French potatoes; Belle de Fontenay, Cornichon or La
    Ratte
1 lb (450 g) carrots
2½ lb (1 kg) chestnuts
1 lb (450 g) salsify
1 onion, finely chopped
7 oz (200 g) chicken livers
approximately ½ pt (275 ml) olive oil
2 egg yolks
8 large pork chops
1 oz (25 g) flour

For the sauce:

pork bones and trimmings
1 onion, peeled and finely chopped
2 carrots
bouquet garni
1 bottle dry white wine
1 oz (25 g) butter
goose fat

Begin with the sauce. Heat 1 tbs of the fat and brown the bones. Add the peeled and chopped onion, carrots and bouquet garni. Cover and sweat for 5 minutes, stirring a couple of times. Cover with half the wine and about ¾ pt (400 ml) water, bring to the boil and simmer for 1 hour. Strain off the bones and vegetables and boil the liquid vigorously to reduce by half. Whisk in the butter and set aside while you prepare the vegetables.

Peel and trim the carrots, potatoes, chestnuts and salsify and blanch each separately for 10 minutes using fresh salted water. Sauté each of the vegetables in goose fat both to brown and finish cooking them. Set aside and keep warm.

In a separate pan melt 1 tbs fat and gently sauté the chopped onion. When it begins to soften add the chicken livers and cook for a couple of minutes; they should be firm but pink inside. Season and set aside while you beat the olive oil into the egg yolks until you have smooth, shiny emulsion and the eggs can take no more oil. Mash the liver, mix in with the onion and mayonnaise and spoon into a serving dish.

Ten minutes before serving fry the chops in fat and assemble on the plate with the vegetables. Keep warm while you make the gravy. Pour off the surplus fat from cooking the chops, sift in the flour and stir to amalgamate. Return to the heat and pour in a dash of the remaining wine and stir briskly. Season generously and stir in the rest of the wine. Boil for a couple of minutes and strain over the assembled meat and vegetables. Serve immediately with the sauce.

HAM WITH DUMPLINGS AND VEGETABLES/LA MIQUE LEVÉE   Serves 6–8

This is a marvellously heartening winter dish that has the great advantage of virtually cooking itself. The liquor is served separately as soup, reserving a little to moisten the meat. In place of the flour dumplings you could make potato gnocchi with 1 tbs of parsley added to the mixture. See page 103.

    2 lb (900 g) firm-fleshed potatoes
    3 lb (1.4 kg) ham
    6 carrots, trimmed and peeled
    1 onion stuck with cloves
    1 small cabbage, cored but left whole
    6 small leeks, trimmed and soaked in water to remove any earth
    6 turnips, trimmed and peeled

    For the dumplings:

    1 lb (450 g) flour, sifted
    2 oz (50 g) yeast, dissolved in a little warm water
    4 eggs, beaten
    1 tbs goose fat or lard
    ½ tsp salt

First make the dumplings. Put the flour into a large mixing bowl and make a well in the centre. Pour in the yeast mixture, the eggs, salt and melted fat and beat it into a dough. Knead thoroughly for at least 15 minutes, roll into a ball and set aside in a warm place in the mixing bowl covered with a damp cloth. Leave for at least 4 hours to double in size. Knead again and form into dumplings.

Put the ham into a large saucepan or casserole and cover with water. Bring to the boil and simmer, skimming occasionally, for 1 hour. Add the carrots, potatoes and onion. After a further 15 minutes add the dump-lings, cabbage, leeks and turnip and cook on for 30 minutes until everything is done. Strain off the liquor, adjust the seasoning and serve as a soup. Arrange the vegetables and dumplings around the ham before serving the main dish.

BOILED HAM WITH VEGETABLES/POTÉE LORRAINE   Serves 6

This is a spicier version of the previous recipe and doesn't require such a huge cooking pan. Serve the broth first as soup accompanied by garlic croûtons.

> 6 medium-sized waxy-variety potatoes
> 1 tbs lard
> 2 onions, sliced
> 4 leeks, sliced and rinsed well
> 1 lb (450 g) ham hock
> 8 oz (225 g) piece lean smoked bacon
> 1 cabbage, cored and halved
> 6 carrots, peeled and cut into chunks
> 3 small turnips, peeled and chopped
> 4 oz (110 g) haricot beans, soaked overnight
> 2 cloves
> 1 bay leaf
> 4 cloves garlic, crushed
> 1 sprig savory
> 6 smoked pork sausages
> 8 oz (225 g) green beans, topped and tailed
> 8 oz (225 g) shelled-weight broad beans
> 8 oz (225 g) peas
> salt, pepper, pinch nutmeg

Select a large heavy casserole. Melt the lard and gently sauté the onions and leeks. Lay the ham on top and cover with water. Bring to the boil and simmer gently, covered, for 45 minutes. Add the bacon, cabbage, carrots, turnips, haricots, cloves, bay leaf, garlic and savory. Cook for a further hour and add the sausages, green and broad beans, peas and potatoes. Season generously with salt, pepper and nutmeg and continue cooking for 30 minutes.

Strain off the liquid and serve with garlic croûtons or reserve for another occasion. Slice the meat on to a large serving plate, arrange with the sausages and vegetables and serve.

SUCKLING PIG IN HERBS/PORCELET AUX HERBES   Serves 6–8

3 lb (1.4 kg) small waxy-variety potatoes
5½–6½ lb (2.5–3 kg) hindquarters of a suckling pig or any joint of
    pork
2 tbs mixed herbs
2 tbs lard
salt, pepper

Parboil the potatoes in their skins for 10 minutes. Drain and peel. Score
the rind of the pork to make diamonds and cover with a paste made by
creaming the herbs into the lard. Put the meat on a trivet in the middle of a
roasting pan and surround with the seasoned potatoes.

Place in a cold oven and bring up to 400°F/200°C/gas mark 6 and cook
for 25 minutes per pound. After about 2 hours of cooking check to see if
the rind has crisped; when it has, turn the potatoes, season them again
and cover the entire dish with foil. Return to a slightly cooler oven
(350°F/180°C/gas mark 4) and complete the cooking.

Remove to a serving plate and carve off the crackling before tackling the
meat. The potatoes will be crunchy and very fattening, thanks to all that
delicious tasty fat.

VEAL OF ARETOUSA/DAMALAKI ARETOUSA   Serves 4–6

In Cyprus Aretousa represents the three virtues of beauty, strength and
patience. I can't quite work out why this dish is so called, but it is delicious.

1½ lb (700 g) Cyprus potatoes
clarified butter
1 lb (900 g) veal cutlets
2 onions, sliced
1 lb (450 g) ripe tomatoes, peeled and chopped
1 glass white wine
1 pt (570 ml) stock
4 bay leaves
salt, white pepper

Peel the potatoes and slice them in half horizontally. Melt some butter in a
large frying pan and gently sauté the potatoes until they are half cooked.
Set aside and fry the cutlets for a couple of minutes on each side.

Take a large casserole dish and pile the potatoes on one side and the meat on the other. Melt a little more butter and sauté the onions until they begin to wilt, then add the tomatoes. Simmer for a few minutes and add the wine, stock and bay leaves. Cook for 5 minutes and pour over the meat and potatoes. Season, cover with foil and then the lid and bake in a slow oven (325°F/170°C/gas mark 3) for 2 hours.

VEAL BIRDS WITH PAPRIKA/ESCALOPES ROULÉES AU PAPRIKA   Serves 6

This is an unusual recipe in that the potato forms part of the stuffing. Serve with a crisp green vegetable and plainly boiled or steamed waxy-variety potatoes.

> 2 long French potatoes
> 3 tbs olive oil
> 3 onions finely sliced
> 1 tbs paprika
> 6 veal escalopes, well beaten
> Dijon mustard
> 12 rashers smoked streaky bacon
> 7 fl oz (200 ml) crème fraîche
> salt, pepper

Heat the olive oil and gently sauté the onion until limp. Stir in the paprika and set aside. Spread each escalope with a thin layer of mustard, two rashers of bacon (without its rind) and a wafer-thin slice of potato. Season and roll up the veal, securing with a toothpick.

Arrange the veal rolls in an ovenproof dish and pour in a scant ½ pt (275 ml) water. Cover and cook at 350°F/180°C/gas mark 4 for 30 minutes. Remove the veal birds to a serving dish. Pour the juices into a saucepan and boil vigorously to reduce the liquid slightly. Stir in the cream, let it bubble up. Pour over the birds and serve.

OFFAL

KIDNEYS IN MADEIRA/POCHKI V MADERE   Serves 2

This dish is a borderline case for inclusion in this chapter because it is a matter of interpretation whether the potatoes are really vital to the dish. It is, however, a delicious way to cook kidneys and is a common Russian dish, generally served as a *zakuska* or starter.

8 tiny new potatoes, boiled and peeled
6 lamb's kidneys
flour
butter
4 oz (110 g) mushrooms, cleaned and finely sliced
½ pt (275 ml) Madeira
¼ pt (150 ml) chicken stock
salt, pepper
1 tbs parsley, finely chopped

Core the kidneys and cut them into thin slices. Season with salt and
pepper and roll in sifted flour. Melt a little butter in a frying pan and fry the
mushrooms for a couple of minutes so they retain some bite. Put the
mushrooms in a suitable casserole and melt 1 tbs butter in the mushroom
pan. Fry the kidney slices quickly over a high heat, turning them to cook
the flour. Transfer to the casserole and deglaze the cooking pan with a
little of the Madeira. Stir in the stock and the rest of the wine. Let it bubble
up and then pour over the kidneys and mushrooms. Season and simmer
for 10 minutes and stir in the potatoes. Cook for a further 5 minutes,
sprinkle on the parsley and serve.

RICHARD OLNEY'S TRIPE AND POTATO TERRINE/POT AU
FOUR   Serves 6

Richard Olney tells the tale of how he was cajoled into recreating this
traditional yet unrecorded recipe from the Ardèche by two Ardèchois
friends. In *Simple French Food* Olney describes how he arrived at the
recipe and I'm glad he went to the trouble. It is a marvellously robust,
delicious and cheap dish that is well worth the effort. This is a marginally
adapted version.

2½ lb (1.4 kg) firm-fleshed potatoes cut into ¼-in (1.5-cm) slices
1½ lb (700 g) beef tripe cut into approximately 2-in (5-cm) squares
1 pig's trotter, large bone removed, split, covered with cold water
    parboiled for 10 minutes, drained and rinsed
8 oz (225 g) pitted black olives, parboiled for 1 minute and drained
3 bay leaves
2 tsp crumbled thyme
1 tbs garlic, finely chopped
2 tbs parsley, finely chopped
flour and olive oil dough
salt

Use a quart (4–5 litre) oven casserole. Line the base with tripe, lay on the pig's trotter, sprinkle with olives, a bay leaf and a little of an aromatic mixture composed of the garlic, thyme and parsley. Season with salt, add a layer of potatoes, then tripe, then seasoning and continue until everything is used up but ending with potato. Press the surface to pack the contents tightly and pour in enough water to cover.

Bring the water up to the boil on top of the stove and seal firmly with a dough made with flour and olive oil. Cook for 4 hours in a slow oven (275°F/140°C/gas mark 1). Prise off the lid, discard and serve.

LIVER WITH POTATOES   Serves 4

This is a comforting sort of dish with the great advantage that once it is in the oven there is nothing else to do. Serve with crunchy mangetouts or French beans and English mustard.

> 1½ lb (700 g) waxy-variety potatoes
> 2 onions, finely sliced
> 2 tbs butter
> 12 oz (350 g) thinly sliced lamb or calf's liver
> 4 tomatoes, peeled and sliced
> 1 tbs marjoram, finely chopped
> 2 tbs parsley, finely chopped
> salt, pepper

Parboil the potatoes in their skins for 10 minutes. Cut into ¼-in (0.5-cm) thick slices. Sauté the onion in a little butter until it turns transparent. Cut the liver into 1-in (2.5-cm) strips and season with pepper. Grease a gratin dish with butter and make alternate layers of potato, onion, liver and tomato, starting with the potato. Season each layer with a sprinkling of marjoram and parsley and salt. Finish with a layer of potatoes, dot with butter and cover with foil.

Bake at 375°F/190°C/gas mark 4 for 45 minutes. Remove the foil and turn the oven up to 400°F/200°C/gas mark 6. Cook for a further 15 minutes until the potatoes are golden brown.

MANGALORE LIVER AND POTATO CURRY/KALEJA ALOO KARHI   Serves 4

This is a spicy version of the preceding, very English dish of Liver and Potatoes and one which I find far more appetising. Serve with plain boiled rice. The dish originates from the coastal village of Mangalore which is just south of Goa in the south-west of India.

> 1 lb (450 g) waxy-variety potatoes, peeled and sliced ½ in (1 cm) thick
> 2 large onions, peeled and sliced
> 3 cloves garlic, chopped
> 4 tbs dried, desiccated coconut
> 3 green chillies, seeded and minced
> 1 tsp each ground cumin and coriander
> ¼ tsp each ground aniseed or caraway seeds, cinnamon and cloves
> 4 tbs ghee
> ¼ tsp black mustard seeds
> 1 lb (450 g) calf's liver, cut thin and sliced into 1-in (2.5-cm) squares
> 1 tbs tamarind concentrate, dissolved in ¼ pt (150 ml) hot water
> 2 tbs coriander leaves, chopped
> 1 tsp salt

Grind the onions, garlic, coconut, chillis and all the ground spices with 2 tbs water. Heat 3 tbs of the ghee and fry the mustard seeds until they pop. Add the liver and stir fry quickly to brown on both sides. Remove with a slotted spoon and set aside. Add the rest of the ghee and get the pan very hot. Turn down the heat and gently stir fry the spice paste to evaporate the water and release the flavours. Return the liver to the pan with the potatoes and pour over the tamarind liquid and salt. Quickly bring the mixture to the boil and then immediately turn the heat down low. Stir in 1 tbs of the coriander leaves and simmer for 2–3 minutes. Transfer to a serving dish and sprinkle with the rest of the coriander.

LAMB

LANCASHIRE HOT POT   Serves 4

Lancashire Hot Pot was traditionally cooked in the bread oven at the end of a baking day when the fire had burned down. The cooking was long and slow. It is also traditional to cook the dish in a deep and narrow-necked earthenware crock. Over the years the recipe has changed slightly; in the days when oysters were pauper's fare the Hot Pot included a dozen and perhaps 2 or 3 sliced lamb's kidneys. Today it is more usual to include field mushrooms and the kidneys are optional. Vital ingredients are the sliced potatoes, lamb chops and onion.

1½ lb (700 g) potatoes, thinly sliced
8 best end-of-neck lamb chops
4 lamb's kidneys, cored and sliced
2 onions, thinly sliced
dripping or butter
salt, pepper

Grease a deep earthenware casserole. Cover the bottom with about a
third of the potatoes, season generously and cover with 4 of the chops,
some of the kidney and onion. Repeat, seasoning each layer and finish
with neatly overlapping potato slices. Pour on sufficient water nearly to fill
the casserole and dot the top with butter.

Bake at 425°F/220°C/gas mark 7 for 30 minutes. Reduce the heat to
275°F/140°C/gas mark 1 and cook covered for 2 hours. Remove the lid for
the last 30 minutes of the cooking so that the potatoes can brown.

MICHAEL SMITH'S INDIVIDUAL LANCASHIRE
HOT POTS   Serves 6

This is a rather posh version of Lancashire Hot Pot in individual dishes.

6 potatoes, each 4 oz (110 g), peeled and finely sliced
2 whole lamb fillets, trimmed and skinned
2 tbs olive or soya oil for frying
24 button onions, skinned
2 inner stalks celery, finely chopped
24 button mushrooms
1 oz (25 g) pearl barley
¼ pt (150 ml) dry white wine, mixed with ¾ pt (400 ml) chicken
    stock
butter
salt, pepper

Have ready 6 ovenproof pots that can comfortably contain 15 fl oz/425
ml. Pre-heat the oven to 325°F/170°C/gas mark 3. Cut each fillet into 12
discs.

Heat a little oil to smoking point. Quickly fry the lamb in small batches
to seal and colour the meat. Place 4 pieces in each pot. Brown the onions
over a fairly fierce heat, adding a splash more oil if necessary. Divide
between the pots and do the same with the celery, mushrooms and pearl
barley. Season each pot with a little salt and pepper. Pour over enough of
the wine and stock to cover and arrange the potatoes neatly in overlap-

ping circles. Dot with butter, cover and bake for 1½ hours. Remove the lids, raise the temperature to 375°F/190°C/gas mark 5 and cook for a further 20–30 minutes until the potatoes are golden brown.

IRISH STEW   Serves 4

Irish stew uses the same ingredients as Lancashire Hot Pot but is generally made with pieces of mutton or lamb as opposed to chops. This is a recipe from a favourite Irish writer, Molly Keane.

>   2 lb (900 g) potatoes, sliced
>   1 lb (450 g) fillet of lamb, cubed
>   2 large onions, sliced
>   salt, pepper
>   parsley, chopped

Preheat the oven to 375°F/190°C/gas mark 5. Line a casserole with alternate layers of meat, potatoes and onion, seasoning each layer well. Finish with potatoes, arranging the slices neatly to cover the top completely. Pour in sufficient water to fill the casserole half way. Cover and bake for 3 hours. Serve sprinkled with parsley.

CAWL   Serves 8–10

This is the Welsh equivalent of Scottish cock-a-leekie and a French potée (see page 230) and is a combination dish of soup and stew. It isn't worth making a cawl for less than 8 and it takes most of the day to cook.

>   1½ lb (700 g) small new potatoes, scrubbed
>   3 lb (1.4 kg) boiling cut of beef and best end-of-neck of lamb left
>   whole
>   dripping or bacon fat
>   2 large onions, thickly sliced
>   2 carrots or parsnips, peeled and sliced
>   1 turnip or swede, peeled and cut into chunks
>   2 stalks celery, sliced
>   bouquet garni, 2 sprigs thyme
>   small white cabbage, sliced
>   3 leeks, sliced and washed
>   1 tbs parsley
>   salt, pepper

Brown the meat all over in the melted fat and transfer to a large casserole. Next, brown the root vegetables and place around the meats. Add the celery, bouquet garni, thyme and cover with water. Bring slowly up to the boil and simmer very gently so there is just a flicker of movement on the surface of the water. Leave to simmer for 3½ hours and add the potatoes. 15 minutes later add the cabbage. Season and discard the bouquet garni. Add the leeks and parsley and simmer for a further 10 minutes.

Cawl can either be served by separating the broth from the meat and vegetables or by giving everyone a little of everything in big soup plates. Serve with bread for mopping-up purposes.

NAVARIN PRINTANIER   Serves 6

This is a lamb stew that relies on spring vegetables for its special character.

    1½ lb (700 g) tiny new potatoes, scrubbed
    3 tbs dripping
    3 small onions, sliced
    3 lb (1.4 kg) breast of lamb, cut into 1-in (2.5-cm) squares
    2 tbs flour
    1 pt (570 ml) brown or vegetable stock
    1 clove garlic
    1 bay leaf, sprig rosemary
    1 lb (450 g) tiny carrots, scrubbed and trimmed
    6 baby turnips
    1½ lb (700 g) peas
    salt, pepper

Melt the dripping and sauté the onion for a couple of minutes before adding the meat. Cook until the meat is browned on all sides and remove both to a plate. Sift in the flour and stir until you have a light roux. Add the stock, stirring continually until amalgamated. Return the meat and onions with the rosemary, garlic, bay leaf and seasoning.

Simmer, covered, for about 1 hour or until the meat is cooked. Add the potatoes, carrots and, turnips and cook for a further 30 minutes. Add the peas. When they are done, the dish is ready.

SAFFRON-BAKED LAMB/AGNEAU AU FOUR   Serves 6

This is a Tunisian dish that is both rich and subtle.

2½ lb (1 kg) waxy-variety potatoes
3 lb (1.4 kg) leg of lamb
3½ fl oz (100 ml) olive oil
juice of 1 lemon
salt, pepper, pinch saffron

Peel the potatoes and cut them in 4 lengthways. Leave them covered in salted water coloured with a pinch of saffron for ½ an hour. Cut up the meat and season. Make layers of potato and meat in an ovenproof dish, sprinkle with oil, the lemon juice and ½ pt (275 ml) of the saffron water. Cover and bake at 350°F/180°C/gas mark 4 for 1½ hours until the meat falls apart.

GREEK ROAST LAMB/ARNI PSITO   Serves 6–8

6 large Cyprus potatoes
3–4 lb (1.4–1.8 kg) leg or shoulder of lamb
4 cloves garlic, sliced or 4 sprigs rosemary
2 tbs lemon juice
½ pt (275 ml) olive oil
salt, pepper, 1 tsp oregano

Make slits in the meat and insert the sliced garlic or bits of rosemary. Rub the skin with half the lemon juice and olive oil and season with salt and pepper. Put the meat in the roasting tray surrounded by the potatoes. Pour the rest of the olive oil, a cup of water and the lemon juice over the potatoes and sprinkle with salt and pepper and the oregano.

Bake at 400°F/200°C/gas mark 6 for 2–3 hours when the potatoes will be browned and the meat well done in the Greek style. Serve with raw cabbage salad.

BAKED LAMB/TAVA   Serves 4–5

This is an aromatic combination of lamb, onion, tomatoes, cumin and bay leaves baked covered with potatoes. The long slow cooking means that the meat is very tender and the potatoes absorb both the meat and tomato juices.

1½ lb (700 g) Cyprus potatoes, peeled and quartered
2 lb (900 g) boned leg or shoulder of lamb, cut into large pieces
1 large onion, chopped
1 lb (450 g) ripe tomatoes, peeled and chopped
2 oz (50 g) crushed cumin seeds
2 bay leaves
2 tbs tomato purée
stock
salt, pepper

Mix the lamb, potatoes, onion and tomatoes in a large ovenproof casserole. Stir in the cumin, bay leaves and seasoning to taste. Mix the tomato purée with enough stock to cover the mixture and pour into the dish. Cover with foil and cook for 2–2½ hours at 300°F/150°C/gas mark 2.

SAUTÉED LAMB/ARNAKI KOKINISTO   Serves 4–5

The generous amount of cinnamon in this oven-baked stew gives a sweet spicy flavour that is most unusual.

2 lb (900 g) potatoes
2 lb (900 g) loin of lamb
oil
2 large onions, sliced into rings
2 cloves garlic, finely chopped
1 lb (450 g) ripe tomatoes, peeled and sliced
2 tbs tomato purée
generous glass of wine
2 tbs lemon juice
stock
2-in (2.5-cm) piece of cinnamon stick or 1½ tsp ground cinnamon
3 bay leaves
salt, pepper

Cut the lamb into chops and brown quickly in a little oil. Repeat with the peeled and thickly sliced potatoes. Put both in a spacious casserole dish and season well. Heat a little more oil and sauté the onions and garlic for 5 minutes and then add the tomatoes and tomato paste. Let it bubble up for 5 minutes and then stir in the wine and lemon juice. Pour the mixture over the meat and potatoes and top up with stock. Tuck in the cinnamon stick and bay leaves, cover with foil and bake for 2½ hours at 300°F/150°C/gas mark 2.

ARAB BAKED LAMB WITH POTATOES   Serves 8–10

When I was about 21 I worked for a couple of months writing a daily magazine for the Tabarka Festival, an international affair organised from Paris with artistes as diverse as Joan Baez, The Kipper Kids, steel bands and local horse gymnasts. The setting was idyllic – on the north-west coast of Tunisia – and by night we dovetailed the eating and drinking between concerts and ended up dancing to strange Tunisian wailing music in one of a surprisingly large number of clubs. By day we recovered on the beach in the sun, maybe taking in an art class or a session to learn photography or mime. At least once a week there would be a big feast of roast lamb with vegetables cooked at the bakery and eaten outside. The memories of the delicious smells, the fiery *boukha* (an eau de vie made from figs), rich, heady wine and impressions of the strange culture clash always swim back when I prepare this marvellous feast.

> 5 lb (2.3 kg) potatoes, sliced
> 2 large onions, sliced
> 2 aubergines, sliced, sprinkled with salt and left to drain
> 1 lb (450 g) ripe tomatoes, sliced
> 2 tsp dried oregano
> 1 large leg of lamb about 6–8 lb (2.7–3.6 kg)
> 6 cloves garlic, sliced
> salt, pepper

Pre-heat the oven to 425°F/220°C/gas mark 7. Lightly grease a huge gratin-type dish or oven tray and make layers with the potatoes, onions, aubergines and tomatoes. Season well and sprinkle with oregano. Trim any excess fat from the lamb and make small slits all over the joint. Post the garlic in slits and season with salt and pepper before laying the lamb on top of the vegetables.

Bake for about 2½ hours turning once during the cooking. Remove the lamb to a serving plate to rest and turn the oven up as high as possible to brown the top layer of vegetables.

ROAST LAMB WITH POTATOES/GIGOT
BOULANGÈRE   Serves 6–8

This is one of my all-time favourite dishes, first encountered in a slightly different form in Tunisia (see the previous recipe). The lamb is perched on top of the potatoes so their juices and fat mingle in with layers of buttered, seasoned and herbed potato slices. The cooking takes a long time because the potatoes and their aromatic mixture are started before the lamb; therefore the whole house smells delicious for hours. It is a marvellous dish for a large party because it requires no attention once in the oven. The garlic can be moderated to taste.

4½ lb (2 kg) potatoes, peeled, sliced and soaked in cold water
1 large onion, finely chopped
3 sprigs fresh thyme
2 bay leaves
6 cloves garlic
4 oz (110 g) butter
4½ lb (2 kg) leg of lamb
salt, pepper

Mix the onion, thyme leaves, crushed bay leaves, three cloves of chopped garlic and a generous amount of seasoning together. Use 1 oz (25 g) of the butter to grease a large earthenware gratin-type dish or roasting pan. Cover the bottom of the pan with potatoes and sprinkle on some of the aromatic mixture. Continue making layers finishing with potatoes. Cover with warm water. Dot with butter and season with salt.

Put the dish into a very hot oven (450°F/230°C/gas mark 8) and cook for between 1½ and 2 hours, until all the liquid has been absorbed. Meanwhile, prepare the lamb. Use the rest of the butter to smear over the lamb. Peel and slice the remaining garlic and tuck either beneath the skin or in slits in the flesh. Weigh the joint and calculate the cooking time allowing between 15 and 20 minutes per pound (450 g) depending on how you like it. Place the joint on top of the potatoes and turn half way through cooking.

To serve remove the joint to a warm serving dish and allow to rest for 10 minutes or so leaving the potatoes in the oven to crisp. Collect the juices that will have seeped from the meat into a jug, carve at the table and let people help themselves to potatoes – there are never enough!

DELHI-STYLE LAMB COOKED WITH POTATOES/ALOO GOSHT
Serves 6

This is a deliciously rich curry with a complex mixture of flavours. Accompany with plain rice and a green vegetable curry.

1½ lb (700 g) waxy-variety potatoes, peeled and quartered
3 onions, finely chopped
½ fresh green chilli pepper, finely chopped
1 clove garlic, chopped
6 tbs ghee or vegetable oil
2½ lb (1 kg) lamb cut from the shoulder into 1-in (2.5-cm) chunks
1 lb (450 g) tomatoes, peeled and chopped
1 tbs ground cumin
2 tsp ground coriander
½ tsp each ground turmeric and cayenne
1½ pts (900 ml) water
2 tsp salt

Sauté the onions, chilli and garlic in the oil until the onion begins to brown. Add the meat, turning it to brown all over. Stir in the tomatoes with the cumin, coriander, turmeric, cayenne and salt. Turn up the temperature and stir fry for 10 minutes until the tomatoes are beginning to collapse and the spices are integrated. Turn down the temperature and add the potatoes and water. Stir to amalgamate and leave partially covered for about 1½ hours until the sauce is thick, the meat tender and the potatoes saturated in the sauce.

SPICED LAMB WITH POTATOES/PAPETA MA KID   Serves 6

This curry comes from Meera Taneja's *Indian Regional Cookery* and is adapted to feed 6. Serve with plainly boiled rice, a soothing cucumber raita or other yoghurt dish and lime pickle.

2 lb (900 g) potatoes, parboiled, peeled and halved horizontally
1½-in (3.5-cm) piece fresh ginger
3 cloves garlic
2½ lb (1 kg) leg of lamb
4 medium onions
6 cloves
2-in (5.0-cm) piece cinnamon
4 large black cardamoms
3 small red chilli peppers
3 tbs oil or ghee
½ pt (275 ml) water
4 oz (110 g) cashew nuts, finely chopped
¼ pt (150 ml) coconut milk
salt to taste

Grind the ginger and garlic into a paste. Chop up the meat into approximately 2-in (5.0-cm) pieces. Rub the paste all over the pieces of meat and leave to marinate for a couple of hours.

Finely chop the onions and cook gently in the oil with the cloves, cinnamon, cardamoms and whole chillies. Stir fry until the onions are soft and then add the meat. Cover and let it cook gently, stirring occasionally, until all the moisture dries up. This will take abut 10–15 minutes. Add the salt and a cup of the water, stir well and leave to simmer for 20 minutes adding a little more water if necessary. Stir in the potatoes and continue simmering until they are tender. Stir the cashews into the coconut and pour over the mixture and cook for a further 10 minutes.

BEEF

CORNISH UNDER ROAST   Serves 4

> 2 lb (900 g) potatoes, peeled and sliced
> 1½ lb (700 g) good quality steak, cut across the steak into 1-in (2.5-cm) strips
> flour
> 2 medium-sized onions, sliced
> water, butter
> salt, pepper

Dip each piece of meat in sifted flour seasoned with salt and pepper. Roll up the slices. Grease an ovenproof dish and cover the bottom with the rolls. Cover with the onions and dot with any fat trimmings from the meat. Season and cover with the potatoes. Pour over sufficient water nearly to cover the potatoes, dot with butter and cover with foil.

Bake at 375°F/190°C/gas mark 5 for 1 hour. Remove the foil and turn up the oven temperature to 400°F/200°C/gas mark 6 for 30 minutes to brown the top layer of potatoes. Serve with lightly cooked cabbage.

PICKLED MEAT WITH POTATO BALLS AND DRIED FRUIT/ SAUERBRATEN MIT KARTOFFELKLOSSEN UND BACKOBST   Serves 6–8

This dish from Germany needs to be planned several days in advance. The meat requires 3–4 days marination and the actual preparation is spread over 2 days.

For the potato balls:

2 lb (900 g) mashed potato
4 oz (110 g) flour
2 eggs
2 oz (50 g) semolina
2 oz (50 g) croûtons
salt, pepper

For the meat and marinade:

2 lb (900 g) stewing steak
1 onion, sliced
1 bay leaf
½ pt (275 ml) vinegar
½ pt (275 ml) water
2 oz (50 g) butter, bacon fat
¼ pt (150 ml) sour cream
flour
salt, pepper

For the dried fruit sauce:

8 oz (225 g) mixed dried fruit
3 oz (75 g) sugar
pinch cinnamon
rind of 1 lemon
butter, flour

Cut the meat into chunks and cover with the onion, bay leaf, vinegar and water and leave in the marinade for at least 3 days, turning once a day. To cook the meat, remove it from the marinade, pat dry and brown all over in a little bacon fat and butter. Place in a casserole dish, season and pour over the sour cream mixed with just under half the strained marinade liquid. Cover and cook very gently for 1–1½ hours. To thicken the sauce, melt 1 tbs of bacon fat, stir in some flour, cook for 1 minute and mix in 2 tbs of the cooking liquid. Whisk to incorporate and stir into the cooking pot.

To make the potato balls, beat the sifted flour, egg and semolina into the potatoes, season and work with your hands to form a firm dough. With floured hands form the dough into balls and press a few croûtons into the middle. Bring a large pan of salted water to the boil and drop in the potato balls. Bring the water back up to the boil, turn down to simmer and cook the balls for 10 minutes. Drain and they are ready to serve.

To make the fruit sauce, wash and soak the fruit overnight in about 2 pts (1 l) of water. The next day add the sugar, spices and lemon rind to the water and simmer gently until the fruit is cooked. If necessary reduce the liquid so that the fruit is merely moist. Stir in a small knob of butter worked with an equal amount of flour, boil and stir continuously to form a thick sauce.

Serve everything separately.

BEEF STEWED IN CIDER WITH CARROTS, LEEKS AND POTATOES/DAUBE DE BOEUF   Serves 6–8

This is a Normandy version of the beef stew normally cooked in red wine that is served throughout France.

    8 large potatoes, peeled and quartered
    4 lb (1.8 kg) stewing steak cut into 1-in (2.5-cm) cubes
    4 tbs bacon fat or lard
    1 clove garlic, chopped
    3 leeks, sliced and washed
    2 tbs flour
    ½ pt (275 ml) cider
    ¾ pt (425 ml) stock
    6 large carrots, peeled and cut into thick slices
    bouquet garni made with 1 sprig thyme, 5 stems parsley and 1 bay
        leaf
    salt, pepper
    2 tbs parsley, chopped

Brown the meat in the bacon or pork fat and add the garlic and leeks. Cook for 10 minutes, then stir in the flour and cook for a further 5 minutes. Pour in the cider and stock and bring the mixture to the boil stirring well to make a smooth liquid. Add the carrots, bouquet garni and simmer for 15 minutes. Add the potatoes and simmer for a further 1 hour. Taste for seasoning and check that the meat is tender. Serve sprinkled with chopped parsley.

FRENCH BEEF STEW/RAGOÛT DE BOEUF   <u>Serves 6</u>

2 lb (900 g) waxy-variety potatoes, parboiled for 10 minutes and peeled
8 oz (225 g) smoked streaky bacon
4 onions, peeled and halved through their fat middle
2½ lb (1 kg) stewing steak, cut into 1-in (2.5-cm) cubes
2 tbs flour
1 pt (570 ml) red wine
bouquet garni
2 shallots
2½ lb (1 kg) carrots
1 lb (450 g) baby turnips
salt, pepper

Cut the bacon into lardons and sauté gently to extract the fat. When they are crisp, remove the lardons with a slotted spoon. Brown the onions, remove and brown the beef in the same fat. Sift in the flour, stir to cook the fat and lift bits that will stick and add a little of the wine. Stir vigorously to make a smooth sauce and add the bouquet garni, the whole unpeeled shallots and the rest of the wine, topping up with water to cover the meat.

Simmer for 1 hour and add the carrots, turnips, potatoes and onions. Bring back to simmer and continue cooking for 30 minutes. Add the lardons, adjust the seasoning, remove the shallots and serve.

FILLET OF BEEF PROVENÇALE/OXFILE PROVENÇALE   <u>Serves 4</u>

This dish was devised accidentally by Swedish chef Julius Carlsons in a restaurant called Bacci Wapen.

2 lb (900 g) waxy-variety potatoes, finely sliced
butter, oil
1½ lb (700 g) fillet of beef
garlic butter (2 oz/50 g butter creamed with 2 crushed cloves garlic)
salt, pepper
parsley, chopped

Sauté the potatoes in batches in oil and butter and transfer to a serving dish. Cover and keep warm. Season the meat and sear in a hot pan for 5 minutes on each side. Transfer to a serving dish, pour over the garlic butter, arrange the potatoes around the meat and return to a very hot oven (450°F/230°C/gas mark 8) for 5 minutes. Serve sprinkled with parsley.

BEEF WITH POTATOES/ALOO KIT BOTI   Serves 6

1 lb (450 g) potatoes, peeled and quartered
1 lb (450 g) ghee
8 oz (225 g) onion, sliced
3-in (7.5-cm) piece of fresh ginger
4 cloves garlic
1 tsp black cumin seeds
6 cardamoms
6 cloves
1 tsp chilli powder
½ tsp turmeric
2 lb (900 g) shoulder of lamb cut into chunks
1 tbs melon seeds
1 tbs watermelon seeds
¾ pt (400 ml) yoghurt
1 tsp salt

Heat the ghee and fry the potatoes golden. Meanwhile grind the onions, peeled ginger and garlic. When the potatoes are done, set aside and strain off all but 3 tbs of the ghee. Stir fry the cumin, cardamoms and cloves and when the seeds pop add the onion mixture. Cook until golden and then stir in the chilli powder, turmeric and salt and cook for a few minutes. Add the meat and brown in the mixture, stirring constantly.

Heat a small frying pan and dry roast the melon and watermelon seeds by frying them without fat until they begin to colour. Grind the seeds and mix into the yoghurt. Stir the yoghurt mixture into the meat and cook gently for about 45 minutes until the meat is beginning to get tender.

Add the potatoes, cover and turn up the heat to generate a lot of steam. After 5 minutes, turn down the heat so that the mixture simmers gently. Continue cooking for a further 10–15 minutes. Serve with Indian bread.

PORTUGUESE MIXED MEAT STEW/COZIDO
A PORTUGUESA   <u>Serves 6–8</u>

2 lb (900 g) potatoes
2 lb (900 g) shin of beef
1–2 lb (450–900 g) piece of bacon or gammon
1 lb (450 g) carrots
1 lb (450 g) turnips
1 large cabbage
1 smoked sausage
1 lb (450 g) rice
salt, pepper

Put the beef and gammon into a large pan and cover with boiling water.
Simmer slowly for 2 hours and add the peeled potatoes, carrots, turnips
and the cabbage cut into quarters. When the pan has returned to a simmer
cook for 30 minutes and add the sausage cut into thick slices. Cook for 15
minutes, adjust the seasoning and check that everything is cooked. Strain
off approximately 1 pt (570 ml) of the cooking liquor and cook the rice.

Arrange the meat and vegetables on a serving plate, the rice on its own.
Keep everything warm while you serve the liquor as a soup.

20.

Side Dishes

---

*'The potatoes never failed us. . . . For each meal, they
looked different and tasted different.'*

Yuri Suhl, *One Foot in America*

BAKED POTATO PURÉE/PASTICCIO DI PATATE   Serves 6

'Mashed potato is the gentile's chicken noodle soup. It's nature's tran-
quilliser, I take it instead of valium.' So said Miles Henderson in Andrew
Payne's *Love After Lunch*.

This dish is the ultimate comfort food. It can be 'enlivened' with garlic
(slip 2 or 3 unpeeled cloves in the pan when you boil the potatoes, then
squeeze out the garlic into the mash), parsley, chives, nutmeg and/or basil
stirred into the mash. *Au naturel* it is the perfect accompaniment to
everything from simply grilled fish, meat and sausages to stews and fancy
dishes.

> 3 lb (1.4 kg) King Edward or other floury-variety potatoes
> 3 oz (75 g) butter
> ¼ pt (150 ml) hot milk
> 2 oz (50 g) grated Parmesan cheese
> salt, pepper

Boil the potatoes in their skins in salted water, drain and dry mash. Add
the butter and hot milk and whisk or beat with a wooden spoon for as
long as you can bear it. Adjust the seasoning and spoon into a buttered
gratin dish.

Top with the Parmesan and bake at 400°F/200°C/gas mark 6 for 20
minutes or until you have a crispy topping.

POMMES DE TERRE MOUSSELINE   Serves 4–6

This is a richer, more substantial variation on the previous recipe, Baked Potato Purée (page 250). It too goes well with almost everything.

    2 lb (900 g) potatoes, boiled in their skins
    9 oz (250 g) butter
    7 fl oz (200 ml) whipped single cream
    4 egg yolks
    salt, pepper, grated nutmeg

Mash the potatoes and whisk in half the butter, the cream and then the egg yolks. Beat for as long as you can bear it, adjust the seasoning and beat again. Make a dome with the potato in a buttered gratin dish. Melt the rest of the butter and pour it over the top of the potatoes. Brown for 5 minutes at the highest temperature your oven can manage.

SWEDE AND POTATO PIE   Serves 6

This is good with sausages and a crunchy green vegetable.

    1 lb (450 g) potatoes, boiled
    2 lb (900 g) swedes, peeled and boiled
    2 oz (50 g) butter
    2 fl oz (50 ml) single cream
    2 oz (50 g) grated Parmesan cheese
    salt, pepper

Mash the vegetables together with the butter, cream, salt and pepper. Whisk or beat with a wooden spoon until they are light and fluffy. Spoon into a buttered gratin dish, top with the Parmesan and bake at 425°F/ 200°C/gas mark 7 for 10 minutes to crisp the top.

DUCHESSE POTATOES   Serves 4

    2 lb (900 g) mashed potato
    2 oz (50 g) butter
    ¼ pt (150 ml) hot milk
    2 eggs
    salt, pepper

Add the butter to the hot milk and beat into the potatoes. Adjust the seasoning and beat in the eggs. Butter an oven dish and either pipe or form little swirls of the potato mixture. Bake for 15–20 minutes at 350°F/180°C/gas mark 4 until the ridges of the swirls are browned.

Duchesse potatoes are especially good with grilled chops but they match almost any meat or fish. Duchesse is what you should use should you ever want to pipe potato on or around something.

POMMES SICILIENNES I   Serves 4

This orange flavoured mash is very good with game, fowl and smoked-cooked foods.

    2 lb (900 g) potatoes, boiled
    4 oz (110 g) butter
    scant ½ pt (275 ml) fresh orange juice
    salt, pepper

Mash the potatoes with half the butter. Whisk in the orange juice and continue whisking until you have a fluffy purée flecked with orange. Season with salt and pepper and spoon into a buttered gratin dish. Make peaks with a fork and dot with pieces of butter. Bake for 15 minutes at 400°F/200°C/gas mark 6 to brown the peaks.

POMMES SICILIENNES 2   Serves 6

    1½ lb (700 g) pommes Duchesse mixture
    1 medium-sized onion
    ½ oz (15 g) bacon fat or lard
    grated rind and juice of 1 large orange
    salt, pepper

Chop the onion very finely and gently brown in the fat. Mix the orange rind and juice, the onion, salt and pepper into the Duchesse mixture (for recipe see page 251–2). Pipe into swirls or pile into a buttered gratin dish. Brown in a hot oven for 15 minutes. This mixture can also be formed into little cakes.

BUTTER BROWNED POTATOES   Serves 2

    1 lb (450 g) very small new potatoes
    2 oz (50 g) butter
    1 tbs flat-leaf parsley, finely chopped
    salt, pepper

Boil or steam the potatoes in their skin until just tender. Drain, peel and in a frying pan that can accommodate all the potatoes in one layer melt the butter and gently sauté, turning frequently, until golden brown all over. This will take between 45 minutes and 1 hour and cannot be hurried. Sprinkle with the parsley, season with salt and pepper and serve.

POMMES DE TERRE À L'ECHIRLÈTE   Serves 4

This is a variation on the previous Butter Browned Potatoes (above) recipe and a classic dish from the Périgord district. It is very good with grilled steak or game.

    2½ lb (1 kg) small new potatoes (large potatoes can be halved
        and/or quartered)
    water or stock to cover
    2 fat cloves garlic
    1 tbs goose lard or pork fat
    salt, pepper

Put the potatoes in a pan with just enough stock or water to cover and add the garlic. Bring the potatoes to the boil with the pan lid on, turn down and allow to simmer until all the liquid is absorbed. Transfer the potatoes and garlic to a frying pan and sauté with the fat until they are browned all over. Season before serving.

NICO LADENIS'S GARLIC POTATOES/POMMES À L'AIL   <u>Serves 2</u>

> 10 tiny new potatoes, boiled in their skins
> 2 tbs very fine, homemade breadcrumbs
> 2 eggs, beaten
> oil for deep frying
> 2 oz (50 g) butter
> 2 cloves garlic, finely chopped
> ½ tsp parsley, finely chopped
> salt, pepper

Skin the potatoes while still hot and roll in the breadcrumbs. Dip in the beaten egg and roll the potatoes in the breadcrumbs again. Heat the oil to 350°F/180°C and deep fry for 5 or 6 minutes until golden. Drain on absorbent kitchen paper and keep warm.

Melt the butter, cook the garlic until golden, season, mix in the parsley and pour over the potatoes.

CARAMELISED POTATOES/BRUNEDE KARTOFLER   <u>Serves 4</u>

This Danish recipe is traditionally served with pork or game.

> 1½ lb (700 g) small new potatoes, boiled in their skins
> 1 oz (25 g) sugar
> 2 oz (50 g) unsalted butter

Skin the potatoes. Using a heavy-based saucepan or frying pan, gently melt the sugar until it turns golden. Add the butter, stirring well and taking care not to burn the sugar. When it is amalgamated add the potatoes to the pan. Continue cooking over a gentle heat, turning the potatoes frequently so they get an even coating of the caramel. This is easier to make if you can fit all the potatoes in one layer.

Serve sprinkled with salt.

PAPRIKA POTATOES 1/PAPRIKA KARTOFFELN   Serves 2–3

1 lb (450 g) potatoes
2 oz (50 g) bacon fat or pork dripping
1 onion, finely sliced
½ tsp Hungarian paprika (double the quantity if the paprika isn't Hungarian)
¼ pt (150 ml) stock
¼ pt (150 ml) sour cream
salt, pepper
parsley, chopped

Melt the fat and sauté the onion. Add the thickly sliced potatoes, season with salt and pepper, add the paprika and stir around for a couple of minutes. Add the stock, cover and simmer very gently for 1 hour. Stir in the cream, sprinkle with chopped parsley.
Serve with frankfurters.

PAPRIKA POTATOES 2/PAPRIKAS KRUMPLI   Serves 4

1½ lb (700 g) potatoes
3 oz (75 g) bacon fat
1 large onion, finely chopped
1–2 tbs paprika
¼–½ tsp chilli powder
¼–½ tsp caraway seeds
1 tsp salt

Melt the dripping and fry the onion until it is transparent. Lower the heat and mix in the paprika and chilli. Peel and slice the potatoes and mix them into the onion. Add the salt, caraway seeds and enough water to cover. Simmer for 20 minutes until the potatoes are cooked.
Serve with smoked sausage and thick chunks of crusty bread.

LEMON DILL POTATOES   Serves 4

    1½ lb (700 g) new potatoes
    1 tbs olive oil
    1 oz (25 g) butter
    1½ oz (40 g) flour
    ½ pt (275 ml) milk
    1 tsp dill seed
    1 tbs parsley, finely chopped
    2 tbs lemon juice
    salt, pepper

Cook the potatoes as usual but add a dash of olive oil to the water. Drain, peel and keep warm. Melt the butter in a saucepan, blend in the flour and gradually add the milk. Stir constantly and as the sauce begins to thicken add the dill seed, the parsley, seasoning and lemon juice. Give the sauce a good beating and pour over the potatoes.
    Serve with simply grilled or steamed fish.

CANARY-STYLE POTATOES/PAPAS ARRUGADAS   Serves 3–4

In the Canaries the potatoes would be boiled in sea water and then served with the spicy *Mojo* sauce. Canary potatoes make a good accompaniment to a dense-fleshed fish.

    1½ lb (700 g) small new potatoes
    3 cloves garlic
    ¼ dried chilli pepper
    1 tsp each cumin seeds and paprika
    ¼ pt (150 ml) wine vinegar
    3 tbs olive oil
    ¼ tsp salt, 4 grinds or pinch ground black pepper
    2 tsp parsley, chopped, to garnish

Scrub the potatoes and boil them in generously salted water. Drain, cut them in halves and put into a serving dish. Pound the garlic, de-seeded chilli pepper and cumin seeds. Mix with the salt and paprika and stir into the vinegar and oil. Season with pepper and pour over the potatoes. Sprinkle with chopped parsley to garnish.

POTATOES IN PORT/POMMES DE TERRE AU PORTO   Serves 6

This is a variation on Pommes Anna (page 80) but far less greasy and cooked over a direct flame. In *New Classic Cuisine* the Roux brothers cook this with truffle peelings but it is very good without and goes wonderfully well with grilled meat.

> 1 ½ lb (700 g) potatoes
> 6 oz (175 g) clarified butter
> 4 fl oz (110 ml) port
> salt

Peel and wash the potatoes. Slice wafer thin (this is easy with a mandoline), pat dry and sprinkle with salt. Divide into 6 piles and, using a small frying pan, melt 1 oz (25 g) of the clarified butter. Put 1 portion of the potato slices in overlapping circles into the pan (this is when you would add a few truffle peelings) and fry for 2 minutes before you turn down the heat and cook gently for 5 minutes. Using a palette knife flip the cake over and cook for a further 5 or 6 minutes. Sprinkle a few drops of port over the cake and cook for a minute more. Serve from the pan and continue with the other portions.

Cooking can be speeded up if you use two frying pans and begin the cakes at 5-minute intervals.

ANTON MOSIMANN'S JACQUELINE POTATOES   Serves 4

A slimmer's Pommes Anna (see page 80); this is from the gourmet slimmers' cookbook *Cuisine Naturelle* by Anton Mosimann.

> 14 oz (400 g) potatoes
> 2 oz (50 g) fromage blanc
> salt, pepper, nutmeg

Peel the potatoes and slice them wafer thin. Put them in a bowl with the fromage blanc and season with nutmeg, salt and pepper. Pre-heat the oven to 375°F/190°C/gas mark 5. Using any small moulds, fill them with overlapping slices of fromage blanc-coated potato and bake for about 12 minutes if the dish is metal, slightly longer if ceramic. Ease the potatoes out with a knife and serve.

MÈRE BLANC'S PANCAKES   Serves 6

One of my greatest gastronomic experiences was a meal at Georges Blanc's restaurant at Vonnas near Bourg en Bresse. While the entire meal was perfection these little pancakes stole the show.

>   1 lb 2 oz (500 g) waxy-variety potatoes, thinly peeled
>   4 fl oz (110 ml) milk
>   4 oz (110 g) flour
>   3 eggs, separated and 1 extra egg white
>   3 tbs double cream
>   clarified butter for frying

Boil the potatoes and mash with a little of the milk. Cool, then mix in the sifted flour, the egg yolks and cream. Whisk the egg whites and fold them into the mixture but don't beat anything too long or too vigorously.

Using a non-stick pan, heat a knob of butter and drop in ¾ tbs of the batter. Cook on both sides, taste and check the consistency; it may need a little more milk. Cook in batches and keep warm in the oven until you've finished the batter. Should you make the batter in advance, it can be stored in the fridge but must be bought back to room temperature before you start cooking.

This and other recipes from Georges Blanc's restaurant La Mère Blanc can be found in *Ma Cuisine des Saisons*, translated and adapted by Caroline Conran.

POTATOES EN PAPILLOTES   Serves 6

'Nicholas Soyer, grandson of the famous Alexis, spent years perfecting the system of paper-bag cookery and published a book extolling its advantages. Indeed they are many. I can vouch for the excellence of this method for new potatoes.' Elizabeth David, in *French Country Cooking*, 1959.

>   24 very small new potatoes, scraped
>   2 leaves mint
>   2 oz (50 g) butter
>   2 pinches salt

Sprinkle the salt over the potatoes, put them and the other ingredients on a fair-sized sheet of greaseproof paper. Fold the paper over and then fold down the edges so that the bag is securely sealed. Pre-heat the oven to

375°F/190°C/gas mark 5 and bake for 35 minutes. As Ms David says, they will come out perfectly cooked, buttery and full of flavour.

POTATOES IN BEER   Serves 4

Not, as you might think, an Irish recipe but one devised by an American living in France. Richard Olney is one of the most gifted, knowledgeable and innovative contemporary cookery writers. This dish might sound unlikely but is one of the most satisfactory uses for half a pint that I know.

> 1½ lb (700 g) potatoes, finely sliced but not rinsed
> 1 onion, finely sliced
> 8 fl oz (225 ml) beer
> 1 oz (25 g) butter
> ¼ pt (150 ml) double cream
> salt

Press alternate salted layers of onion and potatoes into a buttered, deep baking dish, beginning with a layer of onion on the bottom and finishing with a layer of potatoes, arranging the layers of potatoes neatly overlapping so that they take up a minimum of space. Pour over the beer and distribute paper-thin shavings of butter over the entire surface.

Bake for 1 hour, beginning with a hot oven (400°F/200°C/gas mark 6) and turning it down to 350°F/180°C/gas mark 4 after 10 minutes. Ten minutes before removing from the oven, pour the cream evenly over the surface. This is especially good with pan-fried liver.

POMMES DE TERRE À L'ARDENNAISE   Serves 4

Serve with venison or boar.

> 1½ lb (700 g) waxy-variety potatoes
> 6 juniper berries
> 1 clove garlic
> 3 oz (75 g) butter
> 1 tbs olive oil
> 2 tsp salt, pepper

Shred the potatoes and soak them in cold water. Drain and dry them in a tea cloth. Crush the juniper berries, garlic and salt together and sauté in the oil and butter. Add the potatoes, pepper and mix everything together.

Cover with foil and cook gently for about 30 minutes in a frying pan over a direct and moderate flame until a delicious crisp crust has formed on the bottom.

GARFAGNANA POTATOES   Serves 4

    1 lb (450 g) potatoes
    1½ lb (700 g) tomatoes
    2 cloves garlic, finely chopped
    1 carrot, finely chopped
    1 onion, finely chopped
    1 stick celery, finely chopped
    ¼ pt (150 ml) olive oil
    salt, pepper

Peel and chop the tomatoes, peel and cut the potatoes into large chunks. Mix all the ingredients together in a flame-proof casserole and season well. Cover the dish and cook gently over a low flame until the potatoes are cooked, by which time most of the vegetable juice will have been absorbed by the potatoes.

ARTICHOKES WITH POTATOES/ANGINARES ME
PATATES   Serves 4

    1 lb (450 g) new potatoes, diced
    6 small globe artichoke hearts
    2 tbs olive oil
    8 oz (225 g) small carrots, diced
    2 onions, chopped
    1 tbs flour
    2 tbs dill, chopped
    1 tsp salt, ½ tsp pepper

Trim the artichokes and fry gently in the oil. Add the diced and chopped vegetables, the salt and pepper and cook for 5 minutes before stirring in the sifted flour. Gradually add enough water barely to cover the vegetables, stir in the dill, cover and allow to simmer until the artichokes are tender. Serve hot or cold with barbecued meats or fish.

STEWED POTATOES AND PEARS   Serves 4

In Switzerland cooked pears are often served with meat. This Swiss dish is especially good with ham and salt beef.

> 1 lb (450 g) small new potatoes, scrubbed
> 2 oz (50 g) butter
> 1 large onion, sliced
> 8 oz (225 g) dried pears, roughly chopped and covered in water
> 1 tbs honey
> salt, pepper

Choose a heavy-based Le Creuset-type casserole dish for this recipe. Melt the butter, stir in the onions, cover and allow to sweat over a low flame for 5–10 minutes.

Add the pears and their water, the potatoes, honey, several grinds of black pepper and a pinch of salt. If necessary top up the water so that everything is just covered. Cover and cook until both the pears and potatoes are tender. Drain and serve with a knob of butter.

POMMES AMANDINES   Serves 2–3

> 1 lb (450 g) potato, mashed with 1 oz (25 g) butter
> 1 egg yolk and 1 whole egg, beaten with a little milk
> sifted flour
> 1 oz (25 g) flaked almonds, crushed
> oil for frying
> salt, pepper, nutmeg

Beat the egg yolks into the potatoes, season with nutmeg, salt and pepper. Form into little balls about the size of a golf ball, but if the mixture seems sloppy mix in some sifted flour. Dip each ball in the beaten egg and then roll in the crushed almonds. If you are feeling artistic you could mould the balls into little apples and pears (use bits of spaghetti for the stalks). Heat the oil and deep fry until golden, about 5 minutes.

POMMES DE TERRE À LA BARIGOULE   <u>Serves 4</u>

1½ lb (700 g) potatoes
12 small onions
bouquet garni
approximately 1 pt (570 ml) meat stock
1 tbs vinegar
2 tbs olive oil
salt, pepper

Scrub the potatoes if they are new, peel them if they aren't and cut into similar-sized pieces. Put the potatoes, onions and bouquet garni in a pan with the seasoned stock and boil until tender. Strain off the stock and return the potatoes and onions to the pan with the olive oil and vinegar. Simmer for 5 minutes, lightly season and serve.

POTATOES IN WHITE WINE/POMMES DE TERRE AU VIN BLANC   <u>Serves 4</u>

1½ lb (700 g) small new potatoes
2 rashers smoked streaky bacon
1 oz (25 g) butter
1 bay leaf
¼ pt (150 ml or a full glass) white wine
¼ pt (150 ml) stock
salt, pepper

Dice the bacon, blanch in boiling water for a couple of minutes and then put in a pan with all the other ingredients. Simmer until the potatoes are cooked. This is delicious with chicken.

POTATOES IN RED WINE/MATELOTE DE POMMES DE TERRE   <u>Serves 4</u>

1½ lb (700 g) potatoes, sliced
4 oz (110 g) butter
½ pt (275 ml) red wine
2 onions, chopped
salt, pepper, sprig of thyme

Melt the butter in a decent-sized frying pan, pour in the wine, potatoes and onions. Season generously and simmer gently for 35 minutes. Top up with water if it gets too dry.

CANDIED SWEET POTATOES/CONFITS DE PATATE FLAMBÉE
<u>Serves 6</u>

This is a good alternative to cranberry sauce to be served with turkey or boiled ham. A little goes a long way; it will appeal to those with a sweet tooth.

> 2 lb (900 g) sweet potatoes, boiled in their skins
> 2 oz (50 g) butter
> juice of ½ lemon, lime or orange
> 4 oz (110 g) brown sugar
> ¼ tsp grated nutmeg
> 6 tbs rum

Peel and slice the potatoes and arrange them in overlapping slices in a large buttered gratin dish. Squeeze over the citrus juice, sprinkle on the sugar and nutmeg.

Bake near the top of the oven for about 45 minutes at 375°F/190°C/gas mark 5 to caramelise the sugar. Remove from the oven, sprinkle on the rum and set light to it at the table. This dish can also be cooked on a direct flame by cooking all the ingredients, except the rum, in a pan over a very low heat for about 15 minutes. Pour into a serving dish and flame at the table.

SWEET POTATO AND PEAR SOUFFLÉ
<u>Serves 4–6</u>

This is an impressive accompaniment to game and pork.

> 1½ lb (700 g) sweet potatoes
> 2 oz (50 g) butter
> 2 tbs fine white breadcrumbs
> 1 lb (450 g) ripe pears
> 2 eggs, separated
> 2 tbs honey
> juice of 1 lemon
> ½ tsp salt, pinch of ground or 3–4 grinds of fresh black pepper

Bake the potatoes in a moderate oven (350°F/180°C/gas mark 4) for between 45 minutes and 1 hour depending on their size. When completely done split in half and scoop out the flesh. Set aside to cool.

Turn the temperature of the oven up to 425°F/220°C/gas mark 7, butter a large (4–5 pt/2.3–2.8 l) soufflé dish and sprinkle with most of the breadcrumbs. Peel, core and chop the pears and roughly mash the two together before beating in the egg yolks, pepper, salt, lemon juice and honey. In a separate bowl beat the egg whites to stiff peaks and fold into the mixture. Pour into the soufflé dish, sprinkle on the rest of the breadcrumbs and bake for 40 minutes. The top will be brown and crusty and the inside soft.

SPICY POTATOES/MUGLAI ALOO   Serves 6

Serve as part of an Indian meal or as a centrepiece for a vegetarian dinner.

3 lb (1.4 kg) small new potatoes
3 tbs ghee
1 tsp each ground cloves, cumin and coriander
2 green chilli peppers, seeded and chopped
1 tsp fresh ginger, finely chopped
3 cloves garlic
½ tsp turmeric
½ pt (275 ml) water
4 fl oz (110 ml) yoghurt
1 large onion, finely sliced
salt
2 tbs fresh coriander, chopped

Scrub or peel the potatoes, rinse and dry. Melt 2 tbs of the ghee and gently stir fry the potatoes for 15 minutes until they begin to colour. Using a slotted spoon transfer the potatoes to a china dish. Grind together the cloves, chillies, ginger and garlic, stir in the other ready-ground spices, add a little water and salt to form a paste. Stir the paste into the yoghurt and pour over the potatoes. Add the rest of the ghee to the cooking pan and sauté the onion, stirring to make sure it doesn't stick. After a few minutes stir in the water and then the potato mixture. Bring to the boil and then simmer for about 20 minutes until the potatoes are cooked. Two minutes before serving stir in the bulk of the chopped coriander and at the point of serving sprinkle on the remainder.

CAULIFLOWER WITH POTATOES/PHOOL GOBI AUR ALOO KI BHAJI
Serves 4

    1 lb (450 g) new potatoes, boiled
    1 lb (450 g) weight cauliflower florets
    5 tbs ghee
    1 tsp each whole cumin and ground cumin seeds
    1 fresh green chilli pepper, finely chopped
    ½ tsp ground coriander seeds
    ¼ tsp each turmeric and cayenne
    1 tsp salt, pepper

Rinse the florets and dice the potatoes. Heat the ghee in a large frying pan and fry first the cumin seeds and then add the cauliflower. Stir fry the florets and let them brown in places before you cover, turn down the heat and let them sweat it out for 5 or 6 minutes. Add the potatoes, the chilli, seasoning and spices and gently stir it all together. Let it cook on for a further 5 minutes until the florets are cooked but still firm.

Serve with tandoori chicken and nan for mopping-up purposes.

DRY POTATOES WITH GINGER AND GARLIC/SOOKHE ALOO
Serves 5

This is another winner from Madhur Jaffrey and goes well both with Indian food and simply grilled or roasted meats. The diced potatoes end up with a crusty, spicy coating of ginger and garlic. It is best to use a non-stick frying pan.

    1 lb 6 oz (625 g) boiled potatoes
    piece of fresh ginger 1 in x 2 in (2.5 cm x 5 cm)
    3 cloves garlic, peeled
    ½ tsp each ground turmeric and cayenne
    3 tbs water
    5 tbs ghee
    1 tsp fennel seeds (optional)
    1 tsp salt

Dice the potatoes and grind the ginger, garlic, turmeric, cayenne and salt with the water to make a paste. Heat the ghee and when hot put in the fennel seeds. Let them sizzle for a few seconds and then add the paste. Stir fry for a couple of minutes and then stir in the potatoes, turn up the heat and cook until the potatoes have a nice crispy coating. It is important to keep moving the potatoes so that they are evenly crisped. It takes about 10 minutes over a medium high flame.

SPINACH WITH POTATOES/SAAG ALOO   Serves 4

This is a very successful combination that goes well with meat curries and a dish of yoghurt. Frozen spinach works just as well as fresh.

    1¼ lb (550 g) potatoes, peeled and diced
    2 lb (900 g) fresh spinach or 1¼ lb (550 g) frozen
    5 tbs ghee or vegetable oil
    2 tsp whole black mustard seeds
    4 oz (110 g) onion, finely sliced
    2 cloves garlic, finely chopped
    ¼ tsp cayenne
    ¼ pt (150 ml) water
    1 tsp salt, pepper

Wash the spinach, remove the stalks and cook with a little salt in a covered pan over a gentle heat. The remains of the rinsing water will be sufficient liquid. If using frozen spinach, cook in boiling water as per the instructions. In both cases drain and chop the spinach.

Heat the oil and cook the mustard seeds for a couple of seconds until they pop, add the onion and garlic and stir fry for 2 minutes. Add the potatoes and cayenne, let the flavours mingle for a minute or two and then add the spinach, salt, pinch of pepper and water. Bring to the boil, cover, turn down the flame as low as possible and simmer for 30–40 minutes until the potatoes are cooked. Give the dish an occasional stir and if it dries out add a little more water.

This is rather nice with a little yoghurt stirred in just before serving.

POTATOES WITH ALMONDS/ALOO BADAM   Serves 2

This is a delicious and novel idea from the Punjab.

    1 lb (450 g) small new potatoes
    oil for frying
    4 oz (110 g) almond flakes
    2 tsp each ground coriander and roasted ground cumin seeds
    fresh coriander leaves, chopped
    salt

Scrub the potatoes, dry them well and deep fry (350°F/180°C) to a pale golden brown. Drain, allow to cool and pierce them in several places with a skewer. Stuff the holes with almond flakes. Get the oil back up to temperature and deep fry for another 5 minutes until the potatoes are a rich golden brown. Drain and sprinkle with the mixed spices, salt and coriander leaves.

Serve with Indian mint sauce and tandoori chicken.

21.

Sauces and Stuffings

In 1986 *The Times'* cookery writer Frances Bissell wrote a book called *The Pleasures of Cookery*. In the section on vegetables she traces the evolution of sauces and ponders the now totally familiar vegetable coulis, purées and sauces placed under the main ingredient that became a hallmark of nouvelle cruisine. Before giving recipes for her own three favourite vegetable purées Ms Bissell wonders if the wheel will come full circle, 'will we soon be serving a plate of, say, grilled noisettes of lamb sitting in a pool of smooth potato sauce?' Two years later I was very amused to read that Antony Worrall-Thompson, chef/patron of Ménage à Trois had won that year's Mouton Menu competition with seared and herbed fillets of salmon and tuna with red pepper purée and *a potato sauce!*

I don't think though that Ms Bissell need worry that we are heading for potato minimalism. Apart from the Worrall-Thompson sauce and the success of Fredy Giradet's sloppy *pommes purée* that is more of a sauce than a mash, I have only found three potato-based sauces and one Indian chutney that are worth their salt. After all, who needs a potato sauce when you can have a big mound of flavoured mash? Conversely, I have found enough sauces that *complement* potatoes to fill a separate book.

POTATO AND ANCHOVY SAUCE   Serves 4–6

This is marvellous with boiled mutton.

    2 medium-sized, boiled and grated potatoes
    1 medium-sized onion, chopped
    lamb dripping or lard
    6 anchovies, washed and chopped
    ½ pt (275 ml) lamb stock
    2 tbs yoghurt
    salt

Fry the onion in the fat and, when transparent, add the potatoes and anchovies. Add the stock and bring to the boil. Stir in the yoghurt, simmer for 10 minutes and pass through a sieve or thoroughly liquidise. Because tinned anchovies are generally very salty, taste the sauce to check whether additional seasoning is required.

POTATO AND CHESTNUT SAUCE   Serves 8

Serve with pork or game.

  1½ lb (700 g) potatoes
  2 lb (900 g) chestnuts, if using canned be sure to get the
    unsweetened variety
  ¾ pt (400 ml) stock
  ¾ pt (400 ml) milk or dry white wine
  salt, pepper

Boil the potatoes in salted water and pre-heat the oven to 350°F/180°C/ gas mark 4. Score all the chestnuts with a sharp knife and bake them for 15 minutes in batches of 10 at a time. Remove from the oven and, holding each chestnut in a cloth or oven glove, strip off the skin, taking care to remove the membrane. This must be done while they are hot. Simmer the chestnuts in the stock and, when they are completely soft, mash them in the stock.

Meanwhile, peel and purée the potatoes and mix in the soft chestnut mash. Heat the milk. If using wine boil it first to burn off the alcohol. Beat the liquid into the chestnut and potatoes. Continue beating until you have a smooth, fluffy purée the consistency of mayonnaise; if necessary adjust with more liquid and seasoning.

GARLIC CREAM   Serves 4

Serve with dense-fleshed fish.

  1 large floury-variety potato (about 8 oz/225 g)
  6 large cloves garlic
  ¼ pt (150 ml) milk
  ¼ pt (150 ml) heavy cream
  salt, pepper

Chop up the potato, peel the garlic and put them both in a small pan with the milk and cream. Simmer gently until the potato is cooked and most of the liquid has been absorbed. Mash the mixture and whisk it smooth. Season and thin with a little more cream if necessary.

This recipe is adapted from *The Wolfgang Puck Cookbook*; he serves the sauce *under* grilled salmon, surrounded by tomato cream.

INDIAN POTATO CHUTNEY   Serves 6

    1 lb (450 g) waxy-variety potatoes
    4 green chilli peppers
    1 tsp cumin seeds
    juice 1 lemon
    4 fl oz (110 ml) plain yoghurt
    ½ tsp salt, pepper

Cook the unpeeled potatoes in salted water. Drain, peel and dice. Finely dice the chillies and mix the two together in a serving dish. Season, sprinkle on the cumin seeds and pour over the lemon juice. Leave to amalgamate for 10 minutes and carefully stir in the yoghurt.

Serve chilled with any curry.

POTATO FLOUR FOR SAUCES

Sauces made with potato flour (*farine de fécule*) are light, don't cloy the flavour and leave the sauce 'clear'. Use slightly less potato flour than you would if using plain or cornflour. All chefs with traditional French training, and most oriental cooks, use *fécule*, as it's known in French (see page 281).

SAUCES TO SERVE WITH POTATOES

This selection of sauces all complement potatoes particularly well. Serve with plainly boiled, mashed or baked potatoes.

HOT TOMATO SAUCE   Serves 4

This can be served cold as well as hot.

> 6 spring onions, finely sliced
> 1 oz (25 g) butter
> 1 lb (450 g) very ripe tomatoes, peeled, cored and roughly chopped
> pinch of basil or sprig of thyme
> splash of white wine if available
> 1 dsp flat-leaf parsley, chopped
> sugar, salt, pepper

Finely chop the onions and sweat in butter over a low flame until soft. Add the tomatoes, seasoning, basil or thyme and wine. Boil fiercely for 5 minutes to reduce and intensify flavours, add the parsley and simmer for 10 minutes.

This is good with plainly boiled potatoes or with potatoes added to make a stew.

SWEET AND SOUR GREEN SAUCE/SALSA
VERDE AGRODOLCE   Serves 4–6

This is a variation on *pesto* (basil, garlic and olive oil with pine nuts). *Pesto* is widely available at Italian delicatessens, but this sauce isn't.

> 4 oz (110 g) mixed herbs such as basil, mint, flat-leaf parsley, dill or
>   marjoram, chopped
> 2 slices (about 2 oz/50 g) white bread, without crusts
> 6 fl oz (170 ml) wine vinegar
> 2 tbs sugar
> 3 anchovy fillets, washed to remove excess salt
> ½ pt (275 ml) olive oil
> salt, pepper

Blend all ingredients in a mixer, taste and season.

PEPPER SAUCE/SALSA ROMESCO   Serves 4

This is a variation on the great Catalan sauce which Claudia Roden adapted for her book *Mediterranean Cookery*. It is deliciously light, nutty, pungent and spicy.

1 dried red chilli pepper, 2 fresh red peppers
3 large cloves garlic
2 oz (50 g) peeled whole almonds
8 oz (225 g) ripe tomatoes
3 tbs wine vinegar
½ pt (275 ml) olive oil
salt, pepper

Soak the chilli pepper for 30 minutes. Pre-heat the oven to 475°F/240°C/ gas mark 9. All the ingredients are going to be baked and, as the oven is very hot, they must be watched with eagle eyes. Begin with the peppers which take about 20 minutes (the skin will blister and go brown but the flesh will be soft), then the unpeeled garlic (10 minutes), almonds and tomatoes (about 5 minutes).

Peel, core and de-seed the pepper and tomatoes, peel the garlic and set aside while you pound the nuts and garlic to a paste. Liquidise all these ingredients together, season, add the vinegar and finally add the oil at a slow trickle. Continue the motor until everything is amalgamated.

CUCUMBER SAUCE   Serves 6

This is very good served with boiled new potatoes and simply cooked fish when all the ingredients can be served hot or cold.

1 cucumber, peeled and roughly chopped
4 spring onions, finely sliced
2 oz (50 g) unsalted butter
2 oz (50 g) fecule (potato flour)
¼ pt (150 ml) hot milk
1 tbs fresh mint, finely chopped
salt, pepper

Sprinkle the cucumber with salt to draw out the liquid and leave for at least ½ an hour. Rinse and sweat with the spring onions in the butter over a low heat. When soft mix in the sifted flour taking care to leave no lumps, cook for a couple of minutes and stir in the hot milk. Season, cook for 5 minutes and liquidise. Check the seasoning and stir in the mint.

WALNUT SAUCE   Serves 4

1 slice stale white bread, crusts removed (about 1 oz/25 g)
½ pt (275 ml) good chicken stock, or made with 1 Knorr cube
4 oz (50 g) shelled walnuts, roughly chopped

1 clove garlic, crushed
salt, pepper

Soak the bread in the stock and transfer to the food processor. Add the walnuts, process briefly, add the garlic and seasoning and process until smooth. Warm through and check seasoning.

This is particularly good with barbecued chicken and boiled potatoes.

STUFFINGS

OLD ENGLISH STUFFING   To stuff a large chicken

8 oz (225 g) dry mashed potato
2 oz (50 g) diced smoked bacon
1 medium-sized onion, peeled and chopped
4 oz (110 g) sausage meat
1 tsp fresh thyme
salt, pepper

Fry the bacon over a low heat in a non-stick pan. When the fat begins to run add the onion and cook, stirring frequently, until the onion is transparent and the bacon crisp. Stir the onion mixture, sausage meat and herbs into the mash. Season thoroughly.

STUFFINGS FOR GOOSE

Roasting a goose is good news for potato lovers. Goose fat is the ultimate for frying and roasting potatoes and it is sacrilege to waste even a drop!

The rich flesh of the goose is complemented by the soothing foil of a potato stuffing; here are 3 versions. If you decide on some other stuffing for your goose, serve mashed potato garnished with fresh sage or fill little (blind baked) shortcrust tartlets with mash, top with a knob of butter and bake for 5 minutes.

RICHARD SHEPHERD'S POTATO STUFFING
To stuff a 10 lb (4.5 kg) goose

Langan's Brasserie in Mayfair is the only restaurant I know to serve their Christmas goose with the traditional potato stuffing.

1½ lb (700 g) dry mashed potato
2 oz (50 g) butter
2 lb (900 g) onions, sliced
salt, pepper

Melt the butter in a heavy-bottomed lidded dish. Add the onions, season with salt and plenty of pepper, cover and leave to sweat down to a limp transparent pulp. This takes at least 40 minutes and can't be hurried. Mix in with the mash and stuff the goose. This may sound very dull but during the cooking the fat and juices of the goose will seep into the stuffing and the results are unbelievably delicious.

For a deluxe Potato Stuffing, sweat the onions in goose fat instead of butter and mix 4 oz (110 g) finely chopped sage into the mixture.

SUSAN CAMPBELL'S GERMAN
POTATO STUFFING
To stuff a 10 lb (4.5 kg) goose

This recipe is quoted from a German source by Susan Campbell in her *English Cookery New and Old*. This adaptation is by Jeremy Round who published the recipe in the *Independent*.

1½ lb (700 g) potatoes, peeled and cut into small cubes
4 oz (110 g) lean salt pork or bacon, finely chopped
oil for frying
1 medium-sized onion, chopped
4 tbs parsley, chopped
1 tbs each marjoram and sage, chopped
salt, pepper

Boil the diced potatoes for 10 minutes in salted water. Drain. Sauté the pork or bacon in a little oil until crisp. Set aside and, in the same fat, sauté the onion until soft and golden. Mix all the ingredients in a bowl, cool and stuff the bird.

22.

Desserts

SOUFFLÉ DE POMMES DE TERRE

8 oz (225 g) floury-variety potatoes
3 eggs, separated
2 oz caster sugar
½ pt (275 ml) milk
2 oz (50 g) melted butter
salt, pinch nutmeg

Boil the potatoes in their skins with slightly less salt than usual. Peel and mash thoroughly while still hot and then force through a sieve. Whisk the egg yolks and sugar thoroughly before adding the milk, melted butter and nutmeg into the potatoes. Beat the egg whites stiff and fold into the mixture. Butter a soufflé dish, pour in the mixture and bake in a hot (400°F/200°C/gas mark 6) oven for 25 minutes or until the soufflé is golden brown.

Serve with a tart stewed fruit such as rhubarb or plums and cream.

RICHARD BRADLEY'S BAKED POTATO PUDDING   Serves 6–8

The author of my introductory quote was a Professor of Botany at Cambridge University and a keen collector of recipes. The following is one of his particular good finds and makes a fine family winter pudding.

3 lb (1.4 kg) floury-variety potatoes, boiled in their skins
2 large carrots, peeled and finely grated
juice of 2 oranges
1 tbs orange-flower water (fresh orange juice can be substituted but
   won't give such a delicate scented flavour)
2 oz (50 g) butter
2 eggs
1 tsp sugar
salt, pepper

Mash the potatoes thoroughly and beat in the rest of the ingredients until
you have a smooth mixture. Butter a large shallow ovenproof dish and
spoon in the mixture. Bake in a moderate oven (350°F/180°C/gas mark 4)
for approximately 20 minutes until the top is golden brown. Serve directly
from the dish, with cream.

POTATO PANCAKES   Makes 15–20 pancakes

6 eggs
6 oz (175 g) potato flour
12 fl oz (315 ml) cold water
oil for frying
salt

Beat the eggs thoroughly and gradually mix in the sifted flour, a pinch of
salt and the water until you have a pale yellow foamy batter the
consistency of cream. Allow to rest for 30 minutes, beat again before
using.

Heat a splash of oil in a 6-in (15-cm) flat pan (non-stick is particularly
helpful for pancake making) until it begins to smoke. Pour off any excess
oil and quickly pour in enough batter to cover the pan. Cook for a couple
of minutes a side so that the pancake is crisp and golden.

Sod's law is that the first pancake is always a failure. Always wipe the
pan clean and whisk the mixture between pancakes. Serve with whatever
you fancy – cream, maple syrup, lemon juice . . .

POTATO STRUDEL/KRUMPLIS RETES TOLTELEK   Serves 4

Strudel pastry (filo) is sold frozen in many Middle Eastern and mid-
European groceries/delicatessen.

1 lb (450 g) floury-variety potatoes
4 eggs, separated
4 oz (110 g) butter, chopped into small pieces
grated rind of 1 lemon
2 oz (50 g) ground blanched almonds
4 oz (110 g) vanilla sugar
pinch salt
4 sheets filo pastry
melted butter for pastry
icing sugar, sour cream

Cook the potatoes in their skins, peel, mash and sieve while still hot. Allow to cool while you cream the egg yolks with the butter. Mix the lemon rind into the potatoes and then the almonds, egg yolks and butter. In a separate dish whisk the egg whites with the sugar and the pinch of salt to form stiff peaks. Fold the egg whites into the mixture and set aside.

Pre-heat the oven to 400°F/200°C/gas mark 6. Spread out the pastry on a floured surface: you will need 4 sheets of pastry laid on top of one another, each painted with melted butter. Spread on the potato mixture and roll up carefully, tucking in the sides. If necessary secure with more butter and bake for 30 minutes.

Remove to a serving plate, dust with icing sugar and serve with whipped sour cream.

CHRISTMAS PUDDING
Makes two 1 lb (450 g) or one 2 lb (900 g) puddings

4 oz (110 g) dry mashed potato
2 eggs
4 oz (110 g) shredded suet or melted butter
4 oz (110 g) flour
1 small carrot, grated
1 small apple, peeled and grated
1 lb (450 g) mixed dried fruit
1 tbs marmalade
4 oz (110 g) brown sugar
1 tbs golden syrup or black treacle
8 tbs ale, beer, stout, brandy or whisky
1 tsp each mixed spice, cinnamon, almond essence and lemon
    essence

Cream the eggs with the butter or mix with the suet, stir in the sifted flour and, when smooth, the potatoes. Add all the other ingredients and continue mixing until the pudding seems well integrated. Butter two 1 lb (450 g) or one 2 lb (900 g) pudding bowls, fill with the mixture, cover with foil and form a 'head scarf' with some old sheeting so you will be able to lift the pudding out of the steamer.

Steam (on no account letting the water get into the pudding) for a minimum of 6 hours (2 hours in a pressure cooker) and 2 more hours on Christmas Day. The longer you cook the pudding the darker it will be.

SWEET POTATO AND NUT PIE   Serves 6–8

Henry VIII had a great predilection for sweet potato baked in a pie, believing that such a dish would improve his love life. This particular recipe is adapted from *Bill Neal's Southern Cooking*. Jane Grigson includes an almost identical recipe in her *Vegetable Book* but uses walnuts rather than pecans.

        8 oz (225 g) sweet potato, boiled, peeled and mashed
        8 oz (225 g) shortcrust pastry
        4 oz (110 g) butter
        5 oz (150 g) soft brown sugar
        3 eggs, separated
        6 fl oz (170 ml) milk or single cream
        ¼ tsp each freshly grated nutmeg, ground cloves
        ½ tsp ground cinnamon
        4 oz (110 g) shelled whole pecans or halved walnuts
        2 fl oz (50 ml) dark rum, brandy or whisky

Blind bake the pastry in a ⁹⁄₁₀-in (2.3-cm) removable-based tart tin in a hot oven (425°F/220°C/gas mark 7). Remove and leave to cool, reset the oven for 375°F/190°C/gas mark 5.

Cream the butter with the sugar and add the potatoes. Beat the egg yolks and milk together, add the seasonings, 2 oz (50 g) of the nuts which you've roughly chopped and beat in the alcohol. In a separate bowl whisk the egg whites to firm peaks and gently fold into the mixture. Pour into the pastry case and press the remaining nuts around the edge of the pie. Bake for around 40 minutes until the pie has risen and is golden brown on top.

Serve hot or at room temperature with lashings of whipped cream.

BATATADA   <u>Serves 4</u>

This deceptively light Portuguese dessert joins Jane Grigson's curried parsnip soup in the list of dishes with ingredients most likely to fox your guests.

      4 oz (110 g) sweet potato, boiled in its skin
      4 tbs water
      2 oz (50 g) sugar
      6 large egg yolks
      ground cinnamon
      4 oz (50 g) double cream

Mash and sieve the potato as smooth as you can. In a moderate-sized non-stick pan boil up the water with the sugar to make a thick syrup. Stir the potatoes into the syrup and continue cooking for a few minutes, stirring all the time, until you get a translucent, gluey mixture.

Allow to cool and beat in the egg yolks one at a time. Return to a low heat and continue stirring until you have a thick cream that you can 'cut' with the spoon. The moment this happens plunge the pan into cold water to lower the temperature but take care not to get any water into the pudding. Stir in a pinch of cinnamon; taste to check if you need any more sugar or cinnamon.

Divide between 4 ramekins or similar dishes, chill and serve with a swirl of whipped cream and a dusting of cinnamon. Accompany with meringues made with all those egg whites, or almond tuiles.

SWEET POTATO TSIMMES WITH PINEAPPLE   <u>Serves 6</u>

This is a disgustingly sweet dessert much loved by children, especially when they are allowed to cook them.

      4 medium-sized sweet potatoes
      2 oz (50 g) butter
      8 oz (225 g) tin crushed pineapple
      1 tbs soft brown sugar
      packet of marshmallows (for extra dental decay) ·
      1 tsp salt

Boil the potatoes in their skins, peel and mash while still hot. Stir in the butter and mix in the pineapple and a little of the juice, salt and sugar and mix thoroughly. Butter a baking sheet (or 2) and place large spoonfuls at regular intervals. Press a marshmallow on top and bake in hot oven (400°F/200°C/gas mark 6) for 5–10 minutes until the marshmallows are golden brown.

CARIBBEAN SWEET POTATO AND COCONUT PUDDING
Serves 6–8

2 lb (900 g) sweet potatoes
rind and juice of 2 limes (or lemons)
2 egg yolks
6 oz (175 g) soft brown sugar
1 coconut, freshly grated
½ tsp ground cinnamon
3 drops vanilla essence

Peel the potatoes, cut into even-sized chunks and boil with the rind of 1 lime. Grate the second lime before extracting the juice and set aside both juice and rind. Drain and mash the potatoes. Allow to cool.

Pre-heat the oven to 350°F/180°C/gas mark 4, while you cream the egg yolks and sugar. Add to the potatoes and mix in all the other ingredients including the grated rind and juice. Butter an appropriate ovenproof dish, pour in the mixture and bake for 1 hour until the pudding has risen and its top is golden brown.

23

Buns and Cakes

Mashed potato and cakes seem unlikely bedfellows but they are very complementary ones. Cold mashed potato used in place of flour or suet will tranform buns and cakes into light, moist confections. The potato's ability to absorb and reflect other flavours means that cakes made with potato taste of the other ingredients – not of the potato.

Also common in baking is the use of potato starch flour, farina or fecule as it is also known. This flour is made by grinding potatoes and soaking the pulp in clean water to arrive at pure potato starch. In the early nineteenth century the great French chef Carème recorded: 'Wash and scrub 15 pounds of floury potatoes (which gives 2 lb flour). Grate them into a large bowl of water and then change the water. After about 3 hours, in which time the earthy taste of the potato is removed, wash twice more; spread out on silk sieve and set in an oven to dry out. In time you will get a very white flour with a good flavour. Sift before use.' In France it is called *fécule de pommes de terre* or *farine*, in England arrowroot. The flour is widely available (Rakusen's package theirs under supervision of the Beth Din and is kosher) and is bright white, very fine and crackles when you squeeze the packet.

HUNGARIAN POTATO CREAM BISCUITS/TOJASOS BURGONYAPURE
Makes 30 biscuits

2¼ lb (1 kg) floury-variety potatoes
4 oz (110 g) butter, softened
4 egg yolks
oil and butter for frying
salt, pinch ground mace
icing sugar, cinnamon

Boil the potatoes in their skins, peel and purée the pulp while still hot. Leave to cool while you cream the butter and incorporate the egg yolks, mace and salt. Gradually work the potatoes into the butter mixture and continue stirring until you have a smooth mixture.

Heat equal quantities of butter and oil in a frying pan and drop in large spoonfuls of the dough, smooth over and fry both sides golden brown.

Cool on a rack and serve arranged on a doily with a dusting of icing sugar and a pinch of cinnamon.

ZEPHYRS   Makes 30 zephyrs

These are my son Zachary's favourite tea-time treat; I'm never sure if it's because of their delicious melt-in-the-mouth taste or because their name is the same as the naughty monkey in *Babar the Elephant*.

    5 oz (150 g) potato flour
    1½ oz (40 g) plain flour
    4 oz (110 g) butter
    1 egg, separated
    3 oz (75 g) caster sugar
    1 tsp baking powder
    2 tbs dark rum

Cream the butter and work in the egg yolk and sugar. Whip until fluffy and then sift the flours and baking powder into the mixture and beat together. Mix in the rum and set aside while you whisk the egg white into firm peaks. Fold the white into the mixture and place in the refrigerator for one hour.

Pre-heat the oven to 350°F/180°C/gas mark 4 and butter a baking dish. Using 2 teaspoons scoop golf-ball sized mounds on to the baking tray leaving plenty of space between each mound. Bake for 15–20 minutes.

POTATO MUFFINS   Makes 10–16 muffins

    6 oz (175 g) sifted potato flour
    2 tbs soft brown sugar
    1 tsp each baking powder and anise
    4 oz (110 g) sultanas
    3 large eggs, separated
    ½ tsp salt

Mix the flour, sugar, salt, baking powder and anise, toss in the sultanas and stir in the egg yolks. When the mixture is smooth, fold in the stiffly beaten egg whites. Divide between muffin tins which have been buttered and floured and bake for 10 minutes at 400°F/200°C/gas mark 6 and then turn down the temperature to 325°F/170°C/gas mark 3 for the last 5 minutes. Serve hot with butter.

ITALIAN POTATO TEA CAKE

2 lb (900 g) floury-variety potatoes, boiled and skinned
4 oz (110 g) unsalted butter
½ pt (275 ml) cream
1 tbs flour
4 oz (110 g) icing sugar
pinch cinnamon
4 eggs, separated
2 oz (50 g) big breadcrumbs
salt, extra butter

Mash the potatoes and beat in the butter and cream, salt and sifted flour. Rub through a sieve, mix in the sugar and cinnamon and stir in the yolks. Whisk the egg whites to form hard peaks and fold into the mixture so that you end up with a frothy purée.

Butter a 10-in (25-cm) quiche-style dish, pour in the mixture and dot with breadcrumbs dipped in melted butter. Bake for 45 minutes at 450°F/200°C/gas mark 6 until the top is browned. Seat your guests in comfortable chairs and serve slices from the bowl.

POTATO DOUGHNUTS   Makes 20 doughnuts

11 oz (310 g) mashed potatoes
¼ pt (150 ml) milk
¼ oz (10 g) yeast
3½ oz (100 g) flour, sifted
2 egg yolks
1 oz (25 g) butter
At least 4 fl oz (110 ml) oil for frying
¼ tsp salt, sugar

Warm the milk to blood heat and add the yeast. In a large bowl mix together the potatoes, flour and salt. Cream the eggs and butter and together with the yeasty milk add to the potatoes. Work everything together with a wooden spoon until you have a smooth dough. Cover with a cloth and leave to rest for 30 minutes.

On a floured surface roll out the dough and cut out rounds with a pastry cutter. Leave to rise for 5 minutes while you heat the oil to 375°F/190°C. Fry until golden brown, drain and sprinkle with sugar.

SWEET POTATO DOUGHNUTS   Makes 10 doughnuts

2 large equal-sized sweet potatoes, boiled, peeled and mashed
6 fl oz (175 g) coconut milk
3 tbs potato flour
oil for frying
4 oz (110 g) sugar
4 tbs water
pinch salt
icing sugar

Warm the coconut milk and mix with the potato, salt and flour to form a smooth dough. Divide the dough into balls the size of a walnut. Slightly flatten each ball and cut out a hole in the centre. Heat the oil to 375°F/190°C, fry the doughnuts until golden brown and leave to drain and cool.

Meanwhile, heat the sugar and water to form a crystallised syrup. Paint the syrup over the doughnuts, allow to cool and serve sprinkled with icing sugar.

DEVON POTATO CAKE

6 oz (175 g) mashed potato
6 oz (175 g) flour
1 tsp baking powder
2 oz (50 g) butter
2 eggs, beaten
4 oz (110 g) sugar
4 oz (110 g) currants
½ oz (15 g) caraway seeds
pinch of mixed spice

Sift the flour and baking powder into the potatoes and cream in the butter and then the eggs. Stir in all the other dry ingredients and mix well. Turn into a well-buttered flat tin and bake for 30 minutes at 375°F/190°C/gas mark 5. Cut into squares and serve and eat immediately.

POTATO SCONES

8 oz (225 g) seasoned mashed potatoes
4 oz (110 g) sifted flour
1½ tsp baking powder
1 egg, beaten
2 fl oz (50 ml) buttermilk
½ tsp salt, caster sugar, cinnamon

Mix the flour, baking powder and salt into the potatoes and blend in the beaten egg and buttermilk. Beat with a wooden spoon until you have a smooth mixture. Form into either one big scone or several little ones that are ¾-in (1.5-cm) thick and place on a buttered and floured baking tray.

Pre-heat the oven to 400°F/200°C/gas mark 6 and bake for 10 minutes. Turn down the oven to 350°C/180°C/gas mark 4, remove the cake/s and sprinkle with caster sugar and cinnamon and return for 5 more minutes. If you have made one cake, divide into six wedges and serve with butter.

(ONE OF MANY) HUNGARIAN POTATO CAKES/BURGONYAS LINZER

7 oz (200 g) cold mashed potatoes
3½ oz (100 g) butter
10 oz (275 g) flour, sifted
3½ oz (100 g) sugar
3½ oz (100 g) ground hazelnuts
1 small tsp baking powder
1 egg yolk and 1 egg, beaten
jam

Rub the butter into the flour and add the potatoes, sugar, nuts and baking powder. Beat in the egg yolk to make a smooth dough. Pre-heat the oven to 375°F/190°C/gas mark 5 and butter a baking tin. Roll out two thirds of the dough and place on the baking tin. Spread with jam and roll out the remaining dough and cut into strips to make a fretwork over the jam. Brush the strips with beaten egg and bake for 30 minutes.

POTATO-APPLE CAKE

This is an utterly delicious savoury-sweet combination that should be served with thick cream, spoons and forks. It is a perfect high tea dish for a winter's night; preferably served in front of a roaring log fire.

    1 lb (450 g) mashed potatoes
    4 oz (110 g) butter
    4 tbs soft brown sugar
    4 oz (110 g) plain flour
    4 large cooking apples
    pinch dry ginger or cinnamon

Stir 2 oz (50 g) melted butter, the ginger or cinnamon and 1 tsp of sugar into the potatoes. Sift the flour into the mash, mix thoroughly and roll out on to a floured surface. Shape into two rounds, one slightly larger than the other. Butter a baking tray and place the smaller of the rounds on it. Peel and slice the apples and pile on the dough, damp the edges and cover with the larger round. Nip the edges firmly and make a deep X on the top. Bake in a hot oven (400°F/200°C/gas mark 6) for 35 minutes until the pastry is brown and the apples soft.

    To serve, carefully make a hole in the top lid (cutting round the edge rather high up so as not to spill any juice), cover the apples with thin slices of butter and thickly with sugar. Return the lid and bake for a further couple of minutes.

POTATO CREAM

Use in place of icing or to fill a cake.

    8 oz (225 g) mashed potato
    8 oz (225 g) sugar
    1 tbs vanilla sugar
    5 oz (150 g) butter
    2 oz (50 g) ground walnuts
    2 tbs rum, flambéed

Press the potatoes through a sieve twice in order to make them ultra-smooth then, mix in the sugars. Cream the butter and mix with the potatoes and whisk until light and fluffy. Stir in the walnuts and rum.

CHOCOLATE POTATO CAKE

The preceding potato cream recipe (above) works well with this cake.

8 oz (225 g) potato, mashed and finely sieved
4 oz (110 g) butter
2–4 oz (50–110 g) sugar, depending on your sweetness threshold
6 oz (175 g) flour
2 tsp baking powder
1½ oz (40 g) cocoa
few drops vanilla essence
salt

Cream the butter and sugar and mix in the potato. Sift in the flour, salt, baking powder, cocoa, vanilla essence and enough water to make a stiff paste. Pre-heat the oven to 375°F/190°C/gas mark 5. Pour the mixture in to a buttered and floured cake tin and bake for 2 hours.

Allow to shrink and cool before turning out and keep for 24 hours before cutting. Slice through the middle, fill and ice with the potato cream.

ORANGE HONEY SPONGE

I thought this cake was peculiar to my mother until I came across an almost identical recipe in Barbara Maher's wonderful book *Cakes*. A book to entice the most reluctant cakemaker.

2 oz (50 g) potato flour
2 oz (50 g) butter
1 tbs honey
4 eggs, separated
3 oz (75 g) caster sugar
zest of 1 orange
2 oz (50 g) plain flour

Gently melt the butter and honey together and leave to cool while you whisk the egg yolks and sugar to a pale frothy mixture. Mix in the orange zest and beat in the butter and honey. Whisk the egg whites to firm peaks and sift together the two flours. Fold alternate spoonfuls of egg white and flour into the mixture and when complete pour into a greased and floured 8- or 9-in (20.5- or 23-cm) spring-form tin.

Put into a pre-heated low oven (325°F/170°C/gas mark 3) for 40 minutes. Wait 5 minutes for the sides to shrink before turning out on to a wire rack.

When cool fill or coat with potato cream (page 286) but omit the rum and walnuts and cream the juice and zest of 1 orange into the butter.

EUGENIA TORTE

Darra Goldstein adapted this recipe in her book *A Taste of Russia* from a
limited edition cookery book published in the San Francisco Russian
community in the 1930s. It is a cake for special occasions and the
quantities given make a cake that serves 12. But it is especially worth
remembering because it is very quick and easy to make.

4½ oz (125 g) potato flour
4 eggs, separated and 2 extra egg yolks
4 oz (110 g) caster sugar
rind of 1 large orange, finely grated
2 tsp ground unsalted pistachio nuts
2 tsp ground blanched almonds
1 oz (25 g) toasted sliced almonds
3 oz (75 g) thick apricot jam

For the icing:

2½ oz (70 g) finely chopped unsalted pistachio nuts
4 oz (110 g) icing sugar
1 tsp orange-flower water (freshly squeezed orange juice can be
used)
4 tbs double cream

Beat the 6 egg yolks with the caster sugar until thick. Stir in the orange
rind, potato flour and ground nuts. Beat the egg whites until stiff and fold
into the cake batter.

Pre-heat the oven to 350°F/180°C/gas mark 4 and butter two 8-in
(20.5-cm) cake tins. Fit a round of greaseproof paper in the bottom of
each tin and butter the paper. Divide the mixture between the two tins and
bake for 20 minutes. Allow to stand for 10 minutes before you turn on to
racks. Peel off the paper and leave to cool.

When the cakes have cooled, spread one with apricot jam, sprinkle with
the toasted almonds and sandwich it with the other cake. Prepare the icing
by mixing together 2 oz (50 g) of the finely chopped pistachio nuts, the
icing sugar, orange-flower water and cream. Spread the icing on the top
and sides of the cake and sprinkle the remaining pistachios on the top.

DOMINICAN POTATO CAKE

1½ lb (700 g) sweet potatoes, boiled and peeled
1 tbs melted butter
4 oz (110 g) brown sugar
3 medium-sized eggs
3 tbs single cream
1 tbs lime juice
rind of 1 lime, grated
2 tsp baking powder
pinch salt, ¾ tsp grated nutmeg
1 tbs dark rum

While still hot mash the potatoes with the butter and sugar. Beat in the eggs, one at a time and mix in the cream, lime rind and juice. Add the nutmeg, baking powder, salt and rum and blend everything thoroughly. Pre-heat the oven to 325°F/160°C/gas mark 3, pour the mixture into a buttered baking tin and bake for 1½ hours.

24.

Breads

In her definitive work *English Bread and Yeast Cookery*, Elizabeth David points out that were it not for the grain shortages during the Napoleonic Wars, the early decades of the nineteenth century and again in the early 1840s (before the repeal of the Corn Laws) mashed potato in bread making might never have been discovered. Eking out the flour with mashed potato provided surprisingly good results and even in times of abundant grain harvests the combination of flour and mashed potato has stuck. The addition of potato makes a light loaf and one that keeps far longer than a regular one. The flavour is also distinctive and rather addictive. It toasts well and, as Ms David says, it makes exceptionally good croûtons and sandwiches. Use only floury varieties, always cook them in their skins, dry thoroughly and mash without fat or liquid.

POTATO STARTER

The reaction between yeast and mashed potato makes it a fertile fermenting ground. This recipe is used in conjunction with yeast and the resultant bread is quite different from potato bread, but different too from breads made without the starter.

> 1 medium-sized potato, boiled in its skin, peeled, dried and
> mashed.
> 1 pt (570 ml) of potato cooking water
> 1 sachet powdered yeast
> 1 tbs granulated sugar

Place the mash in a china or glass crock and mix in the warm water. Sprinkle the yeast and sugar into the mixture. Leave loosely covered in a large polythene bag for at least 3 days at room temperature. Stir occasionally. Fermentation is complete when it has a pungent, sour odour; the starter should then be tightly covered and refrigerated until required.

The starter will keep indefinitely but every couple of weeks should be revitalised. Beat the mixture well, discard all but 1 cup, let it reach room temperature and then add ½ cup of water and ½ cup of flour. Allow to stand for several hours, cover and then refrigerate.

POTATO STARTER BREAD
Makes 2 small loaves, 6 x 3 x 2½ ins (15 x 7.5 x 6.5 cm)

To simplify this recipe I have used a cup as an object of measurement. Any cup will suffice but use the same one!

    1 cup potato starter
    3 cups flour
    1 sachet dried yeast
    ½ tsp soft brown sugar
    1½ oz (40 g) butter
    1 tsp salt

The night before you wish to make the bread take the starter out of the fridge and bring it to room temperature. Beat in 1 cup of water and 1 cup of flour and return to the fridge.

Sprinkle the yeast and sugar into a cup of warm water. Take 1 cup of the renewed starter and pour into a large mixing bowl together with the salt, melted butter and the yeast and sugar water. Mix thoroughly with a wooden spoon and add 1–2 cups of sifted flour in order to end up with a fairly stiff dough ready for kneading on a floured board. Knead for 5 minutes, put the dough in a large buttered bowl, cover with a damp cloth, and leave to rise for abut 1½ hours. Knead the dough again and divide into 2 loaves, put in buttered bread tins or lay on a greased baking tray. Cover and leave to rise a second time – for 40 minutes or until the dough has doubled in size – and bake for 20 minutes at 425°F/220°C/gas mark 7, then lower the heat to 375°F/190°C/gas mark 5 and bake for a further 20 minutes.

POTATO BREAD   Makes 1 large loaf

This is Dr A. Hunter's recipe, first published in 1805 in his book *Receipts in Modern Cookery; with a Medical Commentary*. Elizabeth David cites it as her favourite potato bread recipe in *English Bread and Yeast Cookery*.

4 oz (110 g) warm, dry mashed potato
1 lb (450 g) white flour
½ oz (15 g) yeast
½ pt (275 ml) milk and water mixed
¾ oz (20 g) salt

Have the flour and salt ready in a bowl, the yeast creamed with a little water, and the milk and water warm in a jug. When your potatoes are cooked, peeled, sieved and weighed, mix them with the flour as if you were rubbing in fat, so that the two are very thoroughly amalgamated. Then add the yeast and the warm milk and water. Mix the dough as for ordinary bread. Leave until it is well risen (about 2 hours), knead lightly, shape and put into a 2–2½ pt (1.5 l) capacity tin. Cover with a damp cloth and leave until the dough reaches the top of the tin. Bake in a moderately hot oven (425°F/220°C/gas mark 7) for 45 minutes.

WHOLEMEAL POTATO BREAD   Makes two 1 lb (450 g) loaves

12 oz (350 g) warm, dry mashed potatoes
2 tsp dried yeast or 1 level tbs fresh yeast
¾ pt (400 ml) warm water
1 tbs molasses
1½ lb (700 g) wholemeal flour
2 tbs sunflower oil
1 tbs salt

Dissolve the yeast into a little of the warmed water and molasses; when it bubbles whisk in the rest of the water. Mix the sieved flour with the salt and rub in the sieved potatoes. Mix the two together until you have a smooth dough. Knead for 5 minutes and work in the oil. Knead again and leave to rise, covered with a damp cloth, for a couple of hours. Knead the dough again and grease two 1 lb (450 g) bread tins. Divide between the tins, cover again with the damp cloth and leave until the dough has risen to the top of the tins.

Pre-heat the oven to 400°F/200°C/gas mark 6 and bake for 10 minutes before reducing the heat to 375°F/190°C/gas mark 5. Bake for a further 35 minutes, remove from the oven and leave for 5 minutes before turning out to cool.

FLAVOURED POTATO BREADS

Potato breads are especially delicious made with nuts, cheeses, herbs, garlic, pre-cooked onion and dried fruits. Follow either of the basic potato bread recipes (pp 291–292) adding between 1 and 2 oz (25–50 g) of your chosen extra ingredient just before you leave the dough to prove. Similarly, rolls and breads can be 'flavoured' with a topping of caraway, poppy, sesame and dill seeds. Wash the top of the dough with water first.

POTATO, CHEESE AND GARLIC BREAD   Makes 1 large loaf

Eat this rich, substantial and aromatic bread straight from the oven. As it cools it gets rather heavy because it has no yeast. The recipe owes much to John Tovey, the inspired chef of Miller Howe in the Lake District.

        12 oz (350 g) warm, mashed potatoes
        1 egg
        2 fl oz (50 ml) milk
        2 cloves garlic, crushed
        2 oz (50 g) Parmesan, finely grated
        12 oz (350 g) self-raising flour
        2 tsp salt

Whisk the egg with the milk, add the crushed garlic, salt and Parmesan. Mix in the mashed potato and finally, the sifted flour. Work everything together into a firm ball, dust with flour and mark the top with wedge lines.

Pre-heat the oven to 375°F/190°C/gas mark 5 and bake for 45 minutes. Serve with soup or plenty of butter and a crisp salad.

BERCHES/POTATO HALLAH   Makes 1 large loaf

There are many claims as to the origin of this plaited loaf. In Northern Germany it is the 'modern' evolution of the tradition of women offering their braided hair to the Teutonic goddess of fertility, while another view is that the plait represents interlocked arms. In Judaism the plait represents the 12 loaves of show bread that were in the temple; so in that case, a precisely prepared plait should have at least 6 humps on each side. The flavour is unlike the packaged sweet hallah widely available. It needs to prove overnight.

1 lb (450 g) warm mashed potato
½ oz (15 g) dried yeast
¼ pt (150 ml) warm water
1 lb (450 g) flour
2½ tsp salt
poppy seeds

Activate the yeast with the warm water and, when ready, mix in the potatoes, salt and sifted flour. Knead the dough for 10–15 minutes until you have a hard dough. Cover with a damp cloth and leave overnight in a warm place to double in size.

Next morning, butter a baking tray and divide the dough into 2. Make a long oblong loaf and place on the tray and then divide the other half into 3 pieces. Roll the 3 pieces into long sausages and make a loose plait. Fashion your plait to fit the top of the oblong loaf, lay it on top and pinch it into position at either end. Cover the loaf again with the damp cloth and leave for 1 hour. Paint the top with water, sprinkle on the poppy seeds and bake for 45 minutes–1 hour at 350°F/180°C/gas mark 4.

SWEET POTATO BREAD   Makes one 8-in (20.5-cm) square loaf

8 oz (225 g) mashed sweet potato
2 dsp dried yeast
4 fl oz (110 ml) warm water
2 dsp honey
2 dsp sunflower oil
2½ oz (70 g) semolina
5 oz (150 g) wholemeal flour
4 dsp butter
½ tsp salt

Sprinkle the yeast on the water, when it begins to froth mix in the salt, honey and oil. Add the potato, semolina and 4 oz (110 g) of the sifted flour. Mix thoroughly, cover with a damp towel and leave to stand for 10 minutes. Cut the butter up into little bits and scatter on the dough, begin to knead and gradually add the remaining sifted flour. Continue kneading for 5-10 minutes until you have a soft dough. If it seems sticky add a little more flour. Butter an 8-inch (20.5-cm) square baking tin and put in the dough. Cover with a damp cloth and leave to rise (it should double its size) for about an hour. Pre-heat the oven to 375°F/190°C/gas mark 5 and bake for 45 minutes.

POTATO ROLLS

This is Elizabeth David's domestic adaptation of Maria Eliza Rundell's 1806 recipe first published in *A New System of Domestic Cookery*. The rolls keep very well and are very quick to make if you use 1 oz (25 g) of yeast and omit 1½ hour's proving.

> 1 lb (450 g) warm, dry mashed potatoes
> ½ oz (10 g) yeast
> ¾ pt (400 ml) water
> ¼ pt (150 ml) milk
> 1½ lb (700 g) flour
> salt

Put the yeast to work with the warm water and mix in the potatoes, the warmed milk, the sifted flour and salt. Knead it well and leave covered with a damp cloth for 1½–2 hours (or ½ hour if using 1 oz/25 g yeast). Knead again and divide into rolls. Place on a greased baking sheet, paint the tops with egg wash if desired, and bake at 400°F/200°C/gas mark 6 for 30 minutes.

CORNISH CHEESE ROLLS

These are soft; a cross between a bread roll and a savoury potato cake.

> 4 oz (110 g) warm, mashed and sieved potatoes
> 8 oz (225 g) flour
> 3 tsp baking powder
> 4 oz (110 g) Cheddar cheese, finely grated
> milk
> 1 tsp salt

Sieve together the flour, baking powder and salt making sure there are no lumps. Gradually mix in the potatoes and cheese, blending the mixture quickly with your fingertips. Add enough milk to make a soft, dry dough, handling the mixture as little as possible. Divide into little mounds and place on a buttered and floured baking sheet. Bake for 15 minutes at 450°F/230°C/gas mark 8.

25.

Drinks

'Excellent,' [James Bond] said to the barman, 'but if you can get a vodka made with grain instead of potatoes, you will find it still better.'

Ian Fleming, *Casino Royale*, 1953.

From the earliest times man has been brewing alcoholic drinks, and the potato, along with maize, has had a major part to play. In ancient Peru they brewed a beer called *chicha* which is still a popular beverage on public occasions. As the potato established itself throughout Europe, in Russia, Poland and Germany it was used in the making of vodka and schnapps. In Scandinavia the potato was the base for their aquavit. But the most famous, reputedly lethal and strictly illegal alcoholic brew is the Irish poteen. In his exhaustive study, *The History and Social Influence of the Potato*, Redcliffe Salaman is reluctant to commit himself to the existence of illicit stills in Ireland 'today' but he gives the following recipe:

'The procedure is to expose medium-sized tubers to frost over several nights, then cut them into slices, soak in water indoors for ten days with occasional stirring, strain the liquor off and add some treacle and yeast. The 'wash', as it is now termed, is allowed to ferment: after an adequate time, it is carefully distilled without being allowed to boil. I owe this recipe to a late very distinguished Irish friend, who obtained it direct from an exponent of the art.'

'Murphy has invented a new method of fishing. He only has to sprinkle a pint or two of poteen into the river and the salmon come up ready canned.' (Irish joke).

POTATO WINES

The potato makes a Rhine-type wine that improves the longer you keep it and on no account should be sampled before six months. I haven't put it to the test, but I read somewhere that if you keep the wine for a couple of years it tastes like brandy but will never have the strength of poteen. Traditionally in Ireland potato wine was called White Root because any sort of potato distilling was and is illegal.

TRADITIONAL IRISH POTATO WINE
Makes approximately 1 gal (4.5 l)

4 lb (1.8 kg) floury-variety potatoes
1½ gal (6.8 l) cold water
3 lb (1.4 kg) genuine Demerara sugar
1 lemon and 1 orange
1 in (2.5 cm) root ginger
1 oz (25 g) wine or baker's yeast

Thoroughly scrub the potatoes, grate or chop into tiny pieces and put in a large saucepan. Add the water, bring to the boil and simmer until the potato is cooked. Strain off the liquor into a large vessel (or divide between two) and stir in the sugar, lemon, orange and ginger. When the sugar has dissolved return to the cooking vessel and simmer for 30 minutes. Leave to cool to room temperature and sprinkle on the yeast. Pour into a fermentation bottle, fit the airlock and leave to ferment. This takes about 2 weeks.

One of the problems of potato wine is that the results are often cloudy because of the high quantity of starch in the tubers. It is possible to buy a starch-destroying enzyme to add to the wine if it is still cloudy a week after the fermentation has finished.

When fermentation is complete, strain into a large scalded vessel, allow to settle for 24 hours and pour into clean, sterilised bottles. Cork and store horizontally for at least 1 year.

H. E. BRAVERY'S MEDIUM POTATO WINE
Makes approximately 1 gal (4.5 l)

This recipe is adapted from the amateur winemaker's book *Home Booze*.

2 lb (900 g) King Edward potatoes
5 pts (2.8 l) water
2¼ lb (1 kg) sugar
1 lb (450 g) raisins
3 oranges
¼ fl oz (5 ml) citric acid
½ pt (275 ml) freshly made strong tea
1 oz (25 g) each wine yeast and nutrient

Scrub the potatoes and grate into 4 pts (2.3 l) water, bring slowly to the boil and simmer gently for 15 minutes. Remove any scum. Put half the sugar into a fermenting pail with the raisins and strain the potatoes into the pan. Stir until the sugar has dissolved, cover and leave to cool to lukewarm.

Extract the juice from the oranges, stir this, the acid and tea into the main liquid. Bring the liquid up to 1 gal (4.5 l) with boiled, cooled water and add the yeast and nutrient. Cover tightly and leave to ferment for 10 days, stirring daily. Strain into a clean vessel. Dissolve the rest of the sugar with 1 pt (570 ml) boiling water, cool and add to the strained liquid. Cover and leave to settle for 3 days. Pour into a fermentation bottle and leave until all fermentation has ceased. Pour into sterilised bottles, trying to leave behind any sediment. Cork and store.

The process of adding the sugar in two stages is an often successful attempt to arrive at clear rather than cloudy wine.

CORNISH BARM

This curious drink should be viewed as sustenance during a fast.

3 oz (75 g) mashed potato
4 oz (110 g) sifted flour
4 oz (110 g) sugar
2 pts (1.1 l) water
1 oz (25 g) raisins

Beat the sifted flour into the potatoes and stir in the sugar. Warm the water and integrate into the paste. Stir in the raisins, bottle and leave for at least one week before using.

26.

Folklore and Fascinating Facts

'What I say is, that if a man really likes potatoes, he must be a pretty decent sort of fellow.'

A. A. Milne, *Not That It Matters*

Brillat-Savarin, one of the most prestigious chefs in history didn't agree: 'I appreciate the potato only as a protection against famine, except for that I know of nothing more eminently *tasteless*.' (*La Physiologie de Goût*, 1825.)

The word spud was first coined in Scotland and originally referred to the three-pronged fork used to lift potatoes.

It is estimated that the Irish potato crop failures of 1845 and 1846 accounted for a population loss of about 2½ million persons.

To cure toothache, carry a potato in a pocket on the same side as the tooth. As the potato dries, the toothache will fade.

Soothe and extract the heat from sunburn or a burn with a raw potato cut in half.

Similarly, use slices of raw potato to refresh puffy eyes. This is particularly effective after tears.

An old wives' tale decrees that a pregnant woman should not eat potatoes, especially at night, if she wishes her child to have a small head.

The favourite food of Paul Cézanne was potatoes with olive oil.

Put small new potatoes in a dry biscuit tin. Cover with dry sand, seal the tin with care and bury in the garden. Mark your spot well and dig them up for Christmas. They will taste as good as summer new potatoes.

On the importance of potatoes today: 'In volume of fresh product, the potato ranks first among the world's most important food crops', *Encyclopaedia Britannica*; '[it is] the world's fourth largest food crop, after corn, wheat and rice', *United Nations Food and Agricultural Organisation*; '[it is]

one of only fifteen food products which feed the entire world', Frances Moore Lappe and Joseph Collins in *Food First*.

Couch-potato is American for a television addict.

Fifteen years ago the US Department of Agriculture set up a research group to find uses for the abundant corn and potato crops that far exceeded the country's needs. The result is 'Super Slurper', a phenomenally absorbent powder capable of soaking up thousands of times its weight of water on contact. One successful use has been in babies' nappies. The powder has been patented worldwide and there are plans to expand into Europe.

In 1983 *The Times* carried a story about the successful testing of a generator that uses a potato as a source of electricity. The experiment was carried out at the Ukrainian Academy of Sciences. Two minute electrodes are inserted into the potato and, hey presto, you get current in a circuit. The Ukrainian researchers say that a single potato will provide electricity for nearly a month.

In 1899 Fanny Bergen recorded in *Animal and Plant Lore*, that 'a dried tuber carried in the pocket or suspended from the neck, is a sure protection against rheumatism.'

It takes 5 tonnes of potatoes to make 1 tonne of crisps.

Bibliography

Ackerman, Roy, *Roy Ackerman's Recipe Collection*, Penguin, 1987
Anderson, Jean, *The Food of Portugal*, Robert Hale, 1987
Avila, Kay, *Take 12 Cooks*, BBC/Macdonald, 1986
Ayrton, Elizabeth, *The Cookery of England*, Penguin, 1977; *The Pleasure of Vegetables*, Penguin, 1983
Barber, Richard, *Cooking and Recipes from Rome to the Renaissance*, Allen Lane, 1973
Beard, James, *Theory and Practice of Good Cooking*, Penguin, 1977
Beck, Simone with Bertholle, Louisette and Child, Julia, *Mastering the Art of French Cooking*, Penguin, 1966
Benghiat, Norma, *Traditional Jamaican Cookery*, Penguin, 1985
Bertholle, Louisette, *French Cooking for All*, Penguin, 1984
Bissell, Frances, *The Pleasures of Cookery*, Chatto & Windus, 1986
Blanc, Georges, *Ma Cuisine des Saisons*, trans. Conran, Caroline, Macmillan, 1987
Boulestin, Marcel and Adair, Robin, *101 Ways of Cooking Potatoes*, Heinemann, 1932
Bourne, Ursula, *Portuguese Cookery*, Penguin, 1973
Boxer, Arabella, *Garden Cookbook*, Weidenfeld & Nicolson, 1974; *Mediterranean Cookbook*, Dent, 1981
Bradley, Richard, *The Country Housewife and Lady's Director* (facsimile edition), Prospect Books, 1980
Bravery, H. E., *Home Booze*, Macdonald and Jane's, 1976
Brown, Catherine and Drew, Robert, *Scottish Cookery*, Robert Drew, 1985
Brennan, Jennifer, *One Dish Meals of Asia*, Times Books, 1985
Bryan, John E. and Castle, Coralie, *Edible Ornamental Garden*, Pitman, 1974
Bugialli, Giuliano, *The Taste of Italy*, Octopus/Conran, 1985
Campbell, Susan, *English Cookery New and Old*, Consumers Association/Hodder & Stoughton, 1981
Carrier, Robert, *Great Dishes of the World*, Nelson, 1963; *Robert Carrier's Entertaining*, Sidgwick & Jackson, 1977
Casas, Penelope, *Foods and Wines of Spain*, Penguin, 1982; *Tapas*, Pavilion Books, 1988
Conil, Jean, *Cuisine Végétarienne Française*, Thorsons, 1985; *Cuisine Fraîcheur*, Aurum Press, 1987
Cornish Recipes Old and New, Bradford Barton, 1970
Craddock, Fanny and Johnnie as Bon Viveur, *The Daily Telegraph Cookbook*, W. H. Allen, 1978; *The Ambitious Cook*, Vol. 3, W. H. Allen, 1985
Craig, Elizabeth, *Hotch Potch*, Collins, 1978
Daly, Dorothy, *Cooking the Italian Way*, Hamlyn, 1958
David, Elizabeth, *French Country Cooking*, Penguin, 1959; *French Provincial Cooking*, Michael Joseph, 1960; *English Bread and Yeast Cookery*, Penguin, 1977; *An Omelette and a Glass of Wine*, Jill Norman, 1985
Davis, Adelle, *Let's Cook it Right*, George Allen & Unwin, 1971
Davis, Hester, *Handbook of Plain Cookery*, McCorquodale, 1982
Der Harounian, Arto, *Classic Vegetable Cookery*, Ebury Press, 1985
Deschamps, Marion, *French Vegetable Cookery*, Robert Hale, 1978

Dimbleby, Josceline, *Favourite Food*, Allen Lane, 1983, Penguin, 1984
Downer, Leslie and Youeda, Minoru, *Step by Step Japanese Cooking*, Macdonald, 1985
Downing, Beryl, *Quick Cook*, Penguin, 1981
Edden, Helen, *Country Recipes of Old England*, Country Life, 1919
Elliot, Rose, *Complete Vegetarian Cookbook*, Collins, 1985
Escoffier, Auguste, *Ma Cuisine*, Hamlyn, 1965
Eyton, Audrey, *The Complete F-Plan Diet*, Penguin, 1982
Farringdon School, *Pot Luck*, Freedom From Hunger, 1964
Fernandez, Rafi, *Malaysian Cookery*, Collins, 1985
Fitzgibbon, Theodora, *The Art of British Cooking*, Phoenix, 1965; *A Taste of London*, Pan,
    1973; *A Taste of Yorkshire*, Ward Lock, 1979
Fleming, Susan, *The Little Potato Book*, Piatkus, 1987
Floyd, Keith, *Floyd on Fire*, BBC, 1986; *Floyd on France*, BBC, 1987
Forbes, Leslie, *A Table in Tuscany*, Webb & Bower, 1985
Fullick, Roy (editor), *The Elle Cookbook*, Michael Joseph, 1981; *The Second Elle Cookbook*,
    Michael Joseph, 1985
Gardnier, Kenneth, *Creole Caribbean Cookery*, Grafton, 1986
Giradet, Fredy, edited by Campbell, Susan, *Cuisine Spontanée*, Macmillan, 1985
Goldstein, Darra, *A Taste of Russia*, Jill Norman, 1985
Green, Henrietta (editor), *RAC Food Routes*, George Philip, 1988
Grigson, Jane, *Good Things*, Michael Joseph, 1971; *English Food*, Macmillan, 1974; *The
    Mushroom Feast*, Penguin, 1975; *Jane Grigson's Vegetable Book*, Michael Joseph, 1978;
    Penguin, 1983; *Observer Guide to European Cookery*, Michael Joseph, 1983; *Observer
    Guide to British Cookery*, Michael Joseph, 1984; *Exotic Fruits and Vegetables*, Jonathan
    Cape, 1986
Guermont, Claude with Frumkin, Paul, *The Norman Table*, Scribners, 1986
Hartley, Dorothy, *Food in England*, Macdonald, 1954
Hazan, Marcella, *The Classic Italian Cookbook*, Macmillan, 1973; *The Second Classic Italian
    Cookbook*, Macmillan, 1978
Hesketh, Christian, Luard, Elisabeth and Blond, Laura, *The Country House Cookery Book*,
    Century, 1985
Hope, Simon, *The Reluctant Vegetarian*, Rider, 1985
Horley, Georgina, *Good Food on a Budget*, Penguin, 1969
Howard, Elizabeth Jane and Maschler, Fay, *Howard and Maschler on Food*, Michael Joseph,
    1987
Hutchins, Sheila, *Grannie's Kitchen*, Granada, 1981
Jaffrey, Madhur, *Madhur Jaffrey's Indian Cookery*, BBC/Michael Joseph, 1982
Johnson, Michelle Berriedale, *British Museum Cookbook*, British Museum Publications, 1987
Johnston, Mireille, *The Cuisine of the Rose*, Penguin, 1984
Keane, Molly, *Nursery Cooking*, Macdonald, 1985
Ladenis, Nico, *My Gastronomy*, Ebury Press, 1987
Lang, George, *The Cuisine of Hungary*, Penguin, 1971
(New) Larousse, Hamlyn, 1960
Leneman, Leah, *Vegan Cooking*, Thorsons, 1982
Lo, Kenneth, *Cheap Chow*, Elm Tree Books, 1976
Leembruggen, Ranse, *Easy Eastern Cooking*, Macdonald, 1986
Lewis, Leon, *Vegetarian Dinner Parties*, Thorsons, 1983
Luard, Elisabeth, *European Peasant Cookery*, Bantam Press, 1986
Lytton Toye, Doris, *Contemporary Cookery*, Condé Nast Publications, 1947
Macnicol, Fred, *Hungarian Cookery*, Penguin, 1978
Maher, Barbara, *Cakes*, Penguin, 1982
Maschler, Fay, *Eating In*, Bloomsbury, 1987
McNeill, Marian, *The Scots Kitchen*, Blackie & Son, 1929
Millau, Christian, *Dining in France*, Sidgwick & Jackson, 1986
Mosimann, Anton, *Cuisine à la Carte*, Northwood, 1981; *Cuisine Naturelle*, Macmillan, 1985
Nathan, Joan, *The Jewish Holiday Kitchen*, Schocken Books, 1979
Neal, Bill, *Bill Neal's Southern Cooking*, University of North Carolina Press, 1985
Nicol, Ann, *Pick Your Own Cookbook*, Freshold, 1987

Olney, Richard, *Simple French Food*, Penguin, 1981; *French Menu Cookbook*, Dorling Kindersley, 1985

Ortiz, Elisabeth Lambert, *Latin American Cooking*, Penguin, 1969; *The Fibre Cookbook*, Jill Norman/Hobhouse, 1982

Pears (57th edition) *Pears Cyclopaedia*

Pirbright, Peter, *Off the Beeton Track*, Binnacle Books, 1946

Pomiane, Edouard de, *Cooking in Ten Minutes*, Faber, 1985

Pourounas, Andreas, *Aphrodite's Cookbook*, compiled and edited by Grosvenor, Helene, Neville Spearman, 1977

Puck, Wolfgang, *The Wolfgang Puck Cookbook*, Random House, 1986

Read, Jan, Manjon, Maite and Johnson, Hugh, *The Wine and Food of France*, Weidenfeld & Nicolson, 1987

Reader's Digest, *Farmhouse Cookery*, Reader's Digest, 1980

Ridgway, Judy, *The Vegetable Year Cook Book*, Piatkus, 1985

Rodale, *Rodale's Good Food Kitchen*, Rodale Press, 1982

Roden, Claudia, *A Book of Middle Eastern Food*, Penguin, 1970; *Picnic*, Penguin, 1981; *Mediterranean Cookery*, BBC, 1987

Rogers, Jenny (Editor), *A Taste of Health*, BBC, 1985

Root, Waverley, *Food of Waverley Root*, Simon & Schuster, 1980

Rosso, Julee and Lukins, Sheila, *Silver Palate Cookbook*, Ebury Press, 1979

Roux, Albert and Michel, *New Classic Cuisine*, Macdonald, 1983

Sahni, Julie, *Classic Indian Cooking*, Dorling Kindersley, 1986

Salaman, Redcliffe, *The History and Social Influence of the Potato*, Cambridge University Press, 1949, 1986

Santa Maria, Jack, *Indian Vegetarian Cookery*, Rider, 1973; *Indian Meat and Fish Cookery*, Rider, 1977; *Greek Vegetarian Cookery*, Rider, 1984

Scott, David and Winata, Surya, *Indonesian Cookery*, Rider, 1984

Sekers, Simone, *Cook's Progress*, Compton Press, 1979; *The Country Housewife*, Hodder & Stoughton, 1983

Sekules, Veronica, *Friends of the Earth Cookbook*, Penguin, 1980

Simon, Nezih, *Eats Without Meats*, Tredolphin Press, 1984

Smart, Elizabeth and Ryan, Agnes, *Cooking the French Way*, Spring Books, 1958

Smith, Michael, *Cooking with Michael Smith*, Papermac, 1981; *New English Cookery*, BBC, 1985

So, Yan-Kit, *Wok Cookbook*, Piatkus, 1985

Spencer, Colin, *Mediterranean Vegetable Cooking*, Thorsons, 1982; *Cordon Vert*, Thorsons, 1985; *The New Vegetarian*, Elm Tree Books, 1986

Spieler, David and Marlena, *Naturally Good*, Faber, 1973

Standard, Stella, *Our Daily Bread*, Lancer Books, 1970

Stevenson, Violet, *Grow and Cook*, David & Charles, 1976

Stubbs, Joyce, *Home Book of Greek Cookery*, Faber & Faber, 1986

Taneeja, Meera, *Indian Regional Cookery*, Mills & Boon, 1980

Torday, Jane, *A Little Book of Old Fashioned Nursery Recipes*, Parsley Publications, 1980

Tovey, John, *Feast of Vegetables*, Century, 1985

Troisgros, Jean and Pierre, translated and edited by Caroline Conran, *Nouvelle Cuisine of Jean and Pierre Troisgros*, Macmillan, 1980

Troy, Diana, *The Breakfast Book*, Allison & Busby, (1985); *The Covent Garden Cookery Book*, Sidgwick & Jackson, 1987

Tull, Anita, *Food and Nutrition*, Oxford University Press, 1984

Uvezian, Sonia, *Best Food of Russia*, Harcourt Brace Jovanovich, 1976

Walker, Clare and Coleman, Gill, *Home Gardener's Cookbook*, Penguin, 1980

Wells, Judy and Johnson, Rick, *The Pie's the Limit*, Penguin, 1983

Wilson, Anne, *Food and Drink in Britain*, Penguin, 1973

Wong, Ella Moi, *Yum Cha*, Angus and Robertson, 1981

Index